GENDER ISSUES

FICTIONAL WORLD OF SHASHI DESHPANDE

GENDER ISSUES

FICTIONAL WORLD OF SHASHI DESHPANDE

Sangeeta Sharma

ATLANTIC

PUBLISHERS & DISTRIBUTORS (P) LTD

Published by
ATLANTIC
PUBLISHERS & DISTRIBUTORS (P) LTD

7/22, Ansari Road, Darya Ganj, New Delhi-110002
Phones : +91-11-40775252, 23273880, 23275880, 23280451
Fax : +91-11-23285873
Web : www.atlanticbooks.com
E-mail : orders@atlanticbooks.com

Branch Office
5, Nallathambi Street, Wallajah Road, Chennai-600002
Phones : +91-44-64611085, 32413319
E-mail : chennai@atlanticbooks.com

Printed in India at Nice Printing Press, A-33/3A, Site-IV, Industrial Area, Sahibabad, Ghaziabad, U.P.

Dedicated to
Mothers and Motherhood

Preface

Shashi Deshpande has been the most versatile and widely read Indian English woman writer since 1980s. The gender bias has been prevalent in the Indian society since time immemorial, which provided her valid reason to depict gender issues prominently in her gynofictional works. Being a liberal feminist, she questions the gender arrangement in the Indian patriarchal society. In her novels she voices her opinion that gender is a social and cultural construct. Her works need to be deconstructed as gynofictional. She has depicted various gender issues such as girl infanticide, girl foeticide, dowry, rape, poor education, neglect of the girl child, the practice of sati, child marriage and widowhood, etc. in her novels like *Roots and Shadows*, *The Dark Holds No Terrors*, *That Long Silence*, *The Binding Vine*, and *A Matter of Time*. She is a keen social observer and is very focused in her depiction of gender issues in the patriarchal Indian society.

Shashi Deshpande is a writer of human emotions and relationships, and her fictional works show the plight of women in the male-dominated society. She has shown in her fictional works those intrinsic values in women which have been flouted by a patriarchal society in India. Unfortunately, Shashi Deshpande has not yet received the critical attention she deserves.

The book, *Gender Issues: Fictional World of Shashi Deshpande* aims at unfolding Deshpande's potential as a candid writer who is genuinely concerned with gender issues. Trapped between tradition and modernity, her women protagonists undergo mental trauma in their quest for identity before they affirm themselves. An attempt has been made in the book to critically analyze the fictional world of Shashi Deshpande as a writer of gender issues in Indian society.

After the reader is introduced to the thematic purpose and perspective, the next chapter focuses on co-travellers of Shashi Deshpande in her fiction. Chapter 3 illustrates through her novel, *The Binding Vine*, the omnipotent power of love. This chapter is followed by a lucid account of women's subjugation in patriarchal society based on *The Dark Holds No Terrors*. The next two chapters critically examine dominant desires of feminine heart and also inner dilemma with reference to *Roots and Shadows* and *That Long Silence* respectively. Chapter 7 shows, through the main character in Shashi Deshpande's *A Matter of Time*, how the 'new woman' tries to emancipate herself as an independent woman.

The book will be useful for students and teachers of English literature, particularly Indian English literature, and researchers in those fields.

Sangeeta Sharma

Acknowledgements

The present work is a synergistic product as various minds as well as many people have contributed to its accomplishment. It is almost impossible to move further without acknowledging the people without whose contributions, my ideas would not have been able to see the light of the day in the form of this book.

First and foremost, I must express my heartiest and sincere thanks to my guide, Dr. Nirupama Sharma who has not only been my supervisor, but also a philosopher mother, and guide in the true sense. Just as the pole star guides the wandering ships in the vast and unfathomable ocean, in the same manner she provides touchstones to her students to accomplish the task at hand. I can never repay the debt that I owe to her.

I take this opportunity to thank Mrs. and Dr. P.K. Sharma for their benevolent attitude towards me.

I am grateful to my hubby, Arbind and my son, Advait for their constant love, affection and support. I am also thankful to my parent from the bottom of my heart who has always given me unflinching help, love, support and encouragement.

Above all, I offer my deep reverence to the Almighty with Whose blessings I have been able to come so far in my life.

Sangeeta Sharma

Contents

1

Introduction: Purpose and Perspective

Gender and literature are very closely related to each other in the sense that neither can be conceived in isolation nor can they be studied apart from society and culture. Gender, as differentiated from sex, has nothing to do with biology. Unlike sex which is biologically determined gender is a social and cultural construct. No wonder, men and women are biologically different from each other, but the sexual differences do not imply inequality and dominance of one over the other. In Indian patriarchal social setup, 'masculinity' is associated with superiority whereas 'femininity' is linked with inferiority, and while masculinity implies strength, action, self-assertion and domination, 'femininity' implies weakness, passivity, docility, obedience and self-negation.

Sex is the creation of God and sexual differences are essential for procreation, but gender is not God's creation. It is the creation of patriarchy and serves the male flair for domination. A patriarchal social set up firmly asserts men's superiority over women and is based not on mutuality but on oppression. Although women have played a vital role in the creation of the society and have been active agents, yet the Indian patriarchal society has always tried to relegate them to the 'margin'.

The subordination of women to men is believed to be older than the civilization itself. The image of women was created by men. It was what he wanted her to be and he never wanted her to be an equal, a co-sharer of all the privileges he was enjoying. Because the image of woman was created not by women or by men and women jointly but by men alone, the standard of womanhood was set for women by men and thus women couldn't have clear perception of themselves. So, woman, presented with an image in a mirror has danced to that image in a hypnotic trance. Thus, patriarchy undermined women sense of self-worth and made them believe that their inferiority was pre-ordained.

Earlier, literature could provide pleasure to the readers (especially male readers) by depicting women as passive, docile, helpless victims at the mercy of men. The inner experiences of women were rendered invisible because they were considered to be trivial and not worth considering. The roles of women were restricted and, therefore, the experiences of the muted female half of the society were not reflected in literature. Since the literary tradition was primarily patriarchal, the woman in male-authored texts was selfless, self-effacing and submissive. But with the rise of feminism, women became aware of the fact that their inferiority is not ordained in heaven and that gender is neither natural nor immutable because it is the creation of patriarchy. It is a construct which can be and needs to be deconstructed. Women have realized that the system of patriarchy which has been with us for a long time, no longer serves the needs of the rapidly changing society where women are trying to emancipate themselves from subordination. Modern Indian women writers are disgusted with the male notion of women's 'proper place' and want to redefine women's own 'selves' as well as their 'proper places'. They have grown intolerant of women's exploitation and victimization by men and they revolt against the marginalization of women. Shashi Deshpande, through her writings, questions the sexual politics and the gender arrangements in the society. She challenges the traditional society's role prescriptions because there is no logical connection between the anatomy of a woman and the roles she is expected to play except that of child-bearing. She highlights, through her writings, that women have grown intolerant of patriarchal oppression whose victims they have been since Eve tasted the forbidden fruit. Women have started their struggle to dethrone the myth of femininity, reject the constructs of the patriarchal thought and to reorder the world.

In her gynofictional works, Shashi Deshpande looks at gender and issues related to it from the socio-cultural and familial angle. She has established through her novels what is quite firmly maintained in gynocriticism that while sex is biologically given, gender is a social and cultural construct. Her works can be deconstructed to understand her notion of equality of men and women. She believes that in the patriarchal society women have been devalued and their basic feminine qualities have been denigrated. In her fictional world, she makes a psychological study of patriarchal relations within the present conditions. A few critics blame that being a woman writer she writes in a biased tone and unnecessarily creates hype around gender issues. But one cannot deny the fact that due to difference in 'gendering', men and women are bound to adopt different characteristics and modes of feeling and temperament. As Gilligan points out that if an observer is a woman, the perspective may be of a different sort. Even Virginia Woolf comments on the difference in male and female writers. "It is probable, however, that both in life and in art, the values of women are not the values of a man. Thus, when a woman comes to write a novel, she will find that she is perpetually wishing to alter the established values...to make serious what appears insignificant to a man, and trivial what is to him important" (Virginia Woolf 1958: 81).

The women writers like Shashi Deshpande have used fiction to explore and share their experiences. The myriad conflicts, which they face in everyday lives, are woven into the fictional world of their creation. In their writings, men portray women as they want them to be. Even Swami Vivekanand, when questioned about the women of India at the Shakespeare Club in Pasadena, California, on 18 Jan., 1900, spoke about the ideals of Indian womanhood (as desired by the so-called patriarchs at the same time humbly admitting that he found his knowledge of Indian women 'not to be so complete'). Therefore, Avadesh Kumar is not wrong when he says:

> Only she, not he, knows what she experiences, so only she can speak of it. (Jasbir Jain and Avadesh Kr Singh 2001: 119)

Thus, it is quite appropriate to deem Shashi Deshpande's writings as more appropriate psychological study of gender issues in India.

Gender studies and gender issues gained momentum in 1960s and 1970s and thus tried to raise women's consciousness against their victimization. The gender issues raised by the Indian women novelists including Shashi Deshpande in their works can be taken as reaction of women to life, their status at home, and to society that has shaped and defined the lives of men and women all over the world. The issues covered by these women novelists include political, economic, socio-cultural, literary, religious and legal sphere of life. Gender issues raised by the novelist show:

> ...an awareness of patriarchal control, exploitation and oppression at the material and ideological levels of women's work and in society in general, and conscious action by women and men to transform the present situation. (Bhasin and Khan 2003: 3)

Thus, it is aptly clear that the gender issues raised by Shashi Deshpande resist presence of sexism, male-domination and patriarchy. Discrimination between the sexes in India begins at the time of birth, or even before it. It starts before the child is born, in the mother's womb. None of the conventional blessings showered upon a pregnant woman mention daughters. A woman in India is made to feel morally obliged to bear a son. Her married life may be a round of frustrating pregnancies. It is not uncommon for people to snigger at families with several daughters: "poor things, they'd been trying so hard for a son but all God seemed to have given them is daughters".

This desire for a male child has been found in virtually all the known cultures, and it has assumed varying intensity and significance through human history. Its obsessive presence in contemporary India is partly historical and partly socio-cultural. It underscores the unchanging rarities of social life and erupts in a cyclical pattern of the most primitive kind. The present-day spate of female infanticide and foeticide are only two of its more extreme forms of current manifestation. A *Times of India's* report (2 May 1993) alleged that the increasing abuse of amniocentesis, along with female foeticide and infanticide, and the facility of pre-selection of sex through spermosorting could mean that in about twenty-five years, the ratio of females to males in Rajasthan could be a mere 1:3. It appears to be only one of the several media warnings that appear to have no effect on the general Indian attitude of preference for the son.

The fact remains that girl infanticide is a common practice in almost all the parts of India. Though orthodox patriarchal regime gives the father absolute control over the lives of his children, yet social practice usually limits this power in the case of the male child. What Simone de Beauvoir has stated in reference to the Western countries also holds true in the case of Indian patriarchal society:

> Every normal new born male is allowed to live, whereas the custom of exposing girl infants is widespread. (Simone de Beauvoir 1989: 114).

Thus, it can be firmly maintained that daughters are the primary victims of infanticide. Killing female children was a 'routine practice' in medieval India and it was probably responsible for the statistical imbalance of males over females. A husband of the first century B.C. instructed his wife:

> If, as well may happen, you give birth to a child, if it is a boy let it live; if it is a girl, expose it. (Adrienne Rich 1976: 185-86)

The presence of such a practice of killing girl child in Indian society even in the ancient times can't be denied as the female sex has been devalued here, since time immemorial. According to a *Times of India* report dated August 23, 1992:

> The methods used to murder female infants include feeding them with the milky extract of the *erukammpal* shrub or paddy grains in hot milk. A new born girl may also have its face covered with a damped towel and then be turned over; drowned in a bucket of water; smothered

with pillows; fed pesticide or overdosed with sleeping pills. (*Times of India* 1992)

There is a certain section in the society that supports female infanticide and refuses to admit it as a sin. They attribute their support to female infanticide for the reason that they (mothers) don't want the pattern repeated in the lives of their daughters. This kind of rationalization has its roots in a close-minded conservatism for which our ancient texts have provided enough fodder. This section of the society believes that the daughter's birth is not welcome not because she is not loved but because she is a source of anxiety. Parents dread the kind of high moral expectations society places upon women, and are anxious not to have a daughter because they will have to be perpetually concerned for her reputation and well-being.

Birth of a daughter in an orthodox patriarchal family is a let-down in some absolute sense. A woman who bears a son, on the other hand, is exalted as someone who has fulfilled her mission as a female. She herself is conditioned into experiencing a sense of achievement at having done so. There are several other factors which make parents feel daughter as a burden and one such factor is that a girl's stay at her father's home is short spanned as she has to go her husband's home after her marriage. Moreover, even if we concede that the girl is an alien in her father's home, it is man-made laws and social strictures that make her so. Right from the birth, a girl is made to feel like a bird of passage in her father's home. Even, allegedly liberal Indian parents are prone to harp on facts like dowry, marriage, security, vulnerability, etc. as reasons for regarding daughter as a liability or a burden. In the Indian society, a girl is generally considered as a compulsion rather than a choice. She learns it quite early in her life that she is a second-class citizen even in her mother's home. If she has brothers, she has to play second fiddle to them. It is she who is roped in to share the domestic chores and she plays mother to her younger siblings. Her breaking-in is all the more rigorous if she happens to belong to an economically deprived class, for even in the best of the worlds the girl-child's needs are generally regarded as dispensable.

In the patriarchal society, self-effacement is considered as a female attribute. The orthodox requirement for the proper conduct of bhojana decree, among other things, is that a person had to leave some part of his food on his plate, and that these remains were to be given to one's *wife, servant or slave*. The assumption that women should willingly submerge even the desire for food until everyone else in the family has eaten has been developed into an imperative which the Indian woman learns to accept from a very early stage. Her own mother, having been lulled to sleep each night on the song of deprivation, is conditioned to regard this as a female legacy which is her duty as a concerned mother to impart to her daughter. Girls in the orthodoxical families are prepared to accept that all the males related to her can control her life but she can't control her own life. She prepares herself for the ultimate goal—marriage—and grooms herself in a way that would make her transition from daughter to wife as smooth as possible. These so-called feminine attributes are the result of relentless indoctrination from the early years of a daughter's life.

The sense of responsibility is ushered into girl's psyche quite early. She is repeatedly made aware that her time in her father's home is short spanned and that there is another home that will one day be hers. In the Indian context, where home, family and community are still so significant in one's relationship with the world, the girl child lives from the start in a kind of 'isthmus of a middle state'. She is told that she would have to leave for her 'real' home one day, but she is also taught to sense that the other place is a hostile one where happiness is chancy, perhaps never to be found. Girls/daughters/women have had no part in policy-making. They can't question man-made strictures or argue against a patriarchal notion with any strength or conviction. A female is never allowed independence of action. An Indian woman is to be under her father's control in childhood, her husband's once married, and her son's when widowed. A daughter's role is null in the scheme of things. The patriarchal society even warns against choosing a brotherless girl for wife. Within the four walls of patriarchal homes, the boy's indiscretions and failings, his whims and tantrums, are more bearable than his sister's. If the family's resources are limited, it is the girl's education which is given the least importance. If both son and daughter wish to opt for a more exclusive or expensive vocational course, the boy gets first preference. Middle-class girls are educated largely as a concession to a superficial social change. In the new executive culture, a personable wife has become a necessary appendage. Matrimonial advertisements frequently mention at least a B.A. degree as one of the necessary assets of a would-be-bride. Large numbers of girl-women are now enrolling for degrees as a result, though many leave half-way if 'good match' is procured. Those who persevere to finish usually abandon all intellectual pursuits after marriage and settle down to the more '*serious*' business of becoming good wives and mothers. The preference given to boys over girls in matters such as education is hardly peculiar to India. But the extent of the insistence on such discrimination has been historically and traditionally prescribed and therefore indisputable even in the present-day. Probably, such sanction reinforces other prejudices and works toward limiting the freedom of choice for the girls in the most situations.

Many of the prejudices prevalent in the patriarchal society are based on biological differences between male and female and which are entirely superfluous. The attitude towards menstruation constitutes the most obvious example of the way in which a purely biological difference has been manipulated and imbued with unfounded biases. Strictures about the treatment of menstruation are recent in nearly all the major world religions. In India, the various religious cultures are unanimously agreed in their reservations about a simple physical process like menstruation. Manu in *Manusmriti* warns man not to lie in the same bed as a menstruating woman or even converse with her. In the patriarchal and gender-biased society, it is believed that having sex with a menstruating woman makes a man loose his wisdom, strength, sight, energy and longevity. Indian woman is still forbidden entry into the kitchen and cannot openly and frankly participate in a religious ritual. They are completely segregated during these three or four days. The general feeling that menstrual blood is somehow polluting and unclean still prevails in the orthodox Indian society. Shashi Deshpande has realistically depicted the plightful condition and treatment of menstruating women in India in her novels.

Shashi Deshpande is a great observer and she has keenly observed the gender bias in Indian society and she has put on horse blinders while depicting the plight of a girl/daughter who struggles hard throughout her life. A middle-class girl, who manages to transcend various social gender limitations, does well in school and university and eventually gets a job, learns all too early that her job is something tolerated for the most part. It is seen as economic boost in some cases, a matter of pride in some other (particularly if the job is a prestigious one), but very rarely as a serious viable alternative to her *real* vocation in life, viz. marriage. That is why a daughter with a job is never let off her share of domestic responsibility. A son, on the other hand, is never expected to help in the routine of domestic chores. Once he begins to earn, he is handled with kid gloves and treated as a creature with a special needs and cares. The girl, in India, has to create a balance between her job outside the house and domestic chores. Her working outside the home is tacitly assumed to be superfluous and dispensable, even if she is professionally successful. It is hardly ever viewed as a possible means of self-fulfilment for a woman.

Child marriages are still rampant in India especially rural India in spite of punitive laws forbidding them. In rural India, it is still advocated that the girl should be married just before puberty or immediately on reaching it. The so-called patriarchs believe that a man ought to give his daughter to "a suitable man" even if she is too young for marriage. Widowers with grown-up children commonly marry young virgins in rural India, even today, without ostensibly arousing either the indignation or protest of the community. On the other hand, widow remarriage is hardly ever heard of, and it is almost inconceivable that it could take place without provoking strong reactions or, at the very least, malicious gossip. The age of the bride and the bridegroom... is only one among several other factors which reassert gender discrimination. The mass of details which specify the suitability of a bride out-weighs those set down for a suitable bridegroom.

Thus, the subject of girl child marriage in Indian society is another issue which highlights continued sexual discrimination that too of the most abhorrent kind. Deshpande has highlighted this issue in her novels. Sakina Yusuf Khan has stated in her article:

> ...at least five hundred child marriages took place in Jaipur district itself on *Akha Teej* day this year, while in other parts of the state, the number reached a few thousand (*Times of India* 1993)

What is most surprising is that all these marriages take place in violation of Child Marriage Restraint Act. *Akha Teej* is Rajasthan's child marriage festival. Even the efforts of the government to stop such marriages by carrying out surprise checks have been in vain as the perpetrators of this practice hoodwink the government by holding the ceremony on some other auspicious day.

Another burning problem prevalent in the patriarchal society is that a daughter is considered as a burden to be disposed of. Most of the families still feel a sense of irrational horror at the thought of a daughter remaining unmarried even if she is economically independent and seems reasonably self-content. The phobia of having an unmarried daughter in the family can be traced to *shashtra* which still exercise insidious influence on the contemporary mainstream consciousness in India. Though *grahasthashrama* is considered as an important phase in a man's life, yet celibacy is permitted if he desires so. But an unmarried daughter is considered as a blot on the family's escutcheon. As P.V. Kane quoted in *History of Dharmshastra* says:

> A man could remain celibate all his life, while at least in medieval and modern time's marriage has been an absolute necessity for every girl. (P.V. Kane 1941: 438)

Those who support this view have a variety of reasons for doing so, primarily economic one as keeping the unmarried daughter for the whole of their lives incurs great expenditure. These retrograde views may be the outcome of a closed world syndrome of the middle-class parents who are prepared to go to any length to get their daughters married off and to ensure that they stay married and do not return to their parents. The girls are not usually permitted celibacy for the reason that an unmarried girl who is not in the first flush of youth is considered, somehow, tainted. Shashi Deshpande touches this issue in many of her novels including *A Matter of Time*.

In the orthodox patriarchal society, privileges of gender are present even within the privileged castes. For example, a Brahmin male can marry a bride belonging to a lower caste but a similar concession is not given to a Brahmin girl. Thus, it becomes apparent that privileges of gender are present even within the privileged castes. Though the union of a Brahmin girl with a non-Brahmin boy is legally permissible, yet the marriage does not get the much desired socio-legality. The fact that a Brahmin female's union with a non-Brahmin boy is not accepted socially is an indication of a way of life born of feudal patriarchy. It shows that notion of the supremacy of male partner in any male-female relationship is universal and deeply embedded in the human consciousness. In Indian society, it is believed that if a man marries beneath his caste, he elevates his wife but a woman marrying beneath her caste is dragged down. Therefore, it is desirable in the patriarchal society that no woman should marry beneath her caste and this notion in itself is biased.

The practice of female circumcision in certain sections of Indian society and in several Muslim cultures throughout the world is cruelly discriminatory both in the motives behind the act and in the community's attitude towards it. The term 'female circumcision' is in itself deceptive for the purpose it describes is enormously different from that of male circumcision. A male child's circumcision is supposed to serve the purpose of enhancing sexual gratification, whereas in the girl its purpose is to obliterate all sexual and erotic enjoyment. Nawal al Saadawi, an Egyptian doctor who was herself circumcised at six, comments bitterly on the 'irony' implicit in the fact that:

> The society looks at the woman as a tool of love and deprives her of the one organ which will make her good at it. (Vrinda Nabar 1995: 86)

For the female, *khatna* is neither an entrance into the community nor a positive sign of adulthood. On the contrary, it is a disciplinary action which is perceived as necessitated by the maturing of a girl. It is something to be done but not to be celebrated as against the circumcision of boys, which is celebrated with all the pomp and show.

Although Shashi Deshpande has not touched this issue in her novels, yet it remains one of the most important gender issues of great concern to the orthodox patriarchal Indian society.

Lots of emphases on a woman's honour as well as the methods and strictures laid down to preserve it mean that as a girl grows up, the burden of shame that accompanies femaleness makes it difficult for her to regard her body as something to be proud of. Ironically, for a culture that lays so much stress on female adornment, we have a traditional horror against the concept of the body as worthy of admiration. In spite of the unabashed nudity of our ancient sculpture, the stress has been laid primarily upon concealment than display. This kind of stereotyped image, which is embedded deep in the creative consciousness is one of the most dangerous cultural prejudices because it is the most difficult to eradicate. Any digression from the accepted norms on the part of woman is condemned as sinful, corruptive and, therefore, undesirable. Another trivial example is the way in which conservatism in dress code continues to shape our ideas of what is decent or indecent. While Indian men have more or less uniformly adopted broadly Western mode of dress, women are still confined to wearing *sarees* or, more recently, the north Indian *salwar kameez*. It may be argued that the jeans and t-shirts generation is very much part of our scene now, but this would be true of only a very small section of even the urban population. Moreover, this *freedom* is by and large tolerated *before* marriage. After marriage, for the most part a woman is expected to revert to the more traditional forms of dresses, especially on formal/religious occasions. Another basic corollary of the code of concealment for a woman is that even today forms of dress could be associated with moral values. In the more conservative parts of India, an elderly woman in trousers would certainly arouse sniggers from men. A slight degree of flamboyance in dress or behaviour is interpreted as ambiguous or inappropriate. Similarly, the girls who do not conform to the traditional mode of dress are termed as 'loose' or 'immoral'. The sexual harassment of college-going girls is routinely justified on the ground that *they ask for it* by dressing provocatively. The onus is clearly on the girl alone. Worse, it is frequently argued that boys/men are *naturally* libidinous and therefore not to be held accountable for their sexual misdemeanours if girls/women set themselves out to 'deliberately' provoke them.

In India, little attention is given to the nightmarish harassment most of the girls face in their growing years. Mostly, this kind of harassment of girls by males (known or unknown to her) goes unnoticed because girls/daughters are conditioned to suppress the harassment out of a sense of fear and shame. Girls in the patriarchal society are taught to think of their growing bodies as shameful and to conceal any signs of natural female curves. Adolescent and teenage girls in India even today instinctively flinch when they see a group of boys approaching them from the opposite direction. They grow expert at holding their books, bags or any thing they have with them as shields to protect themselves from those groping fingers. Although the sexual harassment of adolescent/young girls is more or less global yet the Indian girls are ill-equipped to handle such situations. Her cultural conditioning keeps her rooted in fear, shame and guilt. She is schooled into believing that her relationship with the male sex will be censored and, therefore, the question of discussing any experience of sexual harassment does not arise at all. An unpleasant encounter is usually suppressed, because these subjects are not open to frank discussion. Moreover, she is ashamed, even scared, that she will be accused of having provoked the incident. Thus, Indian society, which is primarily patriarchal in nature, refuses to acknowledge the large-scale prevalence of girl child abuse and incest.

The Indian girl goes through girlhood, preparing for the *big event* in her life: *marriage*. She may have her marriage arranged while she is still a little girl. She may or may not be married off before puberty, but she lives in a sort of limbo (uncertainty) where every freedom and joy is a temporary one. Married, she enters a new phase of bondage and subordination. Vrinda Nabar has written a very beautiful piece in verse to highlight this bondage not of one woman but of entire womanhood:

> Bring out the silver and polished the brass
> Brush off the cobwebs and clean all the glass
> Unlock the pantry, lay out the food
> Keep away grandma, her manners are crude.
>
> We have got a daughter we are willing to sell
> His is the bargain, the profit as well:
> He is coming to see for himself, so he said,
> How she and our money would look in his bed.
>
> Our daughter's a graduate, he's no cause to moan
> She's a well brought up girl with no mind of her own
> She speaks English well, has a fair pretty face,
> And is five-foot four inches by Lord Bhagwan's grace.
>
> Of course she'll be happy, I'll tell you that flat;
> She'll have her own home, produce brat after brat,
> Forget all her youth as she spins out her life
> In waddling behind him, a good Indian wife.
>
> And she'll long to have sons: they are boons from above
> Take it from me that they are proof of God's love
> And when all her daughters are suitably grown,
> She will marry them off as we have done our own.
>
> (Vrinda Nabar 1995: 97-98)

Thus, marriage seems to be the only end towards which, as all the girls are conditioned to believe, they should be moving to.

The sole purpose of the marriage for a woman seems to bear children especially sons to her husband so as to carry on the family lineage. Any woman who fails in doing so is given the onus of her barrenness irrespective of the fact that a man may be even responsible for her inability. Manu believed that woman is the field and man is the seed. It, thus, means responsibility in the process of child-bearing lies more on the shoulders of men. However, the manifestation of social attitudes in matters such as child-bearing show how even conservatism can conveniently look the other way when patriarchal well-being is threatened.

Manu's strictures, if accepted in toto, would mean that the onus of what was procreated rested with man, but even the most rigid traditionalist would prefer to ignore *this* ruling while supporting most others which support patriarchies. Social experience clearly points to the fact that all blame for alleged inadequacies in the processes of childbirth, from actual conception to the sex of the child and its safe delivery is attributed to woman only. Many women in orthodox patriarchal society set off on a series of pilgrimage to propitiate the God so that he may bless her womb with a male foetus. It is usually the woman who is termed as 'barren', not the male who can be responsible for her 'barrenness'. If a woman is unable to conceive a child especially a *male* child, then she is held solely accountable for this inability. Most men are reluctant to test themselves for possible sexual inadequacies. They get most angry what their virility is questioned. Stories of women being abandoned by their husbands for their alleged inability to bear a son are not uncommon.

All the *pativratas* like Sita and Savitri have ever been glorified in the Indian patriarchal culture. Even the contemporary Bollywood movies continue to present sickeningly submissive women who are worshipped by their macho sons because of the way in which they had held the family together in spite of drunken and violent husbands. What is questionable here is not the heroism of a woman who struggles against all the odds to support those she cares for but the sociological assumption that this is the stuff the good woman/wife/mother is made of: acceptance and endurance beyond all bounds of human patience. Such idealization of female martyrdom is the cultural legacy of all those self-denying women of fortitude of whom Sita is the most popular. A family in which the men openly batter their women should really be questioned whether it has any *izzat* left to speak of. But this is never the case: *izzat* seems to be a female-linked commodity. Its preservation is incumbent upon the woman's behaviour alone and it appears to be the male prerogative to ensure that she does not jeopardize its delicate balance at any cost.

In the patriarchal society, a woman is expected to surrender her own existence. After all, a woman is considered as a commodity which is owned by her husband and she has no personality or identity of her own. This patriarchal notion is implicit in the global practice of changing a woman's surname after marriage, which passes the feudal ownership of the woman from father to husband. In some sections of Indian society, however, it is fairly usual even now for the husband to change his wife's *first* name as well. Nothing could be more symbolic of feudal ownership of a woman than this unambiguous assumption that, with marriage, the woman's entire past becomes separate and unconnected with her married life. Moreover, since a name may be seen as conferring a form of identity, distinctiveness, such a practice implies that it is the husband's prerogative to obliterate his wife's identity, if he wishes so, and to give her a new one of his own choice. Girls are conditioned to submit willingly to their husbands' priorities. She is expected to submit to her husband's will even if the price to be paid by her is self-obliteration. This so-called *bhartiya naree* is some one who is self-effacing, self-denying and given to making a door mat of herself. This loss of identity can be perceived in other aspects also. A woman may be a pilot, a captain, an IAS, an Officer, etc., but at every step she is made to realize that she is first a woman than any one else.

Purdah is one of those indigenous symbols whose relevance and validity is strictly female-defined. A physical symbol like *purdah* may signify a whole way of life and, in turn, incorporate several other modes of discrimination. Literally and etymologically, *purdah* means 'curtain' or *ghunghat. Purdah* or curtain signifies concealment of what lies on the other side. The etymological meaning of the term *purdah* in itself is indicative of its gender-related implications. Recent studies of *purdah* system have also shown that its observance does not indicate merely the practice of sexual discrimination but could also signify subtle social as well as class distinctions. Among Indian Muslims, the cut, the style and the material of *purdah* would indicate the woman's status. Thus, in a class society, *purdah* divides not merely women from men but also amongst themselves. It implies proprietary rights over one's woman, and is an affirmation of the need to impose more strict control over them. This *closed-mind* syndrome is quite distressing because it tacitly accepts the most glaring injustices and views them as given and unchangeable. Anees Jung in one of her books has stated that how her efforts to convince an old woman that one-sided observance of *purdah* is arbitrary. Anees tried to convince the old woman quoting from Quran:

> The rule of modesty applies to both men and women.... The need for modesty is the same, both in men and women. (Anees Jung 1990: 33)

But the old woman seemed reluctant to be convinced. Here, *purdah* is symbolic of *closed-mind* syndrome which is misused by males to assert their dominance. The fact remains that however well presented a rationale which argues in favour of *purdah/ ghoonghat,* etc. their essential oppressiveness can't be disguised especially when they are restricted to one half the population of any country/culture and are defined in terms of gender alone. There is very much reason to insist that the men who uphold the continuance of restrictive women-related codes are only exploiting the women who are forced to observe these codes.

Few issues today draw as much attention of researchers, planning groups, grass-root workers and social reformers as the multiple and complex problems pertaining to women. Approaches to the study of women range all the way from the problems of girlhood to the problems of married women. But the one important issue related to women which has been generally ignored and shunned is the problem of the widows. A widow in the patriarchal society has to face the problem of economic, emotional and social adjustment. As such widowhood compels the woman to reassess her own worth and ability in the light of her changed position. One fact that must not be forgotten, in the Indian context, is that the responsibilities of *grahasth ashrama* are well suited to the male order. The second marriage is considered (in case he gets widower) necessary for him as he has to fulfil his obligation as a householder. On the other hand, a widow has supposedly no obligation except sticking to her husband's memories. In Hindu culture, a widow is supposed to wear white, to curb her impulses and emotions and to sleep on a mat instead of cot or bed. The most psychologically devastating effect of widowhood on the widow is that the sight of a widow before setting out of the house is taken to be indicative of certain failure. She is considered as the most inauspicious among all the inauspicious things. Even in today's rural India, tonsuring of widows is the prescribed practice. Some other rituals which depict the gender discrimination in the society are the melodramatic way in which the glass bangles which are symbolic of marital bliss are broken. She is forbidden to eat beetle, non-vegetarian food and wearing red, green or other bright coloured dress or to participate in any socio-religious rituals. Whatever may be the reason for the origin of the rituals such as tonsuring of widows they only accentuates the unequal basis of the male-female position in the society. Widowhood is considered for a woman as a fate worse than death. The most blessed fortune a woman can/could hope for is/was to precede her husband into the grave, to die as a *suhaagan,* with the red-parting in her hair or a *bindi* on her forehead intact. This *suhaagan* mystique still dominates our responses and ways of feeling in the society. The orthodox society gives such an unfair treatment to widows that they are forced to spend their lives as abhorred destitute. The *Ghats* at Varanasi and the temples at Puri are graphic reminders of the pitiable plight of a large number of widows driven out by orthodox society. Every now and then we hear and read about the battles in court widow woman has to fight for her rights in her 'own' home.

The *mangal-sutra*, tied by the husband round the bride's neck during the marriage ceremony, is another gender-based symbol of matrimony. Any attempt to analyze all these practices should take into account the fact that they not merely imply gender discrimination but, worse, they are accessible to a married woman only as long as her husband is alive. A woman once widowed is compelled to stop wearing them willy-nilly. As against the practice, there are no binding symbols of matrimony in relation to a husband/widower. Thus, these practices become discriminatory twice over.

Another issue that seems to be an offshoot consequence of widowhood is the practice of *Sati*. It was legally prohibited in 1829 by the British Governor, Lord Bentick. Though its occurrence is less frequently noticed after its official outlawing, occasional *Satis* are not unknown. Most horrifying case in this regard is that of Roop Kanwar. Several hundreds of people thronged to her village in Rajasthan to witness mutely the incident. Vishal Mangalwadi reported:

> ...the horror of a young girl being buried alive under firewood, screaming for help, receiving none and the fire being relit to ensure her end, with crowds of people watching all the while. (*Indian Express* 1987)

Another fact that infixes the hair of the reader is that is the description that how women are intoxicated and sedated before they are dragged off to become *Satis,* so that they are insensible to their physical pain and don't scream when the flames engulf them. The heart stirring question that arises is that why all such expectations as becoming Sati after the death of the husband, are expected of a woman in a patriarchal society which does not prescribe any such practice for men.

Most of the times, the violence in marital life is triggered off by greed. Many of the harassment cases concerning young married women are dowry related. Dowry is the modernized version of the concept of *stridhan*. It literally means a woman's property. The term was commonly used to refer to gifts given to the daughter by her parents at the time of marriage. In today's consumeristic world, this *stridhan* includes clothes for the bridegroom's family members; acquisitions such as TV, fridge, utensils, car/scooter, furniture followed by a non-stop flow of commodities at every festival, year after year. In spite of the persistent campaign against dowry, such undercover giving and receiving remains unaffected. As long as this practice continued as a sacrosanct and did not cause much emotional inconvenience to girl's family, it was alright. But, with the passage of the time, this expectation of gifts in the form of dowry has turned epidemic as well as endemic. The bridegroom family believes bride's parental home as proverbial magic pitcher which has infinite capacity to produce more, no matter how often it is emptied. The most ugly manifestation of dowry lies in the fact that now dowry has become a precondition of the girl's marriage. The bride's father gives according to his means, frequently out of proportion to them, borrowing if necessary, since he believes that his daughter's prestige and happiness are at stake. The spectre of having one's daughter rejected and unmarried or having the marriage called off at the eleventh hour if the price paid does not match the expectation seems to deaden the scepticism of the most self-avowedly progressive fathers.

Once married, girls are coerced into asking their fathers for additional gifts and tortured if these are not forthcoming. In some cases, they are ruthlessly done away with. The practice of dowry takes a heinous shape when these innocent girls/brides are murdered, poisoned or even burnt alive. The sad truth in most of such cases is that the girls murdered for dowry have tried to apprise their parents of the way things are, but only to be told to endure their tortures silently. The repercussions of having a married daughter returned to her father's home are usually too dejecting for these parents, making them unwilling to listen to their daughter's grievances. These repercussions include the gossip of neighbours and the community, the sense of humiliation and shame, the possibility that such an eventuality would jeopardise the marriage-prospects of their other unmarried daughters by affecting the family honour, and so on. His (father's) responsibility ends with the marriage of his daughter; what happens to her after marriage is her fate (as he thinks). The patriarchal families (including the female patriarchs such as mother, grandmother, etc.) believe daughters to be burdens to be taken off the shoulders. Dowry-related deaths have received considerable attention, but they have not been eye-openers in any revolutionary sense. Dowry is still demanded discreetly or blatantly, and is given. The going rate depends on the boy's profession and his consequent value in the marriage market. Shashi Deshpande has depicted this problem in her novel *The Binding Vine*.

The ordeal of getting a girl married off has acquired grotesque dimensions in the Indian society. Female foeticide/infanticide is among its most tragic manifestations. If the girl survives either of these fates, other horrors await her. The more bizarre consequences of this continuance of a rapacious practice are seen in the suicide of the three young sisters in Kanpur in UP, who hanged themselves to escape the misery and humiliation of being born into a family which could not afford to provide suitable dowries. Due to lack of suitable dowries, they could not hope to find suitable matches. The three daughters mentioned above hanged themselves because they were unwilling to survive in such a system or to see their father humiliated on their behalf. They paid the price for living in an unfair world where their worth was determined by their father's financial status. To quote Vrinda Nabar:

> ...they made their own fatal choice: they opted out of the system while they were able to. They chose death rather than a fate *literally* worse than death. (Vrinda Nabar 1995: 165)

One of the other manifestations of dowry can be seen in the 'sale' of innumerable young Muslim girls to aged Arab visitors, who sexually exploit and then abandon them. The most talked about case in this regard is that of eleven years old Amina from Hyderabad, who was spotted by an air hostess on board. Enquiries revealed that Amina had been married off to a fifty-seven years old Arab national and that, she was unhappy and unwilling to accompany him. Amina was rescued by an air hostess but what about the pitiable plight of other *Aminas* who are *sold* in the name of marriage to be abandoned finally. Later many of these abandoned innocent girls are compelled to take to prostitution to live their lives. The case of Afzal Begam is a much talked one. This girl of fourteen was married to a sixty-two years old Arab who actually *chose* her in preference to her elder sister who was to be his bride, took her to a hotel, deflowered her virginity, and disappeared from her life after a few days, leaving her pregnant. Such a plight of a woman is really a shameful blot on the escutcheon of the patriarchal society whose walls of patriarchy stand firmly on the foundation of gender discrimination.

Another important gender bias that can be seen in the Indian society is that 'sexual experience' is considered exclusively a 'male prerogative'. It could be explored, dissected, and mulled over with infinite enjoyment by men. However, this patriarchal society does not give the same kind of licence to women. If a woman volunteers to discuss or express her opinion of sexual experience, she is termed as a *whore* or *loose*. Writing of the married women in the 1950s, Simone de Beauvoir had observed that a woman is expected to have sexual pleasure only in a specific role, i.e. as a wife. No objections! Especially in the context of Indian woman. But the worst of her situation lies in the fact that she is even denied gratification of her sexual desire within the institution of marriage. Female sexuality is considered as a sexual taboo in the Indian society. There has been no overt change in the Indian attitude to sex and the Indian women. Moreover, since 'arranged marriages' remain the rule, the possibilities for the manifestation of female sexuality remain by and large insignificant. Female virginity is still imperative in an arranged marriage. A wife is supposed to serve her husband with '*tan*', '*man*' and '*dhan*' (as the modern Indian woman has also started working outside the home thereby boosting the family income). At the same time, she is supposed to hide her feelings about sex and most of the husbands don't take into consideration the need of thinking about the sexual fulfilment of their wives. A husband can think of 'having' a extramarital relationship and can have children too in 'that' relation, but a married woman can't even think of extramarital relationship and if she dares to do so she is socially boycotted.

Another important issue that is worth mentioning here is that of subordination and subjugation of women within the four walls of home. The Indian wife is not only a martyr to her husband's needs but also to his family members. In innumerable urban middle-class homes, even today, husbands expect their wives to fetch and carry every thing, from a glass of water to their shoes and socks. Indian parents of a girl are more anxious to avoid the charge that they have not shaped their daughter through the process of self-denial and self-effacement, and thus they begin moulding her from girlhood in the role she would be called upon to play after her marriage. Once engaged, she moves towards a more specific aim: to approximate the ideal wife. If she performs this role well, she is praised even by people with allegedly radical views. To quote Vrinda Nabar:

> In Indian context...motherhood has long been a category which is emphasised, a role which the girl child is conditioned to accept as the end she has been created for. (Vrinda Nabar 1995: 178)

In *Manusmriti*, the mother is given an elevated position even higher than that of a father. But it has remained merely a lip service. In practice, she becomes the subservient doormat in most of the homes. She looks after the needs of others but at the same time is unmindful of her own needs. In case *she* gets widowed/abandoned young, *she* endures all kind of hardships, puts up with all kind of humiliation, and attempts hard to rear her children. She may have a drunken husband who beats her with sickening regularity, or a lecherous employer who tries to molest her, but her fate is clear: *she* represents Indian womanhood and subordination, subjugation, exploitation, suffering and sacrifice are her lot. This kind of *ideal image* has been deliberately imposed on her since girlhood so as to propagate male chauvinism without any protest or resistance. These so-called male chauvinists make her accept that *child bearing* and *child rearing* are her inseparable lot. In fairly progressive homes, even today, the woman is expected to serve the guests and the rest of the household and eating only after males have finished.

The nuclear family is a recent urban phenomenon, and housing conditions in the metropolitan cities are making it increasingly difficult for this new phenomenon (nuclear family) to survive. Many young couples are forced to move in with their parents resulting in a sort of pressure upon the woman especially if she is a working woman. She is answerable to a series of relationships on her husband's side. She is expected to fulfil the dual responsibilities—at home as well as at the working place—passively. The kind of back-breaking drudgery this could involve, may be gauged from the fact that the average Indian housewife lacks even the basic time saving household gadgets seen as essential by her Western counterparts. She goes through a daily routine of washing, cooking and shopping for groceries and vegetables. The archetypal Indian male is not given to worrying his head about the trivia of domestic routine. It is expected that the womanhood will uncomplainingly take care of these even if she has another full time job outside the home. In a typical Indian home, children are seen as the mother's sole responsibility. The father does his share of load by working to support the family and enjoys a special status which even the entry of women into the workforce hasn't eroded. Being sandwiched between the dual roles, she seems to be sapped of her vitality. Her natural affection and desire to nurture is transformed into an exaggerated image of subservience and martyrdom. This typified and glorified image of a so-called ideal woman can be even seen on TV screens. As Vrinda Nabar says:

> *She* is the wonder woman of the new commercials. *She* is Lalita ji, determined to stretch the budget and use money judiciously by opting for Surf from among all the detergents available.... (Vrinda Nabar 1995: 182)

In other words, exploitation, suffering and sacrifice are her lot which she should face bravely and silently. We have seen that the issues of concern to feminists in India are different (to some extent at least) from that of their Western counterparts. Indian feminism is not all about burning bras but asserting 'her' place, not as an entity but as a human being. The word 'feminism' has a negative connotation in the Indian perspective as it had in Western perspective. Any woman is referred to as a feminist whenever she expresses her sentiments of displeasure on being treated as 'door-mat' or as an object of sex. If this yardstick is to be taken into the paradigm, then Shashi Deshpande, an emerging Indian woman novelist is a feminist or a propagandist writer of gender issues. Despite of having only seven novels to her credit, Deshpande has emerged as one of the mainstream women writers in India today. Her work is comparable to that of the established writers like Anita Desai and Nayantara Sahgal who have also registered their protest against patriarchism and male chauvinism in their writings. Her novels are concerned with a woman's quest for self; an exploration into the female psyche and an understanding of the mysteries of life and the protagonist's place in it. Her first novel marks the beginning of the quest of woman for her self. The theme is continued in her later novels and Deshpande's chief concern is with the woman and her external quest. In an interesting interview, Deshpande reveals that all her characters are concerned with their 'selves' and they learn to be honest to themselves. Being true to one's self, not as being true in the sense that nature/culture demands of you, is the wisdom the Deshpande protagonist learns towards the end of each novel.

Comparatively, Shashi Deshpande is a new name on the scene of Indian English writing. However, despite the smaller volume of her writing, her work has drawn critical attention because of her detailed, sensitive and realistic representations of the Indian middle-class women in the domestic sphere. Her concern for women and their oppression is reflected strongly in all her writing. Hers is a well-known name in the literary circle of India and she deserves a special place in the Indian English literature for depicting the quotidian life of an average Indian specially women. What has earned immense respect to her is her uncompromising stance as an Indian writer who writes in English but steadfastly resists the malaise that seems to have afflicted the current crop of Indian writers in English. She refuses to embellish and package her writings to portray India as an exotic land, full of magic and mysticism—a formula that has succeeded in gaining international readership for other Indian authors in English. The present monographic study proposes to make a keen perusal of gender issues specific to Indian society. Before moving further, it would not be out of place to make a brief study of biographical details of Shashi Deshpande.

Born in 1938, in the small town of Dharwad (north of Karnataka in India), Shashi Deshpande is the second daughter of the late Adya Rangachar 'Sriranga', the famous Kannad playwright and a Sanskrit scholar. She spent the first fifteen years of her life in that small town only. Because of her father being a celebrity of Dharwad, she was also known to every one in the small town. Despite being a Brahmin, her father never allowed her (her siblings also) to state that they were Brahmins. There were no elders in the family who could have introduced her and her siblings to the rituals and rites of a Brahmin upbringing. Having inherited her cerebral intellect from her playwright father, Shashi Deshpande started 'reading' and 'thinking' at an early age. She was a voracious reader and about her free and uncluttered upbringing, she says:

> Another thing about my father was that he never made us feel conscious that we were daughters. He never barred us from doing any thing we wanted. (R.S. Pathak 1998: 232)

As a reader, Somerset Maugham and Jane Austen have been the writers of her liking but she denies their conscious influence on her writings. She still admits of reading Jane Austen regularly. As admitted by her in an interview to Vimala Vishwanatha, she says:

> I think Jane Austen had a more lasting influence. I still read her regularly. I don't think there have been any conscious influences on my writings as such. (R.S. Pathak 1998: 233)

But at the same time, she does not deny the influences of feminists like Simon de Beauvoir, Germaine Greer, etc. She admits that a reading of these above-mentioned feminists' works stimulated her. Her reading of them also helped her to resolve her own confusions and put them in order. While reading any of her novels, one can't deny the influence of these writers on her writings as they are frequently mentioned by her. It also reveals her quality voracious readership. She may have inherited her father's intellect genetically but she denies his direct influence upon her as a writer. This difference between father and the daughter comes over the surface when we find that Sriranga's plays are more the plays of ideas whereas Shashi Deshpande's novels are not about ideas only but also about people and the relationships they live in. She says:

> He (father) was dominant, never domineering. On the contrary, if I should criticise, I would say he was somewhat detached from us...never guided us. May be if he had directed us at an early stage, I could have done better. He never did that. (R.S. Pathak 1998: 232)

Shashi Deshpande did not have a close relationship with her father. Shashi Deshpande received her education at Dharwad and

Bangalore now Bangaluru. She took her degrees in Economics and Law. In 1956, she graduated in Eco (Hons.) and that too with a Gold Medal. It was followed by a degree in Law in 1959 from Bangalore University. Though she studied Economics and Law, yet she admits that they never touched her deeply. Later she pursued postgraduation in English literature.

After her marriage to her pathologist husband, she stayed at Mumbai and during her stay at Mumbai she did a course in Journalism from Bhartiya Vidya Bhawan. She did not write any thing except school compositions and letters until she was thirty years old. She spent one year in England (as her husband was on the Commonwealth fellowship). Her husband persuaded her to write about their one year stay in England. So her journey of writing for the sake of writing began with these memoirs. She gave these handwritten memoirs to her father who got them published. After that, she entered an '*Eve's Weekly*' short stories competition and won a consolation prize. That was her first short story. In her own words:

> Then, all the stories started pouring out, as if they had been dammed in for a long time. I have never experienced that spontaneous flow again. It has always been conscious writing after that. (R.S. Pathak 1998: 238)

One of her short-stories titled "The Liberated Woman" won the prize but she realized that the theme was very complex and she decided to extend it in the form of a novel. The result was *Roots and Shadows* which could be published only after her second novel *Dark Holds No Terrors* saw the light of the day. In her own words:

> I wrote because I had to write. I never thought beyond that. Then, after I wrote my first two novels I realized I was becoming a professional and would have to work hard. People kept telling me that I had taken a good hobby. It is a profession. I will go on writing as long as I have something to say. [R.S. Pathak: 1998: 239]

The *Dark Holds No Terrors* was followed by *That Long Silence* which not only won Sahitya Akademi Award for her but also a large number of readers. In her next novel, *The Binding Vine*, she talks about the importance of sisterhood in a woman's life and the problems faced by a woman living all alone on account of her husband's job. *The Binding Vine* was her first departure as her earlier novels are internalized in their thematic tones. In 1996, she wrote *A Matter of Time* in which she writes as a writer of life and its affairs. As a writer this novel is closest to her and it has also received very good response from its readers especially from the foreign readers across the globe.

When we make a study of any 'ism', that ism may be deemed as composed of three facets: sociological, ideological and moral/ethical. Shashi Deshpande's basic concern is with that of the first two. Although the third one is linked to the first two and their inter connection can't be denied, yet Shashi Deshpande as a novelist doesn't pass on any moral/ethical judgements. To say in other words she does not assert militantly the issues like equality of the two sexes but she provides rather tries to provide a mirror to the society highlighting the inequality and gender biasedness prevalent in the society which is chiefly patriarchal in nature. For her to be a feminist in true sense, one (both a male and a female) should liberate oneself from sexist role patterns, domination and oppression.

Works Cited

Beauvoir, Simone de. *The Second Sex*. trans. H.M. Parshley. New York: Alfred Knopf, 1952; rpt. Vintage Books, 1989.

Bhasin and Khan. *Some Questions on Feminism and it's Relevance in South Asia*. New Delhi: Kali for Women, 2003.

Iyenger, Pushpa. "Girls in Salem are Born to Die". *The Times of India*, Aug 23, 1992.

Jain, Jasbir and Avdesh Singh. *Indian Feminism*. New Delhi: Creative Books, 2001.

Jung, Anis. *Unveiling India: A Woman's Journey*. New Delhi: Penguin Books, 1990.

Kane, P.V. *History of Dharamshastra*. Pune: Bhandarkar Oriental Research Inst. Pub., 1941.

Khan, Sakina Yusuf. "No Minor Offence". *The Times of India*, May 9, 1993.

Mangalwadi, Vishar. *Indian Express*. Sep. 19, 1987.

Nabar, Vrinda. *Caste as Woman*. New Delhi: Penguin Books, 1995.

Pathak, R.S. *The Fiction of Shashi Deshpande*. New Delhi: Creative Books, 1998.

Rich Adrienne. *Of Woman Born: Motherhood as Experience and Institution*. New York: W.W. Norton and Company, 1976.

Woolf, Virginia. *Women and Fiction*. New York: Hard Court Brace, 1958.

2

Co-travellers of Shashi Deshpande in English Fiction

English fiction witnessed a revolutionary transmogrification in the late 1960s with the advent of the post-modernist concept providing a new horizon to the realm of literature in general which was languishing in a state of conventionalism in themes as well as in techniques. This landmark change in thematic paradigm had been noticed in the works of many Wollstencraft and Virginia Woolf. Though the voices raised by these earlier Western feminist were universal in tone, yet similar voices in Indian literature can be heard echoing and re-echoing since the time of Savitribai Phule who along with her husband championed the cause of women education. Apart from Savitribai Phule, there was another woman named Pandita Ramabai who raised her voice for women causes. She was educated both in English and Sanskrit and in "High Caste Hindu Women", she argued against the patriarchal reading of the Hindu scriptures. She also raised her voice against the scholarly works of learned Brahmins who encouraged a repressive and demeaning interpretation favouring the suppression of women.

Towards the mid-nineteenth century more and more women began to write in English. Some of them such as Rokeya Hossain created a world of feminist ideologies. In "Sultana Dream", she talks about a world dominated by women; a world which has imprisoned men in a male equivalent of *Zenana* (women quarter). She creates a world that is much better managed than one managed in her own. Women's writing in the twentieth century moved towards a medium of modernisation in which feminist statements were combined with political messages. The writings of women such as Hamsa Wadekar conveyed an honest impression of a world of professional women who were subjected to the brutality and force of patriarchy. Women writers such as Mahashweta Devi combined women causes with political movements. Over the years and throughout the political instability which affected Indian society at large, along with a myriad of other influences which have affected culture, language and social patterns, women's literature in India has evolved to show common experiences, a sense of sisterhood and a range of female experiences that question the recurring face of patriarchy. All of these modern Indian women writers build a platform of universal female experiences. Although the contribution made by Shashi Deshpande in this stream is beyond comparison, yet to move on without making a brief study of other prominent writers will be a loophole in the present study. Another purpose behind making this keep at the related literature would be to know what has been investigated and what is yet to be investigated.

Anita Desai (b. 1937) is one of the pioneers who has given a new direction to the novel-writing by highlighting gender issues in modern India. The combined influence of the great philosophers of the West, and the fast changing elements in the social structure of India had great impact on Anita Desai. Her pre-occupation with Indian women is genuine. As a part of feminine sensibility of a rapidly changing nation, she has an opportunity of sharing the feelings of the women of various circumstances. In her novel *Fire on the Mountain*, Illa Das, a social worker, is projected as a character with all her reactions to the changing customs and cultures of the Indian society. Her sympathetic attitude for the suffering women flows like an undercurrent pervading the fictional world of Desai. Anita Desai's preoccupation with Indian women and their reaction to the far-changing situation in modern India distinguishes her from other women writers. Social comedies and tragicomedies of R.P. Jhabvala, problematic themes of Kamla Markandaya and Nayantara Sehgal's political issues have lost attraction. Anita Desai's women protagonists belong to various age-groups and are in constant conflict with the society. Most of her novels present feminine sensibility full of violent reaction to the situation they belong to. Her concern with emancipation of women and necessary steps to be taken for it, is found on page after page in her novels. Like Lawrence, she also believes in growing awareness among women of their rights and individualities. Always, through their earnest yearning for detachment, her women characters demand more freedom but each one receives the blow

> as though her feelings did not matter to anyone. (Anita Desai 1971: 136)

As a novelist, she seems deeply involved for the upliftment of women who are seen as worst sufferers, highly suppressed and oppressed by social 'tantalisation' or marital discord. Her masterpiece *Cry, The Peacock* is a typically a 'feminine novel', not because it is a story of a woman told by a woman but because it is a fruit of feminine sensibility. Maya, the pivotal character in *Cry, The Peacock* is half-neurotic due to over-attention and excessive breeding in childhood. The novel throws light on various reactions of important women characters under changing social conditions. Maya's sensitiveness obsessed by a childhood prophecy of disaster prevents her, from leading a normal life with her husband. Anita Desai's women characters are no ordinary characters. They are women of sense and sensibility. Maya is delineated as a unique character of suffering. She is representative of a class of women who suffer silently at the hands of men. The loneliness of feminine heart has been highlighted through her character:

> I can't...can't enter that silent darkened room where I should have to alone, gazing at the shadowed ceiling, the revolting fan, with no one for company, not even a stray of light.... (Anita Desai 1963: 163)

Maya, despaired by her helplessness, suffered from loneliness and searches for someone to help her. Maya's cry is the cry of an agonised woman's feeling about being lonely and unwanted. In contrast to Maya, Anita Desai places Nila, 'a new woman' who has courage to admit problems in her marital life and she seeks the help of a lawyer. Through the characters of Nila and her mother, Anita Desai represents—strength and vitality—two important aspects of feminine personality.

Anita Desai's another important novel *Voices in the City* very emphatically voices the method to gain peace and happiness by process of self-denial. Through the character of Monisha, the heroine, the novelist throws light upon stagnancy of prevailing customs by depicting generations of Bengali Women 'spending centuries' in household works. A true picture of feminine world, against which Monisha reacts, is given by the author as follows:

> Lives spent in waiting for nothing; waiting on men, self-centred and indifferent and hungry and demanding and critical, waiting for death and dying misunderstood, always behind bars, those terrifying black bars that shut us in, in the old houses, in the old city. (Anita Desai 2006: 120)

Thus, we find that in her fictional world, Anita Desai gives ample space to women—a neglected class of society. Mrs Desai, by powerful search light of her observation dives deep down and presents the world with her findings which include her prime concern to bare the simmering of emotions within, to bring out sheer womanliness in them, to prove that they are beings not actually devoid of feelings but actually in search of a bit of love and life. Mrs Desai has projected women in sober roles and has tried to focus on the submissiveness of women. By giving primary importance to individual, Mrs. Desai tries to create a balance. She dislikes the militant attitude in women and points out that the role of women changes with change in situations. To say the final word, Maya in a killer's role is as much acceptable to Anita Desai as is Sita in an unruly wife's role.

Kamla Markandaya is one of the most distinguished of the generation of Indian novelists of present generation in English who succeeded the big three—R.K. Narayan, Mulk Raj Anand and Raja Rao. Her work has been notable for an unusual combination of range and intimacy. Kamla Markandaya's novels seem to be fully reflective of the awakened feminine sensibility in modern India as she attempts to project the image of changing traditional society. Woman in different life roles is one of the quintessential themes of her fiction. The narrator in the novel *Nectar in a Sieve* is Rukmani, a rustic woman. The story of her hard peasant life illustrates the truth in Coleridge's line, "work without hope draws nectar in a sieve." Rukmani, the narrator heroine, has a heart that is tempered in love and faith, suffering and sacrifice will not accept defeat. She receives shock after shock, her husband's infidelity and later his death, her daughter's sacrificial going on the street to save the family from starvation, the death of the child. Kunthi, ejection from the house, dismal experiences as a stone-breaker and finally the return to the village with an adopted son—all these factors can't break her spirit. By projecting Rukmani amidst of all her problems, the novelist wants to portray a strong-willed woman character that does not leave hope even in the adverse circumstances. She has eternal faith in the cyclic cycle—calm after storm and spring after winter.

In her another novel, *A Silence of Desire*, Kamla Markandaya proposes that silence of woman is more powerful than her speech. The central character Sarojini is crushed by her inexplicable silence in the beginning of the novel but she is strong-willed enough to assert herself through her silence and is resilient enough to bring harmony and stability to herself and her family. The novelist emphasises the fact that there are times at which one has to maintain silence and there are times when a woman has to speak. Despite their divergent ideological stands, Dandekar and Sarojini lead a harmonious life and are blessed with children. Her secretive errands make Dandekar suspect his wife to be a soiled woman. Sarojini is a strong-willed woman who believes that her westernized husband will never approve of this kind of faith-healing (she goes to a swami to be cured of a tumour) and therefore decides individually. Through Sarojini, Kamla Markandaya depicts a woman who is not completely submissive and asserts her own viewpoint in all matters regarding faith and religion. She is an independent woman who asserts her individuality and emerges strongly to confront male quietly but insistently as wife and mother. In this sense, she marches on the long road of life towards woman's autonomy. She defies male-control and asserts her individuality as a woman. From a submissive and domesticated wife, Sarojini switches on to become an outgoing, liberated, assertive woman intent on shaping her future. Sarojini's visits to swami are symbolic of her assertion of her freedom and her claims to her individual rights. Being a liberal feminist, Kamla Markandaya has tried to create a balance and this balance she tries to project as a solution. In her fictional world, the happiness consists in returning to the fold, to time-worn society and not in running away from this society.

Though Nayantara Sahgal (b. 1937) is more known for the historical and political consciousness in her novels, yet in some of her works, she emerges out as a champion of feminist concerns. This prominent woman novelist seeks to posit the independent existence of women and atrophy all attempts to preclude them from centre-stage of human existence. In her novels, she throws light upon the parlous state of women in the parochial patriarchal society. Her women are victims of conventional society which does not permit women to hold their own identity or ideas. Sahgal has very brilliantly highlighted that women also need like men self-fulfilment, autonomy, self-realization, independence, individuality and self-actualization. Sahgal, not being a militant feminist, feels strongly about female-exploitation and male-sarcasm. Sahgal's first two women, Maya and Rashmi, are still women in stasis but her next three protagonists, namely—Saroj, Simri and Devi—mark a clear advancement from the point of view of self-determination. Quest for identity may be a Herculean task in patriarchal society and once women have strong will and determination, they act as real 'shaktis'. Maya and Rashmi are the products of parochial society where they have been conditioned in such a manner that they pursue their goals away from their homes. In her latter novels, we find women who disseminate the concept of freedom and self-realization and more importantly they do so without the aid of any male-hand. Sahgal's women protagonists of these latter mature works refuse to abide by the fossilized concept of male-supremacy and seek gender equality.

Nayantara Sahgal's Sonali, a strong-willed and emotionally independent woman, in *Rich Like Us*, is the most mature woman-character. As an uncompromising Administrative Officer, her survival instinct is very strong and instead of giving in, she gives up. By projecting the character of Anna Hansen, a Danish woman, the novelist asserts that the thirst for identity is not an Indian woman's problem alone, but a global issue. In Sahgal's last novel, we meet Ranee of Vijaygarh who is out and out a rebel. She breaks all boundaries and makes her own rules. Though she has to live life of agony, yet her mind being free, she lives her life fully. She does not wish to survive as a wife or as a mother only; it is as a person she wishes to survive. Ranee of Vijaygarh, though a nameless character, yet she marks the culmination of the onward march of Sahgal's 'new woman' towards freedom. Though confined in multiple chains, yet this woman shines in the firmament of Sahgal's fiction as the Pole Star. Though she is ignorant of women liberation, she becomes a strong practitioner of the same because she feels a strong urge to insulate her self-respect from the tyrannical forces of parochial traditional society.

Therefore, we find that using her novels as a sharp-edged weapon, Nayantara Sahgal demands social justice for women, her focus being on freedom. Sahgal's protagonists challenge the moth-eaten pretence of tradition, without suffering from loss of identity. In fact, they seem to gain a kind of individuality. They threaten the stranglehold of men and reaffirm their faith in their own potentials. The battle that starts quite demurely with Maya keeps advancing and gaining momentum through Rashmi, Saroj reaches its culmination in Sonali and finally Ranee of Vijaygarh takes it to a glorious height.

R.P. Jhabvala is a prestigious name in Indian fiction especially among women writers. In her novels, she has dealt with gender issues in general and marital discord in particular. Her characters pass through crisis after crisis and most of them are also in quest of better partner searching their hearts within. In her first novel, *To Whom She Will*, Jhabvala presents a strong-willed woman, Amrita, against a weak-willed man, Hari, who lacks courage and confidence. He falls in love with Amrita and wants to marry her but at the same time lacks courage to go against the wishes of his family. In contrast to this unheroic hero, Amrita has been presented as one who knows what she wants out of life. She has full confidence in her decisions and ultimately she decides to marry Hari, irrespective of what her family thought of him.

For her marriage is completely a personal issue and no one else should be allowed to decide their destiny.

> What does my family matter, you know? I would give up everyone and everything for you. Nothing matters, only you. (R.P. Jhavbala 1955: 29)

Amrita believes that their respective families can't come between them and they should never be able to separate them. She has been painted as a self-willed, bold and active like Isabel Archer in Henry James' *The Portrait of a Lady* or like Elizabeth Bennel in Jane Austin's *Pride and Prejudice*. Towards the end of the novel, Hari ultimately marries Sushila, a girl of his family's choice. Jhabvala upholds very strongly this self-willed heroine, Amrita.

In *The Nature of Passion*, Jhabvala does not make any personal comment or remark against dowry and leaves it to the judgement and sensibility of the reader. She shows that even in arranged marriages, discord is noticeable. It is because of this fact in today's set-up of society, dowry is bane. The dangerous devil of dowry has devoured many dear daughters of their parents. It is fully and freely demanded by the boy's family and unwillingly given by the parents of the bride. It is a kind of high premium paid for an insured life for a bride in the groom's house. Higher the groom in status and rank, the bigger is the premium of the dowry. The novelist raises the issue of dowry and holds it responsible for the community feelings in matrimonial issues. In *Nature of Passion*, the novelist shows how the members of Laljee's family totally disapprove of Nemi's affair with a Parsi boy—a boy belonging to a different community. Jhabvala presents another case of disharmony in married life in *Get Ready for Battle*. Guljari Lal and Sarla Devi are a couple married for many years. They live a married life full of dissonance and disturbance. Sarla Devi, a so-called social worker, does not live with her husband who believes in money-making morality and leads a materialistic life. Another pair in this novel is of Vishnu and Mala. Mala is a frank, fashionable and forward woman but she does not like that her husband should mix-up with un-married women. Thus, we can say that central theme of Jhabvala's fiction is the marital discord and this discord has been amply and skilfully depicted by the novelist in her works.

Born in a feudal family of Lucknow, Attia Hosain (b. 1913) spent her childhood in the company of leading intelligentsia. Attia Hosain started writing in a period which was dominated by male-writers and is known as one of the earliest female Diaspora writers from the South-Asian subcontinent. Always, a voracious reader, she resented the distinction made between sons and daughters in the family and the fact that she was not sent to Cambridge as her brother had been. In her novels, she has questioned what had been taken for granted by the other novelists. The portrayal of the woman protagonist Laila, in *Sunlight on a Broken Column*, seems to be autobiographical as Laila struggles for self-empowerment. She struggles to make her own decisions on issues that concerned her most: her marriage, her career and her future. Such attitude of Laila places her at odds with the family and society. Her life changes; life which had been restricted by invisible barriers almost as effectively as the physically restricted lives of her aunts in the *zenana*. Laila, an orphaned daughter of a distinguished Muslim family is brought up in her grandfather's household by orthodox aunts who keep *purdah*. At fifteen, she moves to the home of a liberal but autocratic uncle in Lucknow. Here, for some time she is caught up in politics. Later she gets frustrated, as she is not able to commit herself to any cause. Her own fight for independence is a struggle against the claustrophobia of traditional feminine life, from which she can only back away if she falls in love with a man whom her family has not chosen for her. With its beautiful evocation of India, its political insight and unsentimental understanding of the human heart, *Sunlight on a Broken Column* is classic of Muslim feminine life.

Bharati Mukherjee (b. 1942) is an India-born American who depicts female alienation in the contemporary society in her novels. Her fictional world is full of her discourses, though objective, on male-female dichotomy and about female identity in contemporary society which is basically patriarchal in nature. Titles of her novels indicate her concern for gender issues as most of the titles of her novels draw our attention to the gender of the female protagonist. Titles of first of her two novels—*The Tiger's Daughter* and *Wife* emphasize the colonized condition of her female characters in the patriarchal society. Tara Banerjee in *Tiger's Daughter* (like Rosa Burger in Nadine Gordimer's *Burger's Daughter*) is a daughter while Dimple Basu (wife) is a wife. However, in *Jasmine*, her third novel, there is a marked shift: a refusal to recognize restrictions and a refusal to accept invisibility. While Tara Banerjee seems very much to be an *avtar* of the author herself and Dimple seems to be a more general representative of Indian womanhood, Jasmine is representative of all womanhood.

Bharati Mukherjee's *Jasmine* can be taken as a female bildungsroman; as a novel which specifically traces the development of a female protagonist from childhood through various experiences and crisis, into maturity and more importantly, her self-identity and place in the world. The protagonist in the novel, Jasmine, is born in a family in which daughters are taken as burdens and the resultant fruits of the sins of mother not of father. She has to change her name once she gets married and thus she becomes Jasmine from Jyoti. She shuttles between two identities. Prakash's (Jyoti's husband) desire to change his wife's name from Jyoti to Jasmine is an assertion of patriarchal power, which could be the consequence of subtle, and subliminal desire to control female identity. Death of Prakash further liberates Jasmine and induces her to make all decisions herself. When she reaches America to fulfil her dead husband's wishes, she finds that the melting-pot culture of America offers no magical solution to her status as an outsider. In America, Jasmine is known as Jazzy, Jassy or Jassie which are all derivatives of Jasmine but with a little difference. At this juncture, she stops, to examine her so far tri-coloured identity. For her, Jyoti was now a sati-goddess who had burned herself in a funeral pyre. She visualizes that Jasmine lived for future whereas Jase lives for today. Now, Jase recognizes that in her first two incarnations, she was not able to liberate herself from patriarchal control. Only as Jase, she feels released from male domination on her identity, and free to define herself without any male-reference. And thus Bharati Mukherjeee like many other postcolonial women writers highlights the analogous relationship between men and women in a patriarchal system, and between colonizer and colonized in an imperial system. In this masterpiece of Bharati Mukherjee, the novelist draws our attention to male control of female identity. Jasmine recalls an incident of her childhood days in which a friend of hers, Vimla, sets herself afire because she feels herself to be without a meaningful identity. Vimla is shocked to find that there is no difference in the air inside the pitcher as outside, so also she has no identity other than the borrowed from her husband. Perhaps, this is the rationale behind a system that encourages widows to burn themselves on their husband's funeral pyres. Within the contest of this novel, Vimla is an empty shell. Jasmine identifies her power to shape her own identity. Jasmine's story insists that both inside and outside identities can be female defined. Thus, we can say that Bharati Mukherjee as a novelist of feminist concerns takes up the issues of female identity and individuality.

Gita Mehta (b. 1943) is another prominent woman-novelist and her writings make us realize that the issues related to gender can't be simply ignored. Though the deep-seated theme in her *Karma Cola* (1979) is the East-West encounter, yet the novel reflects the feminine viewpoint. It is true that the work *Karma Cola* is clearly rationalistic in its analysis of the contemporary situation and does not indulge in any gender sentimentality but it speaks of women's heart, though in low tones. Her another work *Raj* covers a turbulent period in Indian history but it is different from other contemporary pieces dealing with the lives of princes and princess in the sense that this masterpiece of Gita Mehta observes the same situation but from the viewpoint of a woman. In this novel, Gita Mehta presents a woman thrown into the fray by relentless fate that snatches away her brother, father, husband and son and leaves her alone to face the realities. The omniscient narrator picks up all the threads of the story and guides us through Jaya's life. The heroine is a mute observer of the events she can't control, be they political whereby the princes were stripped of their power; or pertaining to human weakness whereby her husband and other princes invited their downfall by their vagaries. Gita Mehta depicts the strength in her woman character by placing her heroine in circumstances, which demand her decisiveness, and tests the strength of her character. *Raj* can be termed as a saga of triumph of 'the people' of democratic principles and of a woman accepting the inevitable changes gracefully. Her candidature in the election symbolizes her inner urge for identity and service when she is commanded by her father to be trained in shooting, riding, hunting and tent-pegging, etc., she is opposed by her mother who complains that her husband is trying to make her into a son. Her mother feels that an over-educated girl will be an insult to her in-laws. Gita Mehta also gives the psychological treatment when we find Jaya discarded by her husband who says that he feels afraid that "she won't do...really won't do at all". Even then Jaya does not feel disheartened and she directs all her efforts to please, Pratap Singh, her husband. Finally, when he turns to her, she is disillusioned and dreads his company because she feels that his intimacy soils her as his remoteness had never done. By painting the character of Jaya, an unwanted wife, the novelist presents the pain of living a life without pride; a life which an unwanted wife is forced to live. Thus, Gita Mehta underscores the psychological, mental, emotional and social dilemma faced by a woman though that woman comes out as a winner in the battle of life in which she faces her own people as her enemies.

Gita Hariharan's (b. 1954) *Thousand Faces of Night* is another example of what a husband should not be. Devi's mother arranges her meetings with many boys but Devi finally marries Mahesh. There is nothing to sustain marriage, neither the husband not the wife have any interest in making the marriage work. Devi lives like a stranger in her own home; with a stranger whom she has married. Mayamma, a servant is another important female character in the novel. She is a victim of a heartless husband and whose life becomes worth living only after she came as servant to Parvatiamma, Mahesh's mother. Even Mayamma's philosophy which she had learnt out of her hard experiences does not influence Devi when the latter (Devi) decides to elope with a next door musician.

The firmness of mind and strong willpower of feminine mind has been depicted by Gita Hariharan in the character of Sita, Devi's mother. She is a woman who knows her mind, has clear views on what she wants to achieve. Like the stray branches of Jasmine plant, she prunes in her garden, she prunes her stray thoughts and actions to achieve what she wants to achieve in her life. As a girl, her ambition was to become a great vina player. She achieves that but silences her craving forever when the instrument comes in the way of her being accepted as a good wife and a good daughter-in-law. Sita and Devi of this novel are very unlike the mythological characters of Sita and Devi. Sita in the novel is very firm in character and stoops at nothing which could come in her way. Devi, on the other hand, who carries the name of the Goddess, the Goddess who vanquished demons as if they were flies, is a person without any backbone. The only time, she exhibits some firmness of mind is when she gets into and out of senseless relationships—once with Dan and the next time with Gopal. Both of the relationships are doomed to be nothing other than the temporary answers to the dilemma which Devi faces in her life—dilemma of not knowing what to do with it.

Anjana Appachana's (b. 1956) first novel *Listening Now* has been blamed for being an old-fashioned novel, a Victorian novel with Victorian flaw of probability but the novel is worth reading and worth mentioning from feminine perspective and from the perspective of gender studies. The story is told from the viewpoint of six women. As the narrative's centre is Padma, ostensibly a young widow cast out both by her family and her husband's family, which disapprove of her marriage. She arrives in Delhi along with her daughter, Mallika and her sister. She buys an independent house in middle-class neighbourhood and makes an independent living as a university lecturer. She lives an almost Western life circumscribed by Eastern taboos. Padma herself is a mercurial and passionate woman who lives the life of widowhood and isolation from both families—her own family and the family of her deceased husband. Mallika, Padma's only daughter, is a brilliant but confused child who has a consistent fear of abandonment while Shanta (Padma's sister) is envious and compulsive, with a strong tendency to self-martyrdom. Her mother looks back at her life as almost over and realizes that this world is a dark place to live in. The other two narrators are Padma's neighbours: Madhu has little feeling for her rich husband who indulges with other women and Anu, who is tortured by her mother-in-law but she hides all her grief in her laughter. She is symbolic of the sacrificial woman who is more worried about others' concerns. The novelist projects her as a warm and intuitive woman. The story moves backward from the 1960s to discover Padma's childhood and her tortured romance with Mallika's father. Musing upon her own life, Padma's mother summarizes Indian woman's life. She says that an Indian woman gets married at fourteen; becomes a mother at sixteen followed by numerable children and innumerable miscarriages.

Anjana Appachana's every woman has silence as the only answer to every outrage. *Listening Now* is a large book in every sense, a panorama filled with many insights. This novel illuminates the depth, breadth, and tragic impassibility of the chasm between men and women. This chasm is more clearly visible in India than America. Appachana measures the distortions of this world. Her viewpoint is also supported by Edith Milton who has written:

> Men honour bound to defend their mothers, become their fathers' enemies. Daughters are infantilized by their father's love. And since extra-marital sex involving a decent woman is entirely unspeakable (in fact unthinkable), a woman can be violated casually on the bus or at a festival and have no way to make anyone believe it happened. (Edith Milton 1998)

Thus, the novelist talks about women issues not only in the inner sphere of life but also in the outer sphere.

Arundhati Roy's *The God of Small Things*, apart from being a strong indictment against untouchability, is also a strong document against discrimination between men and women. Roy shows in her masterpiece that inter-religious love is not permissible in the society. Velutha and Ammu become the victims of this 'Love-law' that two beings from different religions should not and must not fall in love. Like Rukmani's in *Nectar in a Sieve*, Ammu's life is a saga of suffering. She is ignored by her parents.

> Her eighteenth birthday came and went unnoticed or at least unremarked upon by her parents. Ammu grew

> desperate. All day she dreamed of escaping from Ayemenem and the clutches of her ill-tempered father and bitter, long suffering mother. (Arundhati Roy 1998: 77)

Ammu and her daughter are non-conformist and can be regarded as feminist characters with a difference from other female characters of the feminist novels. Kamla Markandaya, Nayantara Sahgal, Anita Desai and other feminist novelists have created female characters who either dominate the scene or struggle against all the odds with fortitude to make out their own identity. Arundhati Roy simply presents the tragic tale of women under patriarchal yoke. Though Ammu, Rahel and Margaret do not compromise with their husbands and easily part way from them, they fail to make an independent identity in life. Ammu always remains dependent upon her parents. She along with her twins is the target of negligence, hatred, serenity not only of the society but also of the family. She bears all this but proves herself as an affectionate mother who showers love of both mother and father upon her twins.

Arundhati Roy has done a scathing criticism of gender discrimination. Chacko and Ammu deserve the same punishment but being the male, Chacko is given preferential treatment. As Chacko is a male, so the label divorce does not affect his position in the society. But, for Ammu, her divorced status becomes a bane. The attitude of society towards a divorced woman is reflected upon by Baby Kochamma who reflects upon the view that:

> a married daughter had no position in her parents' home. As for a divorced daughter—according to Baby Kochamma, she had no position anywhere at all. And as for a 'divorced' daughter from a 'love' marriage, well, words could not describe Baby Kochamma's outrage. As for a 'divorced' daughter from an 'intercommunity love' marriage. Baby Kochamma chose to remain quiveringly silent on the subject. (Arundhati Roy 1998: 45-46)

Arundhati Roy presents a horrible picture of husband-wife relationship in a conventional family where the chauvinist male behaves as an autocratic boss of the house. Pappachi, retired govt. official, and an entomologist, regularly beats his wife even at an old age.

> Every night he beats her with a brass flower vase. The beatings were not new. What was new was only the frequency with which they took place. One night Pappachi broke the bow of Mammachi's violin and threw it in the river. (Arundhati Roy 1998: 52)

The novelist shows her deep and subtle understanding of the problem. She shows how Pappachi's professional failure to get the credit of the moth he discovers turns out to be 'a pernicious ghost' that keeps him haunting throughout his life and in turn he beats his wife regularly as an outlet of his professional frustration. Roy's conviction is that men are afraid of women best they outwit men in life. Pappachi's attitude towards his wife is born out of this fear. He abruptly discontinues Mammachi's lesson on the violin when it is reported by the teacher that his wife is exceptionally talented.

Thus, the novel *The God of Small Things* espouses the feminist cause of exposing discriminations between men and women at every level. Roy's female characters are all the more realistic and give an authentic picture of the ground realities. At the same time, she is able to delve deep into the psychic level of women.

Apparently, Manju Kapoor's *Difficult Daughters* is a simple book that weaves a connection between mother and a daughter. This book is not only about difficult daughters but also about difficult mothers. The novelist has portrayed mothers who do not understand their daughters along with the daughters who want to break out into new paths. The novel starts very well and is quite gripping at the beginning with a daughter going on a quest to understand her mother, after her mother's death. The life of a Punjabi family in Amritsar is interestingly depicted and the character of Virmati, the eldest of a batch of eleven children, is skilfully painted. Virmati is the mother to all her sisters and brothers as she is attuned to signs of her mother's pregnancies. She cares for her siblings and bosses over them. As she grows up, she has to protect herself from the comments of an aunt (a mother of 'two' children), who lives next door. Thus, in the beginning, the curious reader comes to know how a young girl reacts to such pressures in her life and how does she manage them.

The novel revolves around two characters, Virmati and Professor. Professor, married to an illiterate woman, falls in love with Virmati. The family objects to the relation and finally she is packed off to Lahore to study further but she is visited regularly by the Professor who makes her pregnant. This man continually talks of his undying love for Virmati but never mentions marriage. The novelist very caustically attacks the results of this relation: first of all she is rejected by her family; then she loses her job and finally she has to undergo the trauma of getting the child aborted. Finally, they marry but then again Virmati has to live an outsider life in his home as he turns blind to her problems. The novelist has successfully depicted a woman who sacrifices everything for the sake of her love and how she is ditched by the man she loves.

Manju Kapoor, in her masterpiece, comes out very negatively about masculine gender. The novel makes the reader doubt if any Indian male is capable of earning any respect. The book can be said to be the seminal thesis of what happens when young women are not able to handle freedom. The book can be taken as unresolved dichotomy of the character of Virmati who on the one hand is very weak, because she just can't kick the professor out of her life and on the other hand she is very strong-willed to resist all kinds of social and family pressure. The novelist projects that the reason for this is not love but lack of love. Virmati as a child received very little love and she is totally overcome by assurances of love by the professor. She is an example of a person in love with 'love' itself. Therefore, Manju Kapoor in her award-winning novel highlights men's exploitation of women; lack of love to the girl-child in patriarchal families and its impact on the psyche of the girl-child.

Meera Mahadevan's *Shulamith* (pub. in 1975) exemplifies a novel in 'shakti' tradition that has the effect of showing the influence of Hindu culture upon Jewish women of India. The novel's main character, Shulamith, experiences a sense of dual fidelity between her devotion to her husband and to her way of life and decides to stay in India when her husband leaves for Israel, but she withers away because she misses him and eventually dies. Another female character in the novel is Mezuzah (sister-in-law of Shulamith), who is allowed initially to date and remain single but finally suffers for violating social norms. Influenced by Western lifestyle, Maizie (Mezuzah) falls in love with a non-Jewish man and becomes pregnant. Her mother would neither let her marry a non-Jewish boy nor let her give birth to a child out of wedlock. Meera Mahadevan explains the forces that compel the westernized young Indian women to embrace their own culture and tradition whenever there is a crisis in their lives. She also makes a satirical attack on the parents who apparently 'liberate' their daughters. Thus, Maizie becomes an image of the suffering woman: her values and personality changes as she transforms first into a subdued, abused, barren wife living in poverty then into a hard-working, self-sacrificial nurse. Meera Mahadevan portrays Maixie and Naomi as victims of a patriarchal tradition and along with she portrays Shulamith as a character to be respected for her integrity. Essentially, Mahadevan has all the admiration for strong-willed women who suffer and learn to endure.

A review of the works of Chitra Fernando (1935-98) will not be out of place. In her works, she has portrayed women who reject traditional family life. In contrast to these so-called 'new women', the novelist has placed the least sympathetic women characters who exploit other women for their own parochial selfish interests. Her novel *Cousins* which was published posthumously in 1998 is the story of Amitha, the central character and how she receives her first sledge hammer blow in life after her father's death. This episode forces her to focus on the realities of real life. By depicting Amitha's days at university, Fernando depicts problems in the life of a woman studying and residing alone in a foreign university. The novelist, then, shows her as a fully grown adult and a working woman who has all the sympathies for the helpless and downtrodden. Amitha realises how people change over the years, including her 'cousins'. This could be the point that the author in her attempt to portray a classical, pseudo, modern society in Sri Lanka successfully achieves her aim in exposing how some sections of the bourgeois society have fallen prey to rigorous false values and the extent to which they suffer from delusions of grandeur. Missilin in *Three Women* is a plain, loyal and hard-working woman servant. Rather than bemoaning that she will never marry; she does not care a jot for men. She has fiery resentment against men for the wrongs they commit against women. In the character of Mrs Ranasingha, "the pious employer of Missilin", the authoress depicts the hypocritical nature of the employer who exploits Missilin because of her obedient nature. Her women characters gain reader's sympathy because of their underdog status. Seela is the most rebellious character who escapes exploitation at the hands of her parents by remaining celibate and she supports herself financially. She is a radical figure who breaks through tradition to build a happy life for herself. She is an assertive individual who asserts her worth. Thus, we can say that Chitra Fernando, in her works, does not reject traditional society but she makes a caustic attack on the greedy and abusive attitude to women in society.

Born in Karachi, raised in Lahore, Bapsy Sidhwa (b. 1938) is the author of four internationally acclaimed novels. This award-winning Pakistani woman novelist is striving hard to bring women issues of the Indian subcontinent into public discussion. She was a young witness to the bloody partition of India and therefore, this important chapter in the history of the subcontinent finds an important place in her writings with a special emphasis on gender-issues. In her masterpiece, *Cracking India*, she gives a vivid description of many women—who were left the victims of rape and torture at the time of partition. Bapsy throws light on how these women on being 'recovered' were not permitted entry into their 'own' homes. Her novels make the reader realize that in the world in general and in this part of the world in particular (Indian subcontinent), "victory is celebrated on woman's body and vengeance is also taken on a woman's body". Maya (Sudhamoy's daughter) is an independent young girl who chooses to go with the system rather than defy it. As the sole-bread-earner of the house, she was concerned about her family's safety and disappointed with her brother for being unable to protect the family when her family's religion had become their biggest enemy. Taslima depicts brilliantly the agony and the pain of being a woman when hatred spreads or the virus of communalism rears its ugly visage. In such circumstances, it is the woman who suffers the most from gruesome act of cruelty done in the name of religion and God. She is assaulted not only physically but also emotionally and her very motherhood becomes the target for the mob. They molest her and in the name of being the self-proclaimed votaries of religion they force themselves upon her so that the next generation is born to their religion. The story of this Hindu girl (Maya) highlights the same hatred, *Lajja* and shame. The gruesome depiction of communal hatred in Taslima's novel through the medium of the exploitation of the women is indeed telling and painful. Every time the girl is molested, she is per force converted to the religion that the perpetrators of the crime belong to, who feel that they have fulfilled their responsibility to their religion by doing so. In the end, we can say that Taslima Nasreen is a militant feminist and her masterpiece *Lajja* is an important document on gender issues.

Sara Suleri is another Pakistani woman novelist who has painted a complex image of the female in the society. She has given biographical details of many women who actually surrounded her in actual life. Although the resolutions of her women are often unclear, yet her portrayal of them shows a demeaning attitude towards men. In many of her works including *Meatless Men*, she marginalizes male roles, a tactic that further enriches her depiction of women. Suleri's attitude towards men is unhesitant voiced by her when in one of her novels she claims that they (men) have the backbone of a shrimp; have a head the size of a bowl and a brain the size of a pea. In *Meatless Men*, Sara Suleri deconstructs the idea of a singular identity of woman and points out the diasporic identity of women as represented within a single woman.

It may be added to conclude that though novels by these so-called feminist novelist are accused to be repetitive in broader perspective and do not offer many varieties of fiction, yet these novels tell the story of predicament and conflict of women. These novelists have 'truly' written about women and while doing so they have done a deep perusal of the values that have given Indian women their image and role towards themselves and the society. The novels by earlier Indian women novelists project the traditional image of women but with the change of time, the portrayal has become realistic. Their characters, like their creators are torn apart by the conflicting forces of society and gender discrimination. These women novelists have very skilfully depicted the plight of 'new woman' particularly by Anita Desai and Nayantara Sahgal. Shobhaa De and Namita Gokhale, on the other hand, have paid attention to the so-called educated 'socialite' women. Thus, we can say that works by these women writers are positive steps towards new dimensions of gender studies. However, it is Shashi Deshpande who touches the so far untouched aspect of feminism: the plight of urban working women who had not been paid attention, they deserve, so far.

Works Cited

Desai, Anita. *Cry, The Peacock*. New Delhi: Orient Paperbacks, 1963.

Desai, Anita. *Fire on the Mountain*. New Delhi: Orient Paperbacks, 1971.

Desai, Anita. *Voices in the City*. New Delhi: Orient Paperbacks, 2006.

Jhabvala, R.P. *To Whom She Will*. London: George Allen and Unwin Ltd., 1955.

Milton, Edith. *The Boston Globe*. May 3, 1998.

Roy, Arundhati. *The God of Small Things*. New Delhi: India Ink, 1998.

3

Sisterhood: A Comfort Not a Solution (*The Binding Vine*)

Feminism and gender issues have been interpreted differently by different people, ranging from a wish to change and challenge the whole existing order of things to the desire to bring about a more balanced and saner equality between the sexes and achieve respectable individual liberty for women with their natural instincts and characteristics intact. Though equality with all its implications at various levels of society is a major gender issue, yet one of the fundamental areas where this equality matters and is desired even by the most conservative propagandists of feminism is in the area of marriage. Categorisation of the female as an object of sex is vehemently opposed. The goal of raising such gender issues is to eliminate existing oppression in the patriarchal society. Feminism as a movement originated in the West but deterioration in the status of women in India paved the way for Indian writers to fight for women's equal access to education and status. This section of writers aim at creating a woman of substance commanding respect and executing her role with dignity, confidence and responsibility.

Shashi Deshpande's clarion calls to modern women in her novel *The Binding Vine* is loud and clear. The patriarchal, chauvinistic and indifferent Indian male role is challenged. The inner most recesses of a woman's heart are brought to light through the perspectives of the protagonist, Urmi. Death of the second child forms the occasion for a journey into the past, into oneself and into future. Using the protagonist, as her mouthpiece, the novelist analyses all the relationships a woman in the Indian society is subjected to. There are moments of revolt, deep-felt anger, desire to set things right, retreat from step which would shatter the sense of well-being and fulfilment mirrored through these relationships. The final resolution is one which points at a relationship that is healthy, satisfying and something that is based on love and the wish to help, rather than drown the soul into the quagmire of the 'dark night'.

The narrator is a woman and gender issues are mainly presented in the novel *The Binding Vine*. The keynote of the novel is struck right at the beginning when Urmi determines not to be plaster cast into a stereotyped image by people around her. If an accidental injury and anxiety makes her fear a restriction in her freedom, an existential experience such as death of her only daughter, Anu, plunges her into morbidity and a masochistic mood which is devoid of all positive values. In the very beginning of the novel, Vanaa reminds Urmi about one incidence in which Urmi had been wounded badly while cycling. The young girl of thirteen, Urmi was not at all worried about her bleeding gashes, but she was anxious that her cycling may be banned. As Vanaa remarks:

> You couldn't walk properly, you hobbled, but you were more concerned with your wheels being out of alignment; you wanted to straighten them out. And when we went to your Baiajji, the first thing you said to her was, "I'm not going to stop cycling, Baiajji, I'm not going to stop". (Shashi Deshpande 1992: 8)

Shashi Deshpande's *The Binding Vine* is an advancement over her earlier novels as it not only uncovers the issues haunting the soul of modern Indian woman but it also shows her (new woman's) handling of these issues. Thus, the novel, in its beginning only, projects that self-assertion is the only way out left for 'new woman'.

In the Indian patriarchal society, girl-child has always been regarded as a burden to bear. In *That Long Silence*, Shashi Deshpande has talked about female infanticide, but in *The Binding Vine*, the novelist also talks about the problem of bringing up a girl-child all alone. In *Dark Holds No Terrors*, Shashi Deshpande has raised a question that why a girl is or should be exclusively the concern of a mother. In the present novel, the novelist offers the answers by projecting the situation when after the death of Baiajji; the survival of Urmi with her grandfather is threatened by many problems. As Urmi says:

> You know, Vanaa, after Baiajji died and Aju wanted us to go on before, he asked me, 'we can manage, can't we?' And I said, so confidently, 'yes, we can manage'. But it was not easy, you know that, Vanaa. No, you don't, you were away then.... You remember that cook of ours? I knew she was stealing, and her son used to leave dirty pictures in my books. (Shashi Deshpande 1992: 173)

Thus, the novelist depicts the problems a girl has to face in case her mother is not around. On the other hand, there is Vanaa who meets a cold treatment from her father. For her father, none except Kishore, her brother, had mattered to him. Vanaa, as a daughter wanted attention of her father. As the novelist remarks:

> Before that he had been a cheerful kind of man, hopefully offering jokes that were hard to laugh at (Going to play bad-minton or good-minton? He asked Vanaa, and me once, seeing us with rackets in our hands). Vanaa, however, never failed to laugh at his jokes. She was a kind girl or was it sycophancy? May be she laughed so that he would notice her. But he never did. For him, there was only Kishore. (Shashi Deshpande 1992)

The middle-class woman, today, is not merely educated; she is also a co-bread earner and supplements her husband's income to maintain the standard of living they aspire to provide for their children. Urmi, the protagonist in the novel, is a college teacher who does not give up her job after her marriage. Many of her relatives suggest her to resign from her job as her husband, Kishore who works in merchant navy and is earning handsomely, can support her financially. However, she does not want to lose her identity and keeps on working. Though Kishore sends her piles of money but she keeps it deposited in bank and spends her own money. Thus, the novelist shows that the new working woman in the patriarchal society has assumed a new role for herself in the wake of changing circumstances. This, however, has not exonerated her from her traditional role and responsibility in family which, in addition to her career-consciousness, has led to severe problems of adjustment and is the main cause of her agony today. The novelist raises the point: If a man is working, he is free from all the domestic responsibilities but a woman is sandwiched between the two roles. Round the clock, a woman is under pressure and ultimately she has no time her herself. In the present novel, Vanaa is exhausted while trying to strike a balance between the two roles. Consequently, there is gap or vacuum created between mother and the daughter, as is evident from a dialogue between Urmi and the Mandira, Vanaa's daughter:

> You know, Urmi aunti, when I grow up, I'm never going to leave my children to go to work.
>
> 'What you will do?'
>
> 'Stay at home and look after them.'
>
> 'When they grow up, they will go away and won't need you. What will you do then?'
>
> 'Then I'll go and work.'
>
> 'Who will give you a job when you are that old?'
>
> I don't care. I'll never leave my children alone.
>
> I realise I have to speak to her. 'Mandira, your mother doesn't leave you alone. That is why she's kept Hirabai for you....
>
> I don't want Hirabai, I want my mother'.
>
> (Shashi Deshpande 1992: 72)

Mandira dislikes being left alone at home to the care of maid-servant, Vanaa feels very disturbed when she comes to know of it from Urmi. Thus, the novelist raises the issue of suffering of daughters of working women who themselves feel the pain because of suffering of their own daughters. But Harish, Vanaa's husband is never worried about being a bit cooperative to her so that she can better manage a balance between her work and home. As Vanaa complains:

> Urmi, why is it nobody thinks of blaming Harish? He is never around, but it is never his fault. (Shashi Deshpande 1992: 75)

Thus, Shashi Deshpande makes a caustic attack on husbands like Harish who enjoy managing the money earned by their wives but pay no heed to the problems faced by their wives. It also shows that it is women who take parenthood seriously, not men.

The novelist has also dealt with the problem of loneliness in marriage. The marriage of Kishore-Urmi was a love marriage. When Urmi's father asks her if she would be able to manage as Kishore will be away most of the times, she says that she will be able to manage. In the beginning, her life is full of ecstasy and she is fearless and confident as her love gives her immense strength. But later this 'killing-loneliness' enters into her life, as she feels:

> But how can Vanaa, secure in the fortress of her marriage to Harish, understand what it is like—marriage with a man who flits into my life a few months in a year and flits out again, leaving nothing of himself behind? Often, after he has gone, I find in myself a frantic grappling for his image, as if in going he has taken that away as well. Then he returns and we pick up the course of our lives from the moment of his return.
>
> ...
>
> I remember a day when Harish and Vanaa were driving me home. I saw Vanaa rest her cheek lightly on Harish's arm,... They looked at each other and I thought, they will make love when they go home. Pain slashed through me and I knew then how vulnerable I was. I tried after that to control the erotic fantasies that invaded me in early hours of the morning,... (Shashi Deshpande 1992: 164-65)

Thus, the novelist raises the issue of loneliness of a married woman who is compelled to stay alone and has to undergo emotional and physical suffering. Instead of being a confident being, as she was at one point of time, she is reduced to 'a fearful being' that is under constant fear of losing her husband. The insight provided by John Gray in *Men, Women and Relationship* seem to be useful in unravelling the cause of Urmi's fear: insecurity in marriage and emotional loneliness:

> Men generally assume that once a woman is fulfilled, she should stay that way. Once he has proven his love, she should know it forever.... From the male point of view, this attitude makes perfect sense. Women find this attitude hard to accept. It is just plain, inconsistent with their internal reality. A woman needs to be reassured that she is special, worthy, understandable and lovable. Men also need to be reassured, but they get that encouragement mainly through their work. Women, however, primarily need reassurance through their relationship. (John Gray 1992: 241)

Gray, an expert in interpersonal communication, is credited with the unique contribution that the difference between men and women is more than biological. According to Gray, men and women feel and respond differently and for a sound relationship between wives and husbands a good understanding of the mental, emotional make-up of the two sexes is necessary, as also is learning the art of asserting and asking for fulfilment. Urmila is not submissive. She does not ask Kishore for more than what he gives her in life. Consequently, she tends to nurture and build up resentment which make her feel that despite a 'love' marriage, her adolescent dreams 'of living happily ever with Kishore' have been modified.

Through the character of Shakutai, the novelist gives us a glimpse of loneliness and abandonment in the life of women living in slums. At the time of her marriage, she was told that the boy lives in Bombay and would take her along with him after marriage. Even after six months, he does not make any effort to take her to Bombay. Shakutai, being the product of the patriarchal society, does not want to be a burden on her father and decides to go to Bombay. There she finds that her husband does not have a regular job and they have to put up in their relative's house. With three children born, the burden of the family falls on her. In spite of her doing all kinds of work to support her family, her husband abandons her for another woman. As an abandoned woman, she faces problems from all sides. Prakash, her son has started revolting against her and she finds it very difficult to meet the demands of her children. In such circumstances, there is none whom she could turn to for help. Her husband, even, does not care to give her emotional support, leave alone the question of financial support. And the paradox is that people in this patriarchal society blame her for it:

> What can you expect, they say, of a girl whose mother has left her husband? Imagine! He left me for another woman, left with these children to bring up. (Shashi Deshpande 1992: 147)

Thus, we find Shakutai to be a lonely and abandoned woman who suffers because of indifferent attitude of her husband.

The most heart stirring kind of loneliness can be observed in the example of Mira who is forced into a loveless marriage and is subjected to marital rape and finally dies after giving birth to her son. The man happens to see her in a wedding and falls in love with her. He gets obsessed with her and through a mutual friend conveys his wishes to his own parents. The proposal is accepted and he does not care to take into consideration Mira's consent for the marriage and hence a bubbly girl like Mira is married to an obsessed man who is not able to 'understand' her. As a result he is unable to reach to her true self. She is subjected to marital rape like Saru in *Dark Holds No Terror* and her rape also goes unpublicised as it takes place within marriage. She also has fear of the 'engulfing night' as she writes about it in her poems:

> But tell me, friend, did Laxmi too
> twist brocade tassels round her fingers
> and tremble, fearing the coming
> of the dark-clouded, engulfing night?
> (Shashi Deshpande 1992: 56)

Thus, Mira has been depicted as a frightened girl whose husband is obsessed about her and does not take care of her feelings. A vivid account of Mira's loneliness can be found in her own words which she had jotted down in her diary:

> Talk, he says to me, why don't you say something, why don't you speak to me? What shall I talk about, I ask him

> stupidly. 'What did you do today, when did you go, what have you been thinking about all evening?' and so he goes on, dragging my day my whole self out of me. But I have my defences; I give him facts, nothing more, never my feelings. He knows what I am doing and he gets angry with me. I don't mind his anger, it makes him leave me to myself, it is a bliss when he does that. But he comes back, he is remorseful, repentant, he holds me close, he begins to babble. And so it begins. 'Please', he says, 'please, I love you.' And over and over again until he has done, 'I love you'. Love! How I hate the word if this is love it is a terrible thing. I have learnt to say 'no' at last, but it makes no difference, no difference at all. What is it he wants from me? I look at myself in the mirror and wonder what is there in me? Why does it have to be me? Why can't he leave me alone? (Shashi Deshpande 1992: 67)

It is not only in her marital life that Mira remains lonely, but also in her relation with her parents who do not consult her about her marriage. Earlier, she feels very shocked when she asks her mother to consult the astrologer who has visited their house and everybody is eager to know his/her future, her mother replies, that her destiny is not beyond her husband's and children's destiny. Later, Mira also feels herself in the same situation. But she is not able to rip her heart open to her mother. She jots down in her diary about her mother:

> My mother is dead. She died happy, they tell me. She saw me married, she saw me pregnant and she was happy. I am supposed to comfort myself with this thought. But, I can find no comfort in it, not for myself, anyway. She is dead, that is the truth.... Yet I am glad I told her nothing. What if I had? What could she have done? Nothing. That was all she could do in her entire life—nothing. 'Don't ask me', she used to say to us. 'Nothing is in my hands'. She knew I was not happy, I know she knew it; but she was afraid to ask me, afraid I would admit it. No I am glad I never told her anything.
>
> ....

> I wish I could have asked her a question. 'Mother', I always wanted to ask, 'why do you want me to repeat your history, when you so despair of your own? But she died and I will never know her answer now. [Shashi Deshpande 1992: 126]

The condition of Kalpana is no different from Mira. She knows that Sulu's husband does have lustful eye on her, but she can't and does not share this unsavoury secret with anybody including her mother.

Traditionally, in the Hindu marriage the position of husband and wife is clearly defined. The husband is expected to be an authoritarian figure whose will should always govern the life of the wife. The wife should regard him as her master and should serve him faithfully. Thus, the traditional concept of superior husband and subordinate wife has had been the guideline of Hindu marriage. The Indian tradition considers the marriage ceremony as one in which the husband and the wife become one however "that one is the husband". In an Indian marriage, it is understood that the wife will merge her name, personality, lifestyle and in fact, her entire life into that of the husband. But as a result of industrialisation, urbanisation, westernisation, women now aspire for:

> Natural companionship, respect, material comforts, satisfaction of emotional and physical needs in marriage.

In the present novel, Shashi Deshpande brings on the surface the inability of the patriarchal society to understand the needs of women and her individuality in marriage. She makes a caustic attack on the traditional mindset which ignores woman's sexuality and considers woman immoral and frivolous even when subjected to physical molestation.

The Binding Vine, Shashi Deshpande's fourth novel, is her boldest statement of a woman's assertion of her own sexuality. As she herself said that one of the themes of the novel was

> about controlling women's minds and bodies. ("Women's Minds and Bodies", *Indian Review of Books*, 2.4 (1993), 26)

It begins with the life of Urmila, an intelligent, independent, outspoken woman who is trying to cope up with the grief of her daughter's death. Taking Urmi as the anchor, Shashi Deshpande has roped in the story of Mira, Kalpana and other characters to show the wrongs including the sexual wrongs done to women in patriarchal Indian society. In her despondency over Anu's death, Urmi stumbles over the diaries of Mira, her dead mother-in-law. Her venture into Mira's life introduces her to traditionally guarded (apparently) life of an Indian woman.

Considering the woman as weak and dependent, the Indian tradition empowers the male members to take control of her life. Mira, is one such woman who becomes a victim of such tradition. A budding poet and an eager student, Mira loses her right to education because a man gets obsessed with the ideal of 'owning' her in marriage. With an obsessive love, the man plots to get married to her, leaving her with no choice. Mira's unwillingness to marry and her interest in studies have no significance for her husband, who nourishes the dream to 'possess' her. Traditionally, marriage is considered as the only goal of a girl's life. Fearful that they may not get a better match, Mira's parents decide to marry her to a man much older to her in age, instead of letting her discover her poetic talents or pursue her studies. Mira's apprehensions about her inability to pursue her studies or poetic career can be seen in her poem:

> Huddled in my cocoon, a somnolent silkworm
>
> Will I emerge a beauteous being?
>
> Or will I, suffocating, cease to exist?
>
> (Shashi Deshpande 1992: 65)

Marrying Mira isn't easy for the man. He cannot propose her directly as his mother would never countenance such a marriage. He induces a mutual friend to suggest his name to Mira's parents as a possible groom for their daughter and finally they are married. At the time of her marriage, like a traditional mother in the patriarchal society, Mira's mother suggests her never to say 'no' to her husband, and this is very well-expressed by Mira in her poem:

> Don't tread paths barred to you
> Obey, never utter a 'no';
> submit and your life will be
> a paradise, she said and blessed me. (Shashi Deshpande 1992: 83)

Mira starts losing her own 'self' and 'identity' as soon as she gets married. She is named as 'Nirmala'. The pain of erasure of her 'self' has been well-expressed by Mira when she finds her 'new name' inscribed on a gold ring:

> A glittering ring gliding on the rice
> Carefully traced a name 'Nirmala'.
> Who is this? None but I,
> My name hence, bestowed upon me.
> Nirmala, they call, I stand statue-still,
> Do you build the new without razing the old?
> A tablet of rice, a pencil of gold
> Can they make me Nirmala?
> (Shashi Deshpande 1992: 101)

The frequent invasion of Mira's physical space leaves her wanting "a room of her own": It is socially accepted that in marriage a husband has a right over his wife's body and it is the duty of the wife to satisfy the physical needs of her husband. This traditional negation of a woman's right over her body and her own sexuality also forms the theme of Shashi Deshpande's short story "The Intrusion". Shashi Deshpande, through this very novel, has criticized the tradition that dictates that the husband has a right to satisfy his biological needs irrespective of the wife's willingness, thus, allowing crimes like marital rape. Mira was married at the age of eighteen to a man who loves her passionately, but she did not find solace in sexual relationship. Urmila finds in the writings of her mother-in-law a clear thread of intense dislike of sexual act with her husband. She writes:

> I have learnt to say 'no' at last, but it makes no difference, no difference at all. What is it he wants from me? I look at myself in the mirror and wonder what is there in me?

> Why does it have to be me? Why can't he leave me alone? (Shashi Deshpande, 1992: 67)

This age-old cry of woman suppressed under the veneer of marriage has begun to find an outlet recently. As Indrani Jaisingh, an eminent lawyer, opines:

> It is assumed that by marrying a man, a woman has given her consent to sexual intercourse with her husband at anytime. Thus, even if he forces himself on her, he is not committing an offence (of rape) as her consent is assumed. In this respect, the women's movement has consistently demanded that the law of rape has to be changed. A recent judgement of court in England indicated that rape within marriage can be an offence. Several states in the U.S. have specially amended their original law to make it (marital rape) an offence. (Indrani Jaisingh 1993: 65)

Thus, the novelist raises the issue of victimisation, endurance and violation of body in marriage in patriarchal Indian society as is evident from Mira's poetry in which she pours her bitter experiences. As Urmi observes after reading Mira's poems:

> It runs through all her writing—a strong, clear thread of an intense dislike of the sexual act with her husband, a physical repulsion from the man she married. (Shashi Deshpande 1992: 63)

Mira's untimely death in child-birth ends her cloistered existence with the man she could not love. But the horrifying impact of patriarchy does not stop here. Mira's husband remarries not for the sake of marriage but for the sake of his motherless child and thus Akka, Urmi's step mother-in-law arrives in the house to suffer indifference to her on the part of her husband who is never able to get rid of memories of his first wife. Akka to him is less a wife, more a mother to his motherless son. The plight of Akka can be well-imagined, who as a bride is told by an old lady that:

> "My brother was crazy about his wife", she said "I've never seen any man like that. And since her death", she said, "it's his son". ... What he really wants now is a mother for that motherless child. (Shashi Deshpande 1992: 47)

Thus, the plight of Akka can be well-imagined as she knows that she is more a mother less a wife. What more can be expected from a man who is obsessed in the love of his first wife and does not care to have a glimpse of what she has scribbled in her diary notebook and piles them up in a trunk?

Priti, another feminist character in the novel, feels excited while talking to Urmila about a landmark judgement in a case filed by a husband against his wife for restoration of conjugal rights. Priti feels excited that the judge has ruled that a wife can't be forced into a sexual relationship with her husband against her will. The novelist, here, raises another important issue that the society can't be changed by merely passing such judgements but by changing social ethos prevalent in the patriarchal society. The girl concerned in the judgement is an actress who is supported by her parents, whereas most of the girls do not get the desired support. To quote the novelist:

> Isn't it radical, absolutely earth-shaking, in this country, I mean? Can you imagine the consequences?
>
> "What consequences?" I asked her. "One judgement by a judge which can be appealed against and over-ruled...."
>
> ......
>
> "How many women do you see going to court on such a matter?"
>
> ......
>
> Naturally her family would like to see her free of her husband so that he won't get any control over that money. Otherwise they would have said, like all parents do, "go back to your husband like a good girl". (Shashi Deshpande 1992: 37-38)

The untold experiences of Mira's life as revealed through her poems disturb Urmi and she identifies Mira's story with that of Kalpana, a lower-middle class girl. Kalpana, a young and attractive girl, becomes a victim of, her uncle, Prabhakar's lust. Prabhakar has his eye set on Kalpana right from the beginning and the day she puts on *saree* for the first time, he is so enamoured by her beauty that he takes her along with him to get her photographed.

Shakutai's sister, Sulu, has her own tragic tale. She is affectionate and helpful in nature. She helps her sister as much as possible and even takes upon herself the responsibility of bringing up Kalpana. Sulu's husband Prabhakar has lust for her, and Sulu under pressure from her husband proposes to Shakutai for Kalpana's marriage to Prabhakar. Sulu gets so suppressed after the episode obviously for the reason that she making such a proposal which is death like to any wife. Kalpana is infuriated on knowing this. She tells her mother about a boy who do not belong to their caste and he is outwardly rejected by her mother, who tells Sulu about Kalpana's affair with that out-caste boy and Sulu, in turn, tells Prabhakar, who out of frustration, rapes Kalpana that very night. When Sulu comes to know of her husband's heinous deed, she commits suicide by burning herself. Sulu had always apprehensions about her husband as she could not give child to him. To quote the novelist:

> Sulu was frightened, she was always frightened because she had no children. She was afraid he would throw her out, take another wife. And then she started getting these white patches on her face, her arms, her neck. He stopped touching her after that. She told me this only yesterday, she kept everything to herself, she never told me her troubles, even about Kalpana—she knew, that first time, that he'd tried to put his hands on Kalpana. But she warned Kalpana not to tell me, not to tell anyone. (Shashi Deshpande 1992: 192-93)

Thus, Sulu like any oppressed wife in lower strata in patriarchal society is compelled to deem it her duty to hide the misdeeds of her husband. She is a lonely woman who thinks herself to be entirely responsible for her issueless status. Although she is no way to be blamed for the misdeed of Prabhakar, yet she punishes herself by igniting herself ablaze. As the novelist writes:

> She finished her cooking, give him his breakfast and then.... The neighbours told me she was like a torch when she ran out, burning from head to toe, they said. (Shashi Deshpande 1992: 189)

Sulu, a dutiful wife, does not forget to serve her husband even on the last day of her life. As Sudhir Kakkar points out in his essay "Feminine Identity in India":

> Getting along with other women in this sphere, learning the mandatory skill of householding, cooking and child care, establishing her place in this primary world; these relationships and these tasks constitute the dailiness of girlhood in India. (Sudhir Kakkar 1998: 50)

Thus, Sulu the poor woman conditioned by the patriarchal Indian society, does not forget to fulfil her duty towards her husband who in not even worthy of being a husband. The kerosene oil, here again is symbolic of pain, betrayal and death.

After talking about control of women's sexuality in marriage, it will not be out of place to talk about control of woman's sexuality outside marriage as it offers the most horrifying picture of control of sexuality of women. As Alison Jagger comments:

> Superficially, women's sexual experiences differ widely from each other; some are prostitutes, some are virgins; some women are raped, while others are protected with obsessive care. Beneath the superficial variety, however radical feminists assert the underlying fact that men control women's sexuality for other own purposes. Radical feminists believe that women, whether they recognize it or not, are the sexual slaves of men. (Alison Jagger 1983: 260)

The novel presents the traumatic experience of Kalpana, a young and beautiful girl, who has been raped by her own uncle. The act of rape is a shattering and cruel invasion of any woman. A bubbly girl like Kalpana, can't cope with the crisis of comatose. The novelist also examines the response of society to the situation. Shakutai, her own mother, believes that if a girl's honour is lost, nothing is left. Even if a girl does nothing wrong, people will always point a finger at her. Shakutai believes that her other daughter will be victimised because of the sake of her sister. The vulnerability of the girl-child is something that affects the rich and the poor alike. Inni, Urmi's mother, confesses her own inability to protect her when she was young and vulnerable.

Surprisingly, it is the male who senses this vulnerability more than the female. Even relationships within the family are no protection against the sexual vulnerability of a girl as seen in the case of Kalpana. Shakutai requests Urmi to take away Sandhya as she feels that she is incapable of taking care of her second daughter, Sandhya. Urmi, the educated, liberated woman with her social contacts and confidence, is the role model in whom she has her hope. That is why she requests Urmila to approach Dr. Bhaskar Jain to make a report so that it appears like a car accident. The novelist reveals how in a patriarchal society, rape carries disgrace for a girl only and the real culprit, i.e. man goes unnoticed. Shakutai, the mother of the victim, does not want an enquiry to be set-up to know the real culprit. She wants the case to be registered as the case of car-accident. She says:

> Ask her, tai, to tell him not to make that report. Even if it happened, what difference will it make now? Why report it? The only thing that will happen is that our name will be mud. I have these two girls.... (Shashi Deshpande 1992: 62)

The novelist has skilfully brought on the surface the inhuman attitude of the patriarchal society to the rape victim as Urmila speaks to her brother:

> Saying that there can be no rape, because it can't be done unless the woman is willing? Yes, I've read that. And the piece by the poet who wants us to "forgive the rapist for he knows not what he is doing". And I have read the letters they say rape happens because women go about exposing themselves. And...oh God! (Shashi Deshpande 1992: 182)

Such a patriarchal and pro-manly attitude discourages the victim and her family to come out with a strong urge to get the real culprit behind the bars. Shakutai, Kalpana's mother in the novel gets very depressed as she herself has suffered all her life because of her husband and now she has to face Kalpana's problem. She is so distressed that once she thinks of committing suicide. The most discouraging moment for her is when she reads all the filth like—Kalpana is a prostitute—in the newspaper. When Urmi advises her not to worry, Shakutai makes a very caustic answer:

> How can I not worry? I have to live with people, I have to live among them. I think I made a mistake, I should have kept quiet. I thought I was helping Kalpana. But sometimes I think only thing that can help Kalpana, now is death. You know, each time I come here, I keep thinking, may be this time, when I come into this ward, I'll see an empty bed, or may be there will be another patient in her bed and they will tell me, "your daughter is dead, she died last night". (Shashi Deshpande 1992: 178)

Thus, the plight and reaction of the parents of victims can be well-imagined. A mother who has given birth to her and now desires death of her daughter then the reaction of others can be well-imagined.

In Indian society, which is chiefly patriarchal in nature, woman is looked upon as a machine which bears children to man. During the early girlhood, a girl is conditioned to play the traditional role of a wife and mother. As a result, she starts enjoying the game '*gharghar*' in which she imagines herself to manage the household affairs efficiently along with taking care of children. This early conditioning prepares her to regard herself as 'a breeding being' and in case after marriage she not able to fulfil this desire (which is imposed upon her by this patriarchal society), she feels shattered and is filled with insecurity and guilt. To quote the novelist:

> Sulu was frightened, she was always frightened because she had no children. She was afraid he would throw her out, take another wife. And then she started getting there patches in her face, her arms, her neck.
>
> ......
>
> She was frightened, always frightened. What if he doesn't like this, what if he wants that, what if he is angry with me, what if he throws me out...? Nobody should live like that, Urmila, so full of fears. (Shashi Deshpande 1992: 192-93)

Shakutai, a representative of female patriarchs, believes herself to be a very unfortunate lady but at the same time she considers herself fortunate enough for having children. The novelist brings on the surface, the attitudinal issue of regarding issuelessness as a curse. In Indian patriarchal society, woman is always blamed for issuelessness as if it is her fault only. Now, even science has proven that there may be some disorder even in the husband; it is also possible that the wife may not be able to give birth to child because of that. Shakutai tells Urmi:

> It seems to me I came into this world carrying a load of misfortune. I thought my Sulu was lucky. I thought, when she married Prabhakar, she at least would have a great life. He is a good man, he doesn't touch drink, not even cigarette.... Yes, I thought her luck is great. But who knows what is hidden in our fate? She says, after a pause, 'God has given her no children'. Suddenly so many things are clear—the tenderness in her voice when she speaks of Sulu, the pity that runs like a refrain through all her talk of her sister. (Shashi Deshpande 1992: 144)

Another important issue that runs like a common string across most of Deshpande novels is the issue of suffering of widows in patriarchal society in India. In most of her novels, Shashi Deshpande depicts the bitter experiences of widowhood. She does believe in depicting the society as it is not as it should be. In Indian patriarchal society, widows are forbidden from participating in festivals, wearing new and gaudy clothes, etc. so as to suppress their sexuality. This patriarchal society expects a widow to remain devoted to the memories of her dead husband. To quote:

> ...the night after Papa's funeral. She wouldn't rest, wouldn't sleep, she talked to us—to us? No, she was scarcely aware of us—the whole night through, of Papa, how they met, of their courtship, their marriage, of things, he said to her, endearments, intimacies. (Shashi Deshpande 1992: 27)

Sexuality and instinct of women have always been controlled by the patriarchs and to fulfil this purpose they use the females in the family whose sexuality, in turn, has been controlled by other elder women that may include mothers or grandmothers. These ladies may be called female patriarchs as they are instruments of patriarchism. Shakutai's outburst brings to light the partisan attitude prevalent in the patriarchal society. If a girl is raped, she alone is censured and victimised. Thus, Shakutai, in spite of all her motherly love and sympathy for her daughter, holds Kalpana's bold independence as the real reason for this catastrophe. When Urmi suggests to her that not Kalpana but the real culprit should be blamed for this catastrophe, Shakutai retorts back:

> What use is it blaming him? Women like you will never understand what it is like for us. We have to keep to our places, we can never step out. There are always people waiting to throw stones at us, our own people first of all. I warned Kalpana, but she would never listen to me. "I am not afraid of anyone", she used to say. That's why this happened to her.... Women must know fear. (Shashi Deshpande 1992: 148)

These so-called female patriarchs believe that the victim should remain silent and anonymous rather than attract notice by making hue and cry in demand of justice. In spite of her nightmarish married life with a husband who neglects her and finally abandons her to live with another woman, Shakutai is much worried about the issue and subsequent effects on marriage prospects of Kalpana. Dr. Bhaskar puzzled over her strange behaviour and comments:

> "Why is the mother so anxious, frantic almost, about her daughter's marriage? Who will marry her if this gets known, she keeps saying. Can't she see the girl's condition!"
>
> "It's not just this girl, there is another daughter."
>
> "How old is she?"
>
> "Twelve, may be thirteen."
>
> "And her mother's worrying about her chances of marriage! That is exactly what I can't understand. Tell me, is getting married so important to a woman?"
>
> I have to think. "Yes", I say finally. "For women like her, definitely". (Shashi Deshpande 1992: 87)

This dialogue between Bhaskar and Urmi, tells about the patriarchal woman Shakutai, who regard that her victim daughter's well-being isn't as important as her marriage. Marriage is so important to her that she is even ready to marry off her lovely daughter Kalpana to a middle-aged man like, Prabhakar. Although, in absence of her husband, she wants to give all possible love and affection to her children, yet it is important to remember that there are limits to her transformation as she too is a product of patriarchy, having assimilated it's power-based value system. As a mother, she attempts to inculcate those very values (which she had acquired as a girl) in her daughters. She is hard with her daughters and wants to prepare them for a hard life. Believing that marriage is the be-all and end-all for a girl, she doesn't mind marrying off her daughter to Prabhakar who is already married. Sulu, Shakutai's sister, is another female patriarch, who doesn't mind Kalpana's marriage to her husband, perhaps for the reason that she is not able to bear child to him because of which out of guilt she is ready to accommodate even a 'second' woman. As Shakutai reveals to Urmi:

> Get me Kalpana, he kept telling her, and you can stay on here, I don't mind. She came to me and I thought it was her idea, that is what she told me. I have no children, she said. If Kalpu marries him, she can be mistress of the house, she doesn't have to do anything, I will do all the work, everything. I thought, what's wrong? At least he's not a drunkard, or a wife-beater or a waster like my husband. (Shashi Deshpande 1992: 193)

Thus for a female patriarch like Shakutai, getting a husband who does not drink is a prized possession for her daughter in itself. Shakutai ignores the fact that though being a perfect housekeeper, Sulu faces unhappiness in marriage. Prabhakar refuses to touch her because of her skin disease. As a favour, he makes her realize that he will not abandon her and lets her cook and clean for him. In return he asks her to make Shakutai's daughter, Kalpana, to marry him. Prabhakar's desire for Kalpana dates back to the time when Sulu and he brought Kalpana to their home with the idea of bringing her up. As Shakutai tells Urmi:

> Even then, when Kalpana went to live with them, he tried to...he wanted...'she gives up'. She was only a child then, she was fourteen and he thought he could.... That is why

> she ran away and refused to go back. But she didn't tell me, why didn't she tell me? And where were my eyes? I should have known, I should have guessed. He used to look at her, he used to say things, he called her, "My beauty", he used to praise her looks. I thought, he is her uncle, he is being affectionate. (Shashi Deshpande 1992: 189-90)

These lines tell about the threat of exploitation faced by young girls from the males related to them. In a survey report, it has been found that in most of the rape-cases in India, girl becomes a victim of some one known or related to her.

Mira, Kishore's mother and Urmila's elder mother-in-law, is a social misfit in the patriarchal society because she happens to be born ahead of her times. Different from all the minor women characters, and being the daughter of a teacher, she is educated, knows English and aspires to become a writer. But in this male-dominated patriarchal society, she does not have the courage to express her desire to become a poetess. She expresses her childhood desire in one of her poems in her diary in which she even, expresses her fear of her ambition being crushed:

> Huddled in my cocoon, a somnolent silk worm
>
> will I emerge a beauteous being?
>
> Or will I, suffocating, cease to exist?
>
> (Shashi Deshpande 1992: 65)

However, in the traditional patriarchal society in which she lives, gender roles are rigidly defined and writing poetry is primarily, a male preserve. She nourishes silently the dream of becoming a writer one day. One day Venu, a promising young poet, is invited to her college to speak to the students. Mira gives much importance to this event as she believes that he may be a mentor to her. But to her amazement, he discourages her to such an extent that she, a born poetess, stops writing poems. To quote:

> And he (Venu) said, yes, she has written.... Why do you need to write poetry? It is enough for a young woman like you to give birth to children. That is your poetry. Leave the other poetry to us men. (Shashi Deshpande 1992: 127)

Thus, this patriarchal answer from Venu, is like a thud on the dreams of Mira, who shares her aspirations with him. Hence, it is the patriarchal society which mars the desires and aspirations of girls and women, the society which applauds men like Venu who are regarded as all time great. This society not only kills the talented poetess like Mira, but it also tries to circumscribe the professional role and identity of a well-educated woman like Urmila who is suggested by people to leave her job as her husband is earning enough. Another example of the talent of women being crushed and female patriarchism can be seen in the example of Bhaskar's mother who had tremendous love for and inclination towards music but her hobby is crushed by her mother-in-law, who like a typical female patriarch, stops her from learning of music. As the novelist remarks:

> My mother loved music, she'd been learning it as a girl. After her marriage, it stopped. I imagine it was my grandmother, who did that. And so my mother turned her ambitions on us, on my sister, rather. She was the one who sang. (Shashi Deshpande 1992: 118)

Thus, we find that traditional women often develop defence mechanism that helps them survive their oppressive situations.

Apart from depicting rape in marital life, loneliness of feminine heart, problems faced by a divorced wife, issuelessness, Shashi Deshpande takes up some other gender issues which appear to be trifle from a patriarchal perspective but actually needs to be given serious thoughts. One of these issues is that a woman's decisions and her choices are taken by men around her. When she is the daughter, her decisions are taken by her father. As a wife her decisions are taken by her husband and when she grows old then her sons take most of the decisions for her. The example in the novel can be seen in the case of Bai Ajji, Urmi's grandmother. She as a girl, is compelled to learn Marathi as it would entitle her for a better groom; as a wife she is compelled to learn English from an English woman as Ajju (Urmi's dada) wants her to learn to speak English so as to match his status. Later she learns Hindi in response to Gandhiji's '*Andolan*'. To quote from the text:

> ...Ajju suddenly decided that his status required his wife to know English she had been taught the language by an English woman.
>
> At first she had resisted, Papa had told me later. And I don't blame her. It was the third time she had to learn a new language. Her father made her switch from a Kannada school to Marathi—he thought it meant a chance of a better husband. Yes, it is true, she said it herself. Then, she went on to Hindi—that was her response to Gandhiji. And after all that, Dada wanted her to learn English. Poor Bai. (Shashi Deshpande 1992: 99)

Thus, we have seen that decision of a woman are taken by men related, one way or the other, and this way she decides to lose her own personality and identity and her own choices. It is not so that this effacement of identity is an easy process. But a girl is conditioned or prepared for this right from the beginning. To quote from the novel:

> I remember, the day the astrologer came home. He read all our horoscopes, told us our futures and we listened as if they were stories about other people. Only my mother's horoscope was not read. "Don't you want to know yours future?" I asked her. And she said—I remember she was serious when she said this—what is there in my life apart from all of you? (Shashi Deshpande 1992: 101)

Thus the point, here, raised by the novelist is how a woman effaces her personality and learns to consider her own well-being in the well-being and happiness of her children and her family only. The novelist brings it on surface that how a girl in a patriarchal society is expected to be self-suppressing of her own personality and identity.

The novelist makes a caustic attack on the so-called 'security' of marriage in the patriarchal society which compels a woman to compromise with the oppressive situation. So is the case with Sulu who agrees to get Kalpana married to her own husband? Her acceptance of a life of humiliation where she would serve Kalpana and her husband after their marriage shows her desperation and lack of choice? Thus, the novelist, painfully reveals that for women like Sulu there is no choice but to cling to a crumbling marriage out of socio-economic security which marriage is supposed to provide. Sulu's desperation becomes the biggest cause of her exploitation where she submits to grave injustice only to retain her married status. On the other hand, men like Prabhakar successfully fulfil their obsessive desires. Even after Kalpana rejects Prabhakar's offer of marriage, he is not deterred and he brutally rapes her. The novelist, makes her observation that the limitations of choice for women in marriage quite implicit in the novel. Urmi also analyzes Akka's marriage. Akka too had little choice but to marry the husband of dead Mira. As Akka, herself, tells to Urmi:

> I was twenty-seven when I got married. In those days, it was old. My family thought I was a hopeless case, I'd be a burden on them forever. When this offer came, they were jubilant. But I was afraid. How could I look after another woman's child?... (Shashi Deshpande 1992: 155)

Therefore, she had to marry a widower, Kishore's father; a man who was obsessed with his first wife. Thus, she was forced to marry a man who wanted a mother for his beloved son more than a wife for himself. It is not that a woman's choice remains circumscribed in marriage only but are even regarded as burden right from the day of their birth. A woman like Shakutai considers girls burdensome. She asks Urmila about the number of children she has. The following dialogue taking place between them is self-revealing:

> "How many children do you have?"
>
> "Only one. A son"....
>
> "And your sister-in-law?"
>
> "She has two daughters."
>
> "Why does God give us daughter...?"
>
> (Shashi Deshpande 1992: 60)

Through the character of Vanaa, Shashi Deshpande presents the selfless life of women who live a life of servitude because tradition has taught them to do so. Vanaa submits to Harish so as to keep her marriage intact. Harish does not co-operate with her in any domestic chores. He is never around whenever she needs him. When Vanaa's little daughter is ill, Vanaa find herself all alone and still Vanaa is devoted to make this relationship work. She always goes by what he says. Urmi, a rebel by nature, feels irritated at Vanaa's constant refrain. 'Harish says'. She is always willing to go along with him in whatever he says. The following dialogue between Vanaa and Urmila reveals hidden layers in the heart of Vanaa:

> "You let him get away with too much, I tell her."
>
> "What do you want me to do?"
>
> "Assert yourself. You don't have to crawl before him, do you?"
>
> "I don't crawl, I do what I want."
>
> "No, you don't. You are scared of him, yes, you are, I've seen you. You don't even dare to call your daughters anything but Mandira and Pallavi, no, not even when you pet them, because Harish doesn't like baby talk..."
>
> I said this when she told me, soon after Pallavi's birth, that they had decided to have no more children.
>
> "Two is enough." But Urmi, she said, her face wistful, "I'd have loved to have had a son."
>
> "You should have told Harish that."
>
> "I did. And he quoted population figures at me. And he said, one, surely I'm not the kind of woman who craves for sons, am I? And, two, what makes me think the next one will be a boy? He is right, only.... I wouldn't have minded taking a chance." (Shashi Deshpande 1992: 80-81)

Thus, Vanaa is symbolic of a traditional woman whose deep-rooted conditioning has been done in the patriarchal society. Like a patriarchally conditioned woman, she wants to have a son, though she has already two lovely daughters. She has desire to have a son but when Harish decides not to take any further chance, she is not able to assert her desire. It shows how the decisions in a patriarchal family are taken exclusively by the husband.

Shashi Deshpande like a true painter of words does show life as it is in her novels instead of painting as it should be ideally in a picture. Like a true social novelist, she has depicted true picture of Indian patriarchal families in which a woman is married off to a man completely unknown to her. Most arranged marriages in India give no opportunity for the couple to know each other and they have fear before initiation of this relaionship. The novelist gives a vivid description of how the niece of Akka appeared to be frightened during her 'first night ceremony'. As the novelist writes:

> What is it like with a man you don't know? The thought came to me at a 'first night ceremony' in Ranidurg, when one of Akka's numerous nieces got married. I remember how almost sacramental the bed seemed, with its cracking new sheets, the pillows with their frilled, elaborately embroidered covers, and fruits and milk like offerings on a table by the bedside. The couple sat stiffly, side by side on the bed, while the women performed an *aarti,* singing the song in subdued notes. In fact, a funeral solemnity hung over all of us during the ceremony. I could not see the girl's face, for she looked steadily down throughout, but I could see that her hands were trembling uncontrollably. And the back of her neck, I can remember that looked like a lamb's, waiting for the butcher's knife to come down upon it. (Shashi Deshpande 1992: 63)

Thus, it is a very frightening experience for a girl to be married to a man unknown to her. Another traumatic experience of girls/women in the Indian patriarchal families is of their seclusion during three days of menstrual cycle. This experience is also horrifying for Saru in the *Dark Holds No Terrors* and its tremor can also be felt in the secluding experience of Mira. Urmila talks about:

> ...the corner room where the women sat three long days, sequestered from the rest of the family, the room with a window which looks out on to the street—'my companion for three days, window in the corner room' Mira calls it. When I read the poem I can see Mira sitting on the floor,

> hair dishevelled, wearing an old saree, her plate and glass by her side. I can see her drawing herself into a huddle each time someone entered, tucking her saree under her feet, drawing it tightly round her shoulders when the children ran in, afraid of polluting them with her touch. And then, when she was alone, looking out of the window, listening to the cries of the hawkers....
>
> Shall I surrender to this Maya-world
> dancing peacock, displaying its feathers?
> Or shall I, defying the market world
> retreat into my shell tortoise-like?
> (Shashi Deshpande 1992: 98)

Analysing the condition of women in marriage, Urmi reviews her own marriage with Kishore. She had gone against her family and her friend, Vanaa, to marry Kishore, but she walks out on him on the wedding night as Kishore looks as if feels trapped by marriage. Her intention in doing so is to prove that her love for him which culminated in marriage is not a binding and will not end his freedom. To prove him wrong she goes to sleep at her parent's house which is adjacent. Thus, regardless of traditions, Urmi dreams of building her relationship with Kishore on the basis of companionship and understanding. But Kishore's job in Merchant Navy disrupts her dream of leading a normal married life. She feels frustrated with his short visits as she can't get time to develop an emotional relationship with him. The long separation from him often fills her with physical longing to have him permanently by her side. Every time he goes "the parting is like death" to Urmi but her hard exterior deceives even her mother as she never lets her mother know her anger and grief. Her efforts to express these feelings to him are always answered by Kishore's passionate lovemaking. But Urmi remains disillusioned and unfulfilled because she realizes:

> But sex is only a temporary answer. I came out of it to find that the lights had come back [...] 'go to sleep', he said. He was kneeling by me his face close to mine, but the closeness was only physical. His voice was cold. I could see the goose bumps on his shoulders, his chest. I did not look

> into his face. I was afraid of what I would see. I turned round and fell asleep. (Shashi Deshpande 1992: 139-40)

Often her sexual needs make her crave for Kishore's permanent presence but his absence leaves her bitter. Sometimes she finds it hard to control her desire and wishes:

> I could put my desires into a deep freeze and take them out, intact and whole, when he returned. (Shashi Deshpande: 1992: 164)

In spite of her love for her husband, Urmi asserts her financial independence. She rejects his money for she as a wife expects more than just monetary support. She longs for the emotional security a husband provides to his wife. Such needs lead her to frustrations and she is never able to reach his emotional centre. Some parts of Kishore evade her as she feels:

> Kishore will never remove his armour, there is something in him I will never reach. I have lived with the hope that someday I will. Each relationship, always important, survives on hope. (Shashi Deshpande 1992: 155)

Urmi's dissatisfaction with the situation between her and Kishore leads to her revolt against the traditional limitations of a wife and she asserts her need. In Dr. Bhaskar Jain, she finds a friend who understands the emotional upheaval through which she is undergoing after Anu's death (Urmi's only daughter). Her husband, Kishore's absence leaves her alone to cope with her grief. But, Bhaskar, the patient listener, understands her emotions and helps her accept her loss. His friendship, which gives Urmi the much needed companionship, comes to an abrupt end with Bhaskar's open declaration of his love for her. Here, once again, Deshpande presents problematized version of the male friend-married woman relationship. Bhaskar grows serious in his intentions towards Urmila. Typically, he surmises that a woman whose husband is away for several months and who never speaks of him couldn't be very happy in her marriage. His patriarchal expectation that a woman staying alone may be wanting sexual favours prompts him to express sexual interest in her:

> "...he leans forward and takes off my glasses."
>
> "What's that for?"

"I want to see your eyes. I want to see you without your shield."

He says this with such feeling, he looked at me with such intensity,..I'm frightened....

"Tell me about your marriage."

"He sees the 'why' in my eyes perhaps, for he says, as if explaining. It's the most important thing to me right now."

"I can say nothing.... Has he realized he does not figure anywhere in the equation of my marriage?"

He waits for a while, then starts the car and drives me home in silence. (Shashi Deshpande 1992: 161-62)

At this juncture, Urmila feels 'cheated' and 'angry'—cheated because she had never thought of Bhaskar as a lover, and angry because she ought to have expected this development as Bhaskar is also the product of the patriarchal society.

Bhaskar's knowledge of the communication gap between Urmi and her husband makes him hopeful. Even if Urmi is tempted, she could not uproot herself from her traditional background. Besides, her love for Kishore has a firm hold on her marriage. The amount of hurt and trouble her affair with Bhaskar will cause also makes her choose the simple and respectful life of fidelity. Overcoming her temptations she finds it much simpler.

Her rejection of Bhaskar for Kishore even if Kishore flits in and out of her life every few month proves that in spite of her dissatisfaction with her marriage she still loves Kishore. Unlike Indu in *Roots and Shadows*, Urmi does not give in to temptations to fulfil her physical needs. She is aware of the complications such a move can bring in her life. Thus, she lives with the hope that her love for Kishore will bring down the barriers between them. Her fiercely independent nature is first seen at the age of fifteen when she chooses to stay alone with her grandfather Aju's dead body (Aju had hanged himself to death) while Kishore goes to fetch some other members of the family. Her rationale is how she could leave her grandfather's dead body until her father comes. In this respect, she is unlike any other protagonist of Shashi Deshpande. The novelist reveals that expressing one's needs and accepting one's vulnerability are not weaknesses but steps to liberation, and that assertiveness and aggressiveness are the desired ideals. Urmila is a strong woman but more aggressive than assertive. Her growth as a character in the book is marked by her gradual realization that to assert is not to deny others their rights, that assertion means to stand up for oneself without hurting others. As a protagonist, therefore, she stands at the other extreme of the spectrum from the rest of the protagonists who are initially passive and whose evolution towards self-assertion from the opposite end, that is, aggressiveness. In the end of the novel, we find her giving up her fears. The roots of her fear of abandonment also lie in her childhood experience of having been sent to Ranidurg to be raised by her grandparents while her brother Amrit is not, an experience that has scarred her psyche deeply. Gray observes:

> Hidden in the unconscious, this feeling of unworthiness generates the fear of needing others. A part of her [the woman] imagines that she will not be supported. (Gray 1992: 53)

When Inni reveals why Urmi was sent to Baiajji for education as one day Inni had left her with a male servant alone, thus shocking her father who never excused Inni for this lapse. Inni reveals to Urmi:

> I was too young, I was not prepared to have a child. And you were not easy, you used to cry all the time, I didn't know how to soothe you. Diwakar was good with you, he was better than me, but Papa said, "How could you leave her alone with a man!" Diwakar! He had been with us since I was a child, that's why Mummy sent him to help me, he was so gentle, but Papa said, "He is a man. Diwakar!" (Shashi Deshpande 1992: 199)

The above dialogue between Urmi's parents reveals the sense of responsibility associated with bringing up of a girl-child and this could be one of the probable reasons for considering a girl-child as a burden. Until now, Urmila used to hold her mother responsible for sending her away to Ranidurg to be brought up by her grandparents. Now, she realizes the pain and agony of her mother who had to part away from her only daughter. Until now Urmi had admired him (her father) very much and considered him 'pragmatic' and firm. It is Amrut, her younger brother who was brought up in his natal home and who corrects her perspective and tells her how their father was a patriarchal, and an authoritarian person. He says:

> Papa was dominating. There is no other word for him. Things were simple to him, "you have to do things my way", and that was it.
>
> "He was absolute master in the house."
>
> "Do you think you have to use physical violence to be brutal? Even to force your will on another is to be brutal." (Shashi Deshpande 1992: 133)

This revelation adds a new dimension to the power-based marital relationship. A man may love his wife, as Urmila's father loves his wife, and yet deny her voice so completely as to cause untold mental torture and suffering. Ultimately, there is realization that a man (Urmi's father in this case) wrongs a woman (Urmi's mother in this case) by imposing his inflexible will on her.

In the course of the novel, Urmi comments and meditates on several gender issues which are normally the concern of the feminists: the girl-child and society, rape and society, woman as obsession to man, marriage in the Indian society, woman and household chores, woman's career and family, relationship between mother and daughter and so on. In this web of loss and despair, experience of existential trauma Deshpande leaves enough space for the glimmerings of hope through the redemptive powers of love. Chesser, in "Cost of Living" as quoted in *Love, Marriage and Sex*, has divided love into three types. These are:

> ego instincts such as self-preservation, sex instinct including the material instinct, and social instinct which in human beings includes altruism. (Chesser 1973: 25)

All the three instincts contribute to make the *The Binding Vine*.

Mira's husband represents the passionate love of men. His one-sided affair with Mira is the love at first sight. He first saw

Mira at a wedding and fell in love with her after which his single-minded object is to marry Mira. His love for her is questionable, bending towards sex as he never succeeds in developing an emotional bond of love between them, but his 'apparent' passion continues even after her death when he brings back a day-old child (his son from Mira) and cares after him.

Urmila and Kishore present the velvety texture and silky smoothness of adolescent love, which is based on infatuation and which they are unable to prolong in the long run. This adolescent joyous feeling of love becomes stale after turning into sex instinct, and Urmi, wrapping herself around with the hard shell of ego, starts losing the strength of love. But she realizes that she has constant longing in her to keep Kishore by her side:

> Fixed forever in our places,
> Face to face two of us,
> Like Siva and his nodding Bull.
> (Shashi Deshpande 1992: 82)

She tries to search the feeling of love again in her relation with Dr. Bhaskar. But this also turns out to be in the end, a transitory relation.

Ego instinct and sex instinct in love work for short time in the life of a man and then they turn to be painful and frustrating if love is not based on mutual understanding. The last type of love as a social instinct has also been presented in *The Binding Vine*. Man being a social animal, comes across many people in his life and *The Binding Vine* is also about the instinct of social love. It binds different human relations, keeps them intact and carries forward the life of human beings. This is the ultimate form of love in which Urmi seeks refuge. In the end of the novel, Urmila remembers:

> And yet I think of Vanaa, heavily pregnant, sitting by me, holding my hand during the pains before Kartik was born, I remember Kishore's face when he first saw Anu, I think of Akka crying for Mira, of Inni's grief when papa told her about his illness, of Papa's anguished face watching her, of the touch of grace there was in Shakutai's hand when she covered me gently at night while I slept, of love with

> which she speaks of her sister, of Sandaya.... Is this it, the spring of life, Mira was looking for? (Shashi Deshpande: 1992: 203)

Mira, desperate of her sexual relations with her husband, dies in the prime of her youth having certain unanswered questions in her heart. The answer we get in the end is the realisation of altruistic quality of social instinct of love. It is this love which has been the main source of teachings in almost all the spiritual scriptures of India since the Vedic Age down to our times. In our religious preaching, we are taught to believe in the omnipotent power of love. Loving our fellows equally and unselfishly we can reach above the petty problems of our individual life, and ultimately a glorious form of salvation comes to us. This is the message of sublime love embedded in *The Binding Vine*, adopting which in their life people can find even today a way to peace in their disturbed life.

Works Cited

Deshpande, Shashi. *The Binding Vine*. New Delhi: Penguin, 1993.

Gray, John. *Men, Women and Relationship*. New York: HarperCollins, 1992.

Jaggar, M. Allison. *Feminist Politics and Human Nature*. New Jersey: Rowman and Allenheld Pub., 1983.

Jaisingh, Indrani. "Survivors: Changing Attitude to Divorce among Women in India". *Uncertain Liaisons*. Ed. Khushwant Singh and Shobhaa De. New Delhi, 1993.

Kakkar, Sudhir. "Feminine Identity in India" Ed. *Women in Indian Society: A Reader*. New Delhi: Sage Publications, 1998.

Kapur, P. *Love, Marriage and Sex*. New Delhi: Vikas Publishing House, 1973.

4

Women's Subjugation in Patriarchal Society (*The Dark Holds No Terrors*)

In Shashi Deshpande's *The Dark Holds No Terrors*, multiple issues concerning women and their conditions have been depicted and described in a form of emotive cobwebs. The novel is a compelling story of a woman's struggle against all odds. First published in 1980, the novel, by the author's admittance, is 'the one most dear to her'. Although Shashi Deshpande has strongly defended her position not to be branded as a feminist author, her work nonetheless vouches for some vital gender issues that can't be ignored. She cites Betty Friedan and Virginia Woolf in her narrative, and in a subtle way brings into focus gender issues of identity, selfhood, autonomy, and of bonding. Referring to B. Friedan, she says that:

> It was easier for her to start the women's liberation movement than to change her own personal life. (Shashi Deshpande 1990: 107)

The novel *The Dark Holds No Terrors* can be taken as feministic forum as it deconstructs and reconstructs the gender roles and inner space, especially in the Indian society. The female protagonist Sarita, in the novel is constantly and often unconsciously in the search of an 'inner space'. Shashi Deshpande treats male-female polarity as natural and for this purpose she uses the motifs of home and family relationships. She projects the post-modern dilemma of a woman who strongly resents the onslaught on her individuality and identity. Sarita faces antagonism mainly from two persons—her mother and her husband. Both of them represent the values and norms established by the patriarchal society. Ironically, a female can be made as an agency for the effective promotion of a male point of view as in the case of Saru's mother. The novel is also different in the sense that other novelists have given the peripheral treatment to the gender issues but Shashi Deshpande gives the nuclear space to the gender issues and explodes the myth of a man's unquestionable superiority and woman being a martyr and a paragon of all virtues. Cheri Register opines that a feminist writing needs to fulfil one or more of the following:

> Serve as forum for women; help to achieve cultural androgyny; provide role models; promote sisterhood; and augment consciousness raising. (Cheri Register 1979)

When we make a perusal of Shashi Deshpande's *The Dark Holds No Terrors* in the light of the above-mentioned statement, we find that this novel has a well-developed plot and it can be taken as an assertion of Simone de Beauvoir's statement that one is not born, but rather becomes a woman. Beauvoir believes that it is the civilization that produces this creature (woman) which is described as feminine. However, Shashi Deshpande's novel is different from the feminist works of the West which present male protagonist providing secondary roles to women. However, Shashi Deshpande's protagonists are women who ponder over their situations and their relation to others.

Unlike many Indian women novelists, Shashi Deshpande talks about the biased attitude of parents in upbringing a girl child. Though this attitudinal issue is universal in tone, yet the voices heard are Indian, particularly in her *The Dark Holds No Terrors*. One cannot expect anything less from a novelist who was influenced by the writings of Jane Austen and still she loves to re-read her works very much. *The Dark Holds No Terrors* (1980), the first of her published works, is based upon her own observation when she saw a couple...the wife had a better job and there was an obvious tension between them. Shashi Deshpande, at the first place, wrote a story on the same theme and titled this story as "Liberated Woman" which won her Femina short-story contests. She re-wrote this story about seventeen times and still she felt that she had not got it right. So, when we take into consideration this fact, we realize that the work is about a woman who suffers not only at the hands of her parents but also at the hands of her husband.

To begin with, *The Dark Holds No Terrors* is the story of Sarita reflecting on her small town upbringing, a domineering mother, a jealous husband and a failing marriage. She finally realizes that there is more to life than dependency on husband, parents and social acceptance. Very dexterously, Shashi Deshpande throws light on silence, loss, confusion, disappointment and silent cruelties of married life of this claustrophobic woman, Sarita. The novelist narrates the story of a career woman who as a child was abused emotionally by her mother and now is being abused sexually by her husband. In doing so, the novelist brings several gender issues in context to Indian patriarchal system on surface.

Shashi Deshpande makes a caustic attack on Indian patriarchal system in which a girl-child faces parental rejection only for the reason that she was born as a girl and that too because of no fault of hers. Saru's relationship with her brother has been given a special treatment. She is not given any importance and is always ignored in favour of her brother, Dhruva—no ceremony for her but no occasion is missed to celebrate for Dhruva (her brother), be it his birthday or his naming-ceremony. As a child, Saru was told the story of mythological Dhruva, who was pushed off his father's lap and who gave himself up to steadfast meditation so that he became the constant North Star. One day out of her childish logic, Saru pushes Dhruva off her father's lap so as to see if he also becomes a star like a mythological Dhruva. If she had been a son, then this incidence would have been told and retold to the relatives and acquaintances with the vestige of a smile but she was unfairly punished for this action of hers as if she had committed a major crime. This discrimination does not stop here only. It recurs annually in the form of birthday celebrations of Dhruva. There was always joyous excitement in the house on the occasion of Dhruva's birthdays. His birthdays are celebrated with much fanfare and performance of religious rites but her birthdays lack all the religious rites. Later, after the death of Dhruva, her birthdays go unacknowledged as if it was she who had killed him. This discrimination on the part of parents has been portrayed very skilfully by Shashi Deshpande:

> There was always a *puja* on Dhruva's birthday. A festive lunch in the afternoon and an *aarti* in the evening during which Dhruva, as an infant, sat solemnly on Baba's lap, ...my birthdays were almost the same...but there was no *puja*. (Shashi Deshpande 1990: 168-69)

Even this small scale celebration on her birthdays stopped after the death of Dhruva. Her birthdays passed over in silence until her friend Smita gifted her a pair of earrings. On receiving this small gift Sarita, an ignored girl, feels more amazed than pleased. She as a girl-child has to spend her childhood as a lonely child as there was none whom she could talk to and there was none whom she could confide in. Her father never spoke to her, though he used to have frequent conversations with Dhruva. His 'indifference' may be considered as an indirect expression of patriarchy that is emotionally injurious. Physically and socially, there are different measures that patriarchy employs in placing women and marking their space. Perhaps this reserved attitude on the part of her father was because of an old-fashioned attitude that daughters are their mother's business. Surprisingly, she is more a liability to her own mother who surprises her by gifting a pair of earrings, made of gold, on her fifteenth birthday. Saru's mother presents this gift to her daughter not for the reason that she cared for her daughter's feelings but for the sake of people that what they will think about a grown-up girl of fifteen without any earrings or bangles made of gold.

Sarita undergoes great humiliation and neglect not only on the account of special treatment given to her brother by her parents but also on the account of their indifference towards her. For her parents, she was more a liability less a daughter. The novelist, here, discusses that how a girl is brought up more like a 'daughter' than a child. Although some of the critics attribute this gender-biased attitude of Saru's mother to her own very unhappy childhood. Sarita's maternal grandmother had been deserted by her husband, leaving her with the burden of bringing up two daughters, one of whom had been Sarita's mother. The woman and her daughters had been sheltered by her parents 'unwillingly'. Saru's mother's childhood had influenced her adult personality. Perhaps, her childhood feelings of insecurity and being 'unwanted' had conditioned her to an extent that she started regarding girl-child as a burden. The novelist has very well expressed this point of view by presenting a dialogue between Saru and her parents when she decides to pursue her career in medicine. Had she been a boy, her parents would have taken pride in her achievement of scoring a first class, but so is not the case. She has to fight literally for her career and she is prepared for this battle. The novelist comments:

> But she is a girl.
>
> Yes, I am a girl. But it is more than that. I am not Dhruva.
>
> Well, plenty of girls go in for medicine.
>
> Yes, but they are the girls whose fathers have lots of money. You don't belong to that class. And don't forget, medicine or no medicine, doctor or no doctor, you still have to get her married, spend money on her wedding. Can you do both? Make yourself a pauper, and who will look after you in your old days?... Let her go for a B.Sc.... You can get her married in two years and our responsibility will be over. (Shashi Deshpande 1990: 144)

Thus, the novelist brings on the surface the gender biasedness that has made its niche in the psyche of traditional parents, who believe their daughters to be burdens needed to be put off. For such parents the education of their daughters is of least importance. Sarita's mother goes a step further when Saru's father mentions her choice of education. She says:

> What gives her the right to choose? Have we no say in the matter?... I know you will have to spend for her wedding as well. We cannot ever evade that responsibility. (Shashi Deshpande 1990: 144)

This is not only the freedom to choose one's career that a woman is ripped off but also the freedom to choose her own life partner. If a girl decides to marry by her own choice or to marry outside her caste; she is thought to be a threat to the so-called 'family honour'. If an educated and economically independent woman like Sarita is not allowed by her parents to marry by her own choice then the plight of illiterate or semi-literate woman can be well imagined. Girls like Saru who protest and marry against the wishes of their parents are never welcome in their families. They are never 'forgotten and forgiven'. Sarita and Manohar hope that someday they will be forgiven but Saru's mother even does not want to see her again in her life. She develops so much hatred for Sarita that she does not want to go to see a doctor as Sarita is a doctor by profession. Mrinal, Madhav's sister, who is so much fed up by the treatment she receives at her parental house that she is ready to marry anyone. Madhav tells Sarita:

> She hates our village and the kind of life she is leading. Going on and on with the same things, day after day. Get the water, look after the kids, help mother.... Oh, she is fed up, she says she wants to get away to. 'I don't care how'. She says she is prepared to marry anyone who will take her away from there. Father is looking for a bridegroom for her, but he will never think of consulting her or asking her what she would like. [Shashi Deshpande 1990: 122]

Thus, the novelist highlights the issue of pitiable condition of girls in their own parental homes and discloses at the same time domestic-chores' burden on the shoulders of the young girls. At the age when they should be occupied with playing themselves, they are given the responsibility of taking care of their younger siblings.

Shashi Deshpande is not a militant feminist and being a liberal feminist she takes up many issues which have been left untouched by the so-called radical feminists of the West who believe men to be entirely responsible for the plight of women. Not in mood to appease the foreign readers, the novelist depicts the issues deeply rooted in Indian patriarchal system. In order to do so, Shashi Deshpande, talks about the so-called female patriarchs. Sarita's mother is one of the female patriarchs in the novel *The Dark Holds No Terror*. The novelist explores that the male-oriented society conditions females in such a manner that these so-called 'female patriarchs' work against even those of their own gender. Through this novel, Shashi Deshpande conveys an important message that suppression, subjugation and exploitation are not confined to the male-female relationship only but also exist between a female-female relationship as well. Sarita, the protagonist in the novel, grows up to be a victim of her mother's gender-biased attitude. As a child, she is fully aware of her mother's preference for the son. She is not able to comprehend her mother's behaviour towards her. She is partially if not completely aware of the fact that she is merely a liability or a responsibility that can be ridden off by marrying off. Saru's mother, like a traditional Indian mother, is worried about her daughter's complexion or her appearance instead of her education. Sarita as a girl gets constant reminders of her destiny to get married and leave her father's home. The dialogue between Saru and her mother is as following:

> Don't go out in the sun. You will get even darker.
>
> Who cares?
>
> We have to care even if you don't. We have to get you married.
>
> I don't want to get married.
>
> Will you live with us all your life?
>
> Why not?
>
> You can't.
>
> And Dhruva?
>
> He is different. He is a boy. (Shashi Deshpande 1990: 45)

The conversation reveals a mother's anxiety lest anything should mar her daughter's appearance or complexion and make it difficult to get her married. In the emphasis on a fair complexion, that must not grow dark and an appearance that should remain attractive (because men like it so), lays a concrete example of de Beauvoir's observation that a woman is defined with reference to a man. A girl is conditioned since her childhood that physical appearance is the only criterion for being selected or rejected in marriage. If a girl is not beautiful then her parents are not able to find a very good match for her. Shashi Deshpande, here, wants to highlights the problem of a girl of marriageable age. It fills a girl with the feeling of fear of rejection. Many number of advertisements for fair complexioned girls can be found in matrimonial advertisements published in Indian newspapers. Tillie Olsen sees in such socialization the origin of a girl/woman's silence and oppression because it is a slow, corrosive form of mental colonization and pacification:

> The leeching of belief, of will, the damaging of capacity begins so early. Sparse is the literature on the way of denial to small girl children of the development of their endowment as born human: active, vigorous bodies; exercise of power to do so, to make, to investigate, to invent, to conquer obstacles, to resist violations of the self, ...little has been written on the harms of instilling constant concern with the appearance; the need to please.... (Eagletoro 1992: 54)

Kamla tai (Saru's mother) tries her best to persuade her husband not to send Saru to a medical college. She, like male patriarchs, believes that girls belong to an altogether different family. The socialization of these female patriarchs has been done in such a manner that they look upon girls only as future wives. Veena Das says in this regard:

> Daughters are comparable to something kept in trust for another (amanat). You have to care for them, love them and you will be held responsible for them but you are destined to loose them. Once a daughter is properly married and goes to her own house it is like a debt that has been paid. (Veena Das 1992: 93)

Another example of female patriarchism can be seen in the novel in the character of Mai kaki, who praises Saru's mother for suffering silently (as she suffers from cancer). Kamla tai does not reveal to anybody about her suffering as Mai kaki narrates to Saru:

> She never told anyone about what was happening to her. The amount she ate...I will tell you, a sparrow would have eaten more. Your father never noticed because she never ate with him. (Shashi Deshpande 1990: 99)

This silence between Saru's parents outlines the emotional margins in the couples' relation and the way Mai kaki praises it, tells of women as a part of 'mute group'. To Mai kaki—the destiny of Saru's mother, who suffered silently, seems to be much better than her own destiny as she has to live as a widow. Mai kaki believes herself to be very unlucky as she survives her husband and is therefore unloved, unwanted and useless. She curses herself for being alive when her husband is no more. Here, Shashi Deshpande wants to assert that widowhood is taken as the worst calamity in the traditional patriarchal society. A widower can live without his wife but life gets catastrophic for a widow as T.N. Madan observes:

> ...the death of her husband is seen as altering the social identity of a woman. (T.N. Madan Vol. 9)

Another issue, of gender-discrimination, that is highlighted by the novelist is that though these so-called 'female patriarchs' work against those of their own gender, yet they are looked down upon by the staunch male-patriarchs. Saru's classmate Padmakar, on the one hand, wants 'favours' from Sarita and on the other hand, he has no respect for his own wife who has devoted her life to none but her husband and his family. She is disliked by her husband for the reason that she talks all the time about children and the family only while this behaviour on her part shows her concern for the family and him. She just cooks what he likes and never calls her husband by his name. By depicting the relationship of Padmakar with his wife, the novelist raises the issue that devotion and submissiveness of women are taken to be 'social backwardness' by the so-called male-chauvinsts. The novelist also wants to send the message that women can earn respect for themselves not by following the traditional path as followed by Padmakar's wife but by asserting their individuality when required.

The novel *The Dark Holds No Terrors* explores the sexual vulnerability of women and the exploitation as a sex-object, which is sanctioned by marriage in the patriarchal system. The intercourse in the novel amounts to rape but it goes unpublicised since it occurs within marriage. In patriarchal terms, particularly in India, sexual violence against women is a means of 'subjugating' or 'taming' the woman into passivity. Saru is apprehensive of the sexual act after marriage and is reluctant to engage in sex as she hints at postponing their stay-together (after marriage) on the pretext of her studies. She dislikes the idea of staying in one room 'chawl' with Manohar, who cannot pay for better with the little he earns. At this point of time, Saru knows that consummation is inevitable but she wants to postpone it on account of her studies. She is apprehensive about sex but the first experience is absorbing for her and she is satisfied (in her professional life) by treating people around her. After passing out from the medical college, Saru is happy to treat people in small colonies. The episode of factory-explosion changes their lives completely. After treating the patients of factory explosion, Saru is very tired and she does not change her blood-stained white coat and thus the people in the neighbourhood come to know that she is a doctor. Now onwards, whenever they go out together, she receives more wishes and smiles. This is the moment which changes her life and consequently changes their lives. Manohar starts feeling subjugated and subordinated and therefore feels frustrated. Unable to compete with her in the professional sphere, he marks his superiority in bed. There it begins, the physical exploitation, as depicted by Shashi Deshpande:

> It was because I was tired, always too tired after my long day at the hospital.... And there were times when he was rough and abrupt with me, I put it down to the ardour of his love.
>
> In any case, these occasions were rare enough then. So rare that I could easily forget them. But now I know that it was there it began...the esteem with which I was surrounded made me inches taller.... Now I was the lady doctor and he was my husband.
>
> a+b they told us in mathematics is equal to b+a. But here a+b was not definitely equal to b+a. It became a monstrously unbalanced equation, lopsided, unequal, impossible. (Shashi Deshpande 1990: 42)

The woman in this narrative does not find a freedom or assurance of self in the successful acquisition of 'room of her own'—Shashi Deshpande does not play out a Woolfian thesis—rather, the woman who gains entry to this room looses her self; she is thrown into an existential crisis. Interestingly, Saru's professional life is described as a facade behind which her true self hides. Thus, after the incidence of factory-explosion, Manohar who was a loving husband until now turns a cruel husband who asserts and satisfies his 'male-ego' by making her a prey in bed. He believes her to be exclusively 'his property', an inorganic thing, a non-living and hence exercises his sexual rights over her. Therefore, he forces himself upon her brutally and she usually wakes up to find herself being violated in midnight. After this episode, Manohar establishes his superiority in the relationship; he humiliates her and treats her like an inanimate object. The point to be noted is that her assent in the matter is not necessary to him. It seems as if she has been 'provided' to him for 'exclusive use' through the legal channel of marriage.

In the novel *The Dark Holds No Terror*, Shashi Deshpande has portrayed and highlighted the vulnerability of women and physical exploitation along with humiliation. Deshpande rejects prudery to probe an intimate experience of women. She is primarily concerned with women and does not hesitate to uncover issues such as women's sexuality which has remained neglected so far in Indian English literature or has been held as a taboo in Indian women's writings. The best part of Shashi's depiction of women's sexual issues in India is that it has not a tinge of vulgarity in it. The impact of the hammer, with which the novelist strikes while depicting women's exploitation in marriage, can be seen in the following line:

> Terror waited for me in our room. I could not escape it. (Shashi Deshpande 1990: 79)

The point to be noted here is that Manu who is otherwise a very accommodating husband, turns 'hostile' and 'manly' towards her whenever he faces a challenge to his 'manhood'. For example, when Manu and Saru go out for shopping a few things they need at Ooty (they have planned a holiday at Ooty), and they meet Manu's colleague and his wife, his friend comments that they could not afford such a holiday as his wife is not a lady doctor. That very moment, Saru 'realises' that 'terror' awaits her in bed that night. The novelist gives voice to her protagonist and depicts:

> I woke up to darkness and an awareness of fear. Panic. Then pain. There it was, for the second time, what I had just lulled myself into believing was just a nightmare. The hurting hand, the savage teeth, the monstrous assault of

> a horribly familiar body and above me, a face I could not recognise.... Then I began to struggle. But my body, hurt and painful, could do nothing against the fearful strength which overwhelmed me.... And then, mercifully, the end, the face still hovering over mine, changing as the body relaxed, becoming the familiar known one of my husband's. (Shashi Deshpande 1990: 111-12)

Her body is now reduced to an 'outline' in chalk. It exists in the multiplication of various forms of pains: pain of loss, pain of suffering and pain of mental trauma. To Sarita it is not the cruelty of her husband that fills her with grief, but also:

> The thing she knew she had lost forever...the eternal female dream of finding happiness through a man. It would never come alive for her again.... And it was like a silent mourning wail inside her. (Shashi Deshpande 1990: 24).

The circles of pain that surround a woman may not possibly redeem her. But pain, ultimately, becomes a means of self-discovery that enables Sarita to take the decisive step of leaving her house, children and husband. The dichotomy in the nature of Manohar can be noticed when he gets up the next morning and behaves as usual as if nothing had happened the previous night. It seems as if he has come to his normal self after asserting his superiority and manhood in bed. In another incident, Saru gives interviews for a special issue on career women brought out by a women magazine. The interviewer makes a casual query to Manu how it feels when his wife earns not only the butter but most of the bread as well. This question initiates the sense of insecurity in Manohar. The lover in him dies and this feeling of insecurity reaches the point of culmination with the interviewer's query. He is unable to come to terms with the fact that he is a failure in life. Manu lets his wounded male pride manifest itself in the form of sexual sadism. He believes that the bed is the only place where he can assert his animal power over her.

It is not the case that Shashi Deshpande wants to depict physical exploitation as the only possible aspect of marriage in the Indian society; she wants to project that marriage has been used rather misused as a licence by Indian men to assert their superiority and the subordination of women. As she herself in an interview with Lakshmi Holmstrom says that as far as she as an author is concerned, the important issue is the degradation that women experience and continue to experience apart from this so-called subordination and inequality. As told to Lakshmi Holmstrom:

> But to me feminism isn't a matter of theory: it is difficult to apply Kate Millett or Simone de Beauvoir or whoever to the reality of our daily lives in India. And, there are such terrible misconceptions about feminism by people here. They often think it is about burning bras and walking out on your husband, children or about not being married, not having children, etc. I always try to make the point now about what feminism is not, and try to say that we have to discover what it is in our own lives. our experiences. And I actually feel that a lot of women in India are feminist without realising it. I am surprised at how much our lives have changed in recent years. (Interview to Lakshmi Holmstrom in *Fiction of Shashi Deshpande* edited by R.S. Pathak; Creative Books, New Delhi, 1998: 249)

A deep perusal of *The Dark Holds No Terrors* enables the reader to glimpse the dynamics of Indian patriarchy, and what feminists scholars have termed as 'gender politics'. This novel of hers not only exposes the oppressive condition of women within Indian society but also helps to identify the areas of conflict and tension in the domestic world that the educated, middle-class Indian woman has to face today. The behaviour of the male characters of Shashi Deshpande is typically 'chauvinistic behaviour' and in reaction to their chauvinistic behaviour, her female characters start their quest for selfhood. To some of the readers, the novel seems to be one-dimensional depiction of molestation in marriage but there are several other issues which mark their presence and which need to be perused carefully.

We have seen that depiction of physical exploitation in marriage has been done skilfully by the novelist. A woman's desire is not taken into consideration by these chauvinistic men. Manu is unable to bear the fact that he is a failure and his wife is a remarkable success in life; Manu lets wounded male pride manifest itself in the form of sexual sadism. Shashi Deshpande has very vividly depicted this act of Manohar a mean and loathsome fellow, who basks in her glory by day and ill-treats her at night. The novelist writes:

> The beginning was abrupt. There had been no preparation for it.... The nightmare was compounded of lips and teeth as well. Hands and teeth? No, hammers and pincers.... I struggled to utter the usual words of protest, to say.... Not now, stop it. But the words were strangled in my throat. The face above mine was the face of a stranger.... A man I did not know.... It was monstrous invasion of my body. I tried to move, twisting my body wriggling under the weight that pinned it down. The small pains merged all at once into larger one.... I began to fight back, hopelessly, savagely, and suddenly.... The body that was not mine relaxed.... It was more as if my mind had deserted my shamefully bruised body, disowning it, making it insensate.... I turned my head slightly, fearfully and saw him beside me, snoring softly. No more a stranger but my husband. (Shashi Deshpande 1990: 11-12)

Shashi Deshpande depicts the character of Manohar with a purpose of depicting men who are having dwarf careers in comparison to their wives'. Sarita's career is Manu's problem but he shudders at the idea of her giving up her job. Manohar has this realization that they will be in financial crisis if she leaves her job. As a mediocre man, he tricks of cajoling her by offering to take her out for a movie. That night he treats her like a young lover making love to his beloved. He can't dream of going back to the shabby middle class way of life. So he lets pass her relationship with Boozie with half-shut eyes. Saru knows that Boozie is the fairy god-father who with the wave of his magical wand can make things easier for her. Saru also knows it very well that one does not help anybody without selfish interest but the urge to achieve more in life compels her to accept Boozie's ways. She knows he is the ladder whom she can make use of. Manu knows every thing about Saru and Boozie and even then he decides to keep his mouth shut because he knows that he himself in incapable of taking more out of life. The novelist writes:

> And there was Manu coming to me, saying
>
> "He is here."
>
> "Who?"
>
> No need to ask, really. No need for him to reply.
>
> ......
>
> Invite him in. And look after him. I knew there was plenty of talk about me and him. I knew what they said about my rapid climb since the day I met him.
>
> ......
>
> He (Boozie) put his two hands on my shoulders and shook me gently. I could feel the stares. Every one's except Manu. Who would not look at us? (Shashi Deshpande 1990: 93-94)

At this point anybody may expect Sarita to hate Boozie for spoiling her reputation but she hates Manu for the reason that he does not react at all to her relationship with Boozie. The only possible explanation for this inert response of Manu may be that in his sub-conscience, he has this realization that Sarita is the primary bread-earner of the family. But the 'man' inside him can't let it pass so easily and that night he tries to 'possess' her. Saru's relation with Boozie may also be taken as symbolic of her inner desire to acquire an identity and individuality of her own for which she uses Boozie as a ladder.

Apart from depicting gender issues like biased attitude of parents and marriage as a licence of physical exploitation, Shashi Deshpande depicts the loneliness of a feminine heart from the perspective of a psychological novelist. She, as a novelist of gender issues, has explored the plight of women particularly Indian women from all possible angles. Using Saru as her mouthpiece, the novelist depicts how an Indian woman feels lonely during her girlhood and this loneliness provides her nothing but insecurity. Shashi Deshpande's Sarita feels lonely not only in social and family sphere but also in emotional sphere. As a child, she is not able to rip her heart open to her parents who also do not try to talk their daughter so as to know what lies in her heart. She never discloses to her parents what she wants to become in her life, though her classmates know about it as they read her autobiographical essay written for a competition. It is only when she clears her intermediate exam, that she talks to her parents about her future plan to pursue medicine as her career. She knows that mother's answer will be a firm 'no' and that day she feels as if she has to face an ordeal while talking to her parents for their consent for her professional studies. At this juncture, we can see a lonely girl struggling hard to pursue a career of her own choice. We find Saru again lonely when we find her pondering over whether to marry Manu or not. At this juncture also, we find her facing the situation all alone as there is none whom she can talk to or can confide in. Finally, when she finds her mother strongly protesting over the issue, Sarita makes her mind about marrying Manohar. If her parents had been open to her then she could have changed her decision as she would have discussed the matter with her parents. But parents, in general, in India are not open to their daughters. Ultimately, Sarita decides to marry Manohar more for the reason that her mother has opposed and reacted in a very cold manner. Sarita answers all the queries about Manohar in a cool manner as depicted by the novelist:

> What caste is he?
>
> I don't know.
>
> A Brahmin?
>
> Of course not.
>
> Then, cruelly.... His father keeps a cycle shop.
>
> Oh, so they are low caste people, are they?
>
> ......
>
> I hope so. (Shashi Deshpande 1990: 96)

Sarita feels lonely not only as an adolescent girl but also as a girl of marriageable age; loneliness is her destiny as a wife also. At this juncture, the novelist also wants the reader to realize that if a girl does not get support from her parents, then she might take wrong decisions in her life. Saru feels very happy immediately after marriage but gradually this happiness, too, starts shrinking. Lover in Manu changes to the stranger of night. She is so scared of nights as if some terror awaits her in her bedroom. She cannot talk to anybody about this strange terror. At one moment of time, she thinks of divorce but even in her imagination, she finds herself lonely and thus incapable of talking to the lawyer. The novelist depicts Saru's imaginary discussion with the lawyer whom she approaches for the divorce:

> Can I divorce my husband?
>
> Any reason?
>
> He is cruel.
>
> How? Will you be specific? Please give details.
>
> (Shashi Deshpande 1990: 97)

Though no lawyer would talk like this, yet Saru finds it difficult to talk to anybody about her problem. When Sarita comes to know about her mother's death, she decides to go to her father's place. Apparently, she goes to condole her mother's death but in fact she goes there with the purpose of ripping her heart open to her father. Every one believes that Sarita has rushed home to comfort the afflicted father but in the core of her heart, she knows that she has come to her father to comfort and rid herself of her loneliness. The novelist writes:

> The urge to confide in someone, to talk to someone, was growing in her. Often she had found herself staring at people, weighing them up, thinking.... Are you on my side? Are you? And even more often, waking up at night with a start, thinking.... I am alone. Knowing, with a kind of cold hopelessness, that it was not a dream, but real. That she was awake, not dreaming, and was truly was alone. That there was no one who could comfort her. That, perhaps, there never would be anyone. (Shashi Deshpande 1990: 43)

Sarita, representative of professional woman of modern India, feels the same kind of loneliness and emptiness in her professional life also. She feels herself to be a ventriloquist's dummy who smiles, laughs and talks because of ventriloquist. Her ventriloquist is her profession which makes her move on but in a selfless way. In between seeing patients, she keeps on doodling on blank paper so as to escape from her role of a professional. To quote the novelist:

> Always the fear that one day Nirmala (her assistant) would look in and find no one behind the table. Just a white coat containing nothing. Emptiness. The mounting terror that one day there would be no ventriloquist, giving me the right lines to say, the right faces to make. (Shashi Deshpande 1990: 22)

When a patient leaves her chamber and before another patient moves in, Saru goes on doodling circle within another circle. This doodling on her part is symbolic of emptiness, loneliness and seclusion in her life. If we make a Winnicottian study of the novel (pl. refer to D.W. Winnicot's psycho-analytic theory—which believes that it is the quality of maternal care in the early stages of the infant life that determines whether the infant will start off well in life), we feel that Sarita has a fear about her professional role. In the words of the novelist:

> There is this strange new fear of disintegration. A terrified consciousness of not existing. No, worse. (Shashi Deshpande 1990: 2)

In this opening scene about Saru's professional life (according to Winnicot), she keeps up all the pretences because there is nothing else apart from these pretensions in her otherwise vacuous life. Sarita's 'false self' has been so careful to hide her 'true self' that she is now unable to find it. To find her 'true self', Sarita goes back to her primitive environment to try and locate the self that she had lost years back to a mother who had monstrously impinged on her tender mind with myriad distortions of a patriarchal order that she herself had imbibed from her own damaged childhood. The mother had directly transmitted her legacy of dispossession to her daughter. A little later in the novel, Sarita refers to this lost self as a bone that a dog buries deep in the ground, and then is unable to find it for a while.

Same kind of vacuum and loneliness can be seen in the life of Kamala, Saru's mother. She does not complain to her husband about her own suffering. She suffers from stomach-cancer and is not able to tell her husband about it. She does not take enough food and does not reveal it to her husband. As Mai kaki tells to Saru:

> She never told anyone about what was happening to her. The amount (she ate)...I tell you, a sparrow would have eaten more. Your father never noticed because she never ate with him. (Shashi Deshpande 1990: 108)

When Mai kaki advises her to see a doctor, Kamala refuses and her refusal is appreciated by the so-called female patriarchs like Mai kaki. She appreciates her for the reason that Kamala is not like the new generation women who rush to see a doctor for every small reason.

The set up of Indian society is changing at a very rapid pace. Gone are the days when man alone used to be the bread earner for the family. Nowadays, women are working shoulder to shoulder along with men. As a result of working in outer domain, women are enjoying financial independence. Even the financial independence has not been able to elevate her status in the family. She earns but does not get freedom to manage her finances. It is her father or husband who makes most of decisions for her. As a daughter, it is her father who makes decisions about her studies or marriage, etc. and as a wife her decisions are taken by her husband. A woman has to face subordination and harassment not only at her working place but also within the four walls of her home. A man's duty is over as soon as he comes back home, but wife has to finish the domestic chores. A working woman gets sandwiched between her career and her role as a wife, mother and daughter-in-law. Though a woman works outside the home, yet she is expected to manage all the domestic chores all alone. Shashi Deshpande uses her characters as her mouthpiece to highlight the problems of working women. Sarita, the protagonist in the novel is MBBS doctor but like any other woman, she feels anxious whenever she gets late in reaching home. She feels worried not only because of children but also for the reason that she has to give an account of her time to her husband. In today's society, men expect women to earn equally but they are not prepared to shoulder their responsibilities. On the other hand, a woman is made to feel contrite (to feel guilty) if she is not able to do domestic chores in a satisfactory manner. One day Sarita gets late in returning back from the clinic and she feels very anxious while entering into the home. The novelist writes:

> When I came home I found him sitting with a brooding expression on his face that made my heart give painful, quivering little jumps. What is it now? Oh God what is it now? What have I done? What has someone said?
>
> "Did Nirmal ring you up?"
>
> ......
>
> "Yes".
>
> It wasn't that then. What else?
>
> "Renu"? "Abhi"? Are they in bed?
>
> That was obvious, but I had to talk, to go on proving my penitence, my contrition. (Shashi Deshpande 1990: 78-79).

Thus, Shashi Deshpande depicts that how working woman is under constant pressure to prove herself not only at the working place but also to prove her efficiency at home. In case, she is not able to work up to others' expectations she is filled with guilty feelings. A woman is made to feel guilty not only at home but also at her working place. Sarita receives a very bad treatment when she commits a mistake in doing a lumbar puncture; she is badly chided by Boozie, a senior doctor. He makes a caustic attack not only on her professional identity but also on her womanhood. She feels so humiliated as if her clothes are being torn off in the public place. If a man would have been there in place of Saru, Boozie would not have dared to give such a treatment. The novelist writes:

> And why could not you do it? What have you learnt in your five years here? Nothing, it seems. I don't want incompetent, clumsy, uninterested females cluttering up this place. Go home and play with your rolling pins and knitting needles. Even a moron could have done this simple thing. Why do you come here when you aren't interested? (Shashi Deshpande 1990: 89)

This monologue by Boozie tells of the kind of treatment a woman has to meet at the working place. A woman may be as much or even more efficient as any man but she is chided as soon as she commits a mistake though unknowingly. Thus, the novelist depicts very dextrously the mental harassment of women at the working place. But at the same time the effort made by Sarita to stop herself from shedding tears on being chided by Boozie is symbolic of the inner strength, a woman needs to have to confront such a situation. This is the reason that Saru decides to stay calm as she does not want to project herself as a weepy professional.

Another ugly picture of exploitation is painted by Shashi Deshpande in the form of Saru-Boozie relationship in the light of her rapid climb in her professional career. She was an intelligent student in her under graduation days, yet she knew that to make a niche for herself in M.D. she would have to please Boozie. He has his 'favourite' girl student in every batch. Boozie 'loves' the company of girls and needs the company of young women everyday. In lieu of this company, he helps these young women in his own ways. Sarita knows that her relation with Boozie is the talk of the town but she ignores all these talks for the reason that she cannot get success in her career without his help. The novelist wants to assert that a woman, as much as talented she may be, has to take the support of a man. Sarita needs money to set up a consulting room and Boozie gives her the required money. She feels very angry when her husband does not react on knowing that Saru has received money from Boozie. The novelist writes:

> I have got money.
>
> "How?"
>
> 'Boozie' gave it to me.
>
> He could have asked me then.... Why?
>
> And I would have told him.... What would I have said? But the occasion did not arise because he never asked me. And, there was, perversely, no relief in me, but contempt that he didn't. (Shashi Deshpande 1990: 92-93)

Saru is taken as a prized possession by her husband. She has to bear all the domestic responsibilities along with taking care of her professional ascent and growth it is the income that has tilted in favour of Sarita, not in favour of her husband, Manohar, once a promising and a charismatic young poet whom she married, as a runaway girl against the wishes of her parents. In her many acts of violations of societal norms, Sarita defies her parents in studying medicine and becoming a doctor.

Shashi Deshpande has highlighted in *Dark Holds No Terrors* that an urban working woman belonging to the middle class is oppressed at all the levels including domestic, professional and marital levels and she seems to have lost her control over her own life. During the childhood, she is told that she is an *ammanat* of the other house and thus she grows up with the feeling she will own her own house when she gets married. But this belief receives a jolt when she gets married and goes to her husband's house and finally, realizes that she has no place of her own. In the childhood only, she is told about Sita and Savitri and she is taught to emulate them to become an ideal wife. As a wife and a mother, she has no identity of her own. Her existence is geared towards pleasing her husband and bearing him children. As Alison M. Jagger says:

> With the partial exception of mothers, the male culture defines women as sexual objects for male pleasure.... As a daughter and as a wife, a woman's sexuality is carefully controlled so that she may not bring dishonour to her family. (Alison M. Jagger 1983)

Woman gains respect and status only when she grows old. This again is contingent upon her having born male children or possessing money. She is considered as an object of sexual gratification. Often, as a result of having no outlet for her hostility and aggression, she turns into an oppressor of other women, especially her daughter-in-law. As a widow or even as a childless woman, she is excluded from the larger cultural fabric of society. The novelist asserts that women have been conditioned as if the happiness of their husbands is the sole purpose of their lives. Madhav's mother feels punished as her husband stops talking to her when Satish (Madhav's brother) runs away from the house. Her husband is angry with her only for the reason that she didn't reveal to him that Satish had threatened to run away from the house. When Sarita is curious to know about the punishment given to Madhav's mother by his father, Madhav tells her that his father has stopped taking food cooked by his mother. As the novelist writes:

> Was there a punishment? She should have laughed, but the boy's expression made it obvious he considered it cruel. For some reason, she thought of the women in the Sanskrit story from her school text. The woman who would not disturb her husband's sleep even to save her child from the fire. A woman, so blessed, it was said, that *Agni* himself came and saved the child. Now she thought...who wrote that story? A man of course. Telling all women for all time...your duty to Me comes first. And women, poor fools, believed him. So that even today, Madhav's mother considers it a punishment to be deprived of a chance to serve her husband. And yet...if I could believe in that...if I could put my duty to my husband above all else...? (Shashi Deshpande 1990: 203)

Thus, we find that women, Indian women in particular, have been conditioned to serve their husbands with utmost devotion. Saru's real plight lies in her awareness that her only aim in life is not to please her husband. Had she identified herself with the traditions, she would have been at peace with herself, but she refuses to do so. It is not so that Shashi Deshpande, here, offers a solution but she wants to depict the real predicament of an educated and earning woman in today's society who is thoughtful of what she wants out of life. Thus, we find that the novelist wants to show that a woman's existence is shaped by her position as a person of minimal consequence to society. She explores the different levels of oppression and their overt and covert manifestations. Her concern is for woman and how she fares in the society, Indian society in particular.

Depicting the lives of Sarita and her mother, Deshpande seems to depict that changing one's personal life in the given social condition is the most challenging job for a woman. The novelist contests a typical male view that the man is at the centre and the woman is always on the periphery. The novelist deconstructs and interrogates patriarchy's axiomatic and universal assumptions through the character of depicting a male world view and being anti-woman in his place:

> Well, look at the way he made the women always subordinate to the men.
>
> But that's how it was, wasn't it?
>
> But it is not just their roles. It is the way he made the woman's personality merge into the stronger colours of a man's personality. Look at Hamlet, Lear, Othello. And look at Ophelia, Cordelia, Desdemona. Poor, feeble shadows. And when you come to a conflict or a climax, the woman recedes into the background. Just look at the way he disposed of Lady Macbeth. How splendidly she starts off, really! But so much positiveness, so much action is too much for the poor female and so she bows out. (Shashi Deshpande 1990: 156)

Although a minor character makes this observation, yet it resonates throughout the narrative.

Shashi Deshpande has depicted man-woman relationship with all dextrousness. Her male characters are to be analyzed in terms of their relationship with the protagonist. In the novel *The Dark Hold No Terrors*, Boozie has a definite romantic air about him and he fits the description of the popular women's magazine's hero. Sarita is drawn towards him because he is audacious and rich (unlike her husband, Manu). When Boozie displays interest in her, she gets attracted to him as he has all that she has aspired for in a man—money, position, fame, power and romance. As their relationship grows, she deceives herself into believing that theirs is only a teacher-student relationship. The novelist writes:

> (I)t was Pygmalion-Galatea story all over again.... How fast I learnt things, apart from paediatrics...from him. It was he who taught me to dress with elegance and simplicity, he taught me to speak good english...how to read and what.... (Shashi Deshpande: 1990: 91)

Here, the novelist does not make it clear whether it is a relationship of mentor-creator and protégé-creation. It is hinted by the novelist that Sarita is attracted towards Boozie not only for the professional but also for emotional reason as she is provided a sense of security by Boozie, something which her husband fails to do. As John Gray opines:

> Men generally assume once a woman is fulfilled, she should stay that way. Once he has proven his love, she should know it forever,... From the male point of view, this attitude makes perfect sense.
>
> Women find this attitude hard to accept. It is just plain inconsistent with their internal reality. A woman needs to be reassured that she is special, worthy, understandable and lovable. Men also need to be reassured but they get that encouragement mainly through their work. Women, however, primarily need reassurance through their relationship. (John Gray 1992)

Thus, we can say that Saru enters into this relationship with Boozie, primarily, with the purpose of professional help and later on turns to his help for the security which her husband is not able to provide her and finally she withdraws from the relationship. Sarita allows Boozie to shape up her career but at the same time she expects Manu to reprimand her for allowing Boozie to do so; this attitude on her part symbolizes the traditional need of women in patriarchal society to be controlled and protected by a male. She wants to be dominated by Boozie and expects a sense of protection from Manu.

Thus, we have seen that *The Dark Hold No Terrors* by Shashi Deshpande is different from most of the Indian novels dealing with gender issues. In most of these novels, the gender issues are offered a peripheral treatment. Such novels end up glorifying the stereo typical virtues of Indian women, like patience, devotion and abject acceptance of whatever is meted out to her. This novel explodes the myth of man's unquestionable superiority and the myth of women being a martyr and a paragon of all virtues. In other words, we can say that this novel has set a new phenomenon in Indian English Fiction—a novel based on problems faced by a career woman. Sarita visits her father and it provides her an opportunity to review her relationship with her husband, her father, her own children, her dead mother and her dead brother. Towards the end of the novel, we find her having a better understanding of herself and others. Now, she has ample courage to confront the reality. This is the message, the novelist wants to impart through this novel. Confronting the reality does not scare Sarita anymore. The dark no longer holds any terror to her. During her stay at her father's house, she makes an agonising search for herself and during this search, she feels that in her childhood she was made conscious of her gender as a child, as a young girl, as a wife and even as a professional. Sarita's mother's adoration of her son at her daughter's cost is the rallying point for the novelist to bring her feminist ideas together. The novelist wants to highlight the preference for boys over girls in Indian homes. The message is clear that this preference is inextricably linked with the psyche of Indian parents. The possible reason behind this could be that sons bring in dowry and this would have contributed to the development of the thought of the Indian psyche that the birth of a son is auspicious as he carries on the family lineage. As Sarabjit K. Sandhu has remarked:

> ...the male child is considered more important than a girl because he is qualified to give *agni* to his dead parents. The soul of the dead person would otherwise wander in ferment. (Sarabjit K. Sandhu 1991: 41)

It has been noticed that Shashi Deshpande reveals social aspect of keen sibling jealousy born of a mother's undue fondness for the son. The novelist wants to project or depict that this sort of blatant discrimination leads to a sense of insecurity and hatred among daughters toward their parents. Y.S. Sunita Reddy observes:

> In this connection, Saru's mother's attitude is typical of most of Indian mothers and a common enough phenomenon in the Indian context. (Y. Sunita Reddy 2001: 51)

This attitude of Sarita's mother may be taken as one of the reasons for Sarita being a mute spectator to the accidental death of her brother by drowning. All her life, the memories of her mother, accusing Saru of intentionally killing Dhruva, haunt her. As a result of her mother's accusations, Saru, too, on her part has a guilty conscience as she considers herself responsible for having remained a mute spectator to her brother's death by drowning. She never refutes the charge levelled against her by her mother. A few critics believe that Dhruva's demise had always been her subconscious desire and there is a very thin demarcation between her wish and its fulfilment. In the novel, the novelist reveals the social aspect of sibling rivalry. The discriminatory behaviour on the part of the parents makes girl-children feel unwanted. This feeling of being unwanted gives a sense of alienation and estrangement among daughters. The novelist opines that this gender discrimination is very much prevalent in Indian set up, irrespective of geographical or chronological space. In the novel, the feeling of being unwanted is so acute that Sarita begins to hate her own existence as a girl or as a woman. On attaining puberty, she scornfully says to her mother:

> If you are a woman, I don't want to be one. (Shashi Deshpande 1990: 62)

Very inhuman treatment is meted out to her during her monthly ordeals. She is treated like an untouchable, segregated from the other members and is made to sleep on a straw mat with a cup and a plate exclusively meant for her to be served in from a distance. As a result, she is engulfed with a sense of a shame and prays in desperation for a miracle to put an end to it. This segregation on the part of the family fills girls with a feeling of shame. This feeling of shame and unwantedness produces hatred in the hearts of girls during their impressionable years. As a result of this suffocating atmosphere in her home, Saru wants to leave home for Bombay to seek medicine as a career. Devoid of love and security, girls want to be loved and a hope to get love and attention, they get entrapped by false lovers and these girls rush into marriage unconditionally. Indian parents are also to be partly blamed for creating such circumstances that lead to the girls' taking such steps. These girls become aware of their decisions as soon as they face the hardships that are awaiting them. In case of Saru, she realizes very soon that she has rushed into marriage and she gets fed up by dingy one room set and other financial constraints. Earlier she was happy and contented to live on Manu's salary but in her new role as a career woman, she becomes discontented. She resents:

> For me, things now began to hurt. [...] a frayed saree I could not replace, a movie I could not see, an outing I could not join in. I knew now that without money life became petty and dreary. The thought of going on this way became unbearable. (Shashi Deshpande 1990: 92)

Through this unseen confrontation between Saru and Manu, the novelist wants to highlight that man-woman relation is based not only on love and emotions only but also on need and attraction. The novelist wants to assert that when 'need and attraction' take the place of 'love and emotion' in a relationship, then that relationship is not able to bloom for a longer time. In the beginning, Sarita gets 'attracted' towards Manohar and ultimately she ends up becoming 'a need' for Manohar. At this point of time, love and emotion vanishes from their relationship. Increase in social and economic status of women has also an impact on conjugal relationship. As soon as a woman is earning less than her husband, it is fine. But as soon as she starts earning more than her husband, troubles start pouring in. Manu, in the novel is happy as long as Saru is treating patients from neighbourhood. She is the representative of the new woman in Indian society who denies remaining contented and she has ambition to move higher and higher in life by establishing herself as an efficient doctor. As a result, she gets contentment in her career and this contentment in her career is no match to her growing discontentment at home. This feeling of discontentment at home arises out of discontentment in the mind of Manu, who feels himself inferior in front of his wife, who enjoys a better status than him. Certain incidents aggravate the already strained relation between them and as a result, he does not behave like a husband but like a rapist. He feels helpless and effeminate when the interviewing girl incidentally asks Manu that how does it feel when his wife is earning not only the butter but most of the bread also. Although he is a cheerful normal man during day time but he turns into a rapist at that night, so as to assert his manhood which seems to be in danger during day.

To present the other issues related to the married life, Shashi Deshpande contrasts Saru's life with the lives of her two school friends—Sunita and Nalu. Sunita leaves no effort to pose as a happier married woman. All the while she talks about her intimacy with her husband as if she were a non-entity without him, which only invokes pity in the eyes of the reader. Nalu also questions her as to why she lets her husband change her name from Sunita to Anju:

> Do you have to surrender so easily? (Shashi Deshpande 1990: 117)

Nalu is contemptuous of Sunita's constant references to her husband and hates her for her submissive attitude of satisfying every whim of his. Nalu tells her:

> Well, I refuse to call you Anju or Gitanjali or whatever. To me you are Sunita and will always be Sunita. (Shashi Deshpande 1990: 118)

Saru contrasts Nalu with the Nalu of her college days who was full of enthusiasm. But now bitterness has crept into her. Saru feels that it would be wrong to say that Nalu is bitter because she never married or never bore a child. Shashi Deshpande suggests that it would be equally stupid to call a married woman 'fulfilled' because she got married and has children.

Shashi Deshpande has presented this contrasted lives of Saru, Nalini and Sunita with the purpose of projecting that a wife, a mother and a spinster had their own share of joys and sorrows, and it is almost difficult to conclude that as to who is more happier or fulfilled. While the married women are shown to be dissatisfied with their marriage, the unmarried ones are shown to have their own sufferings and anxieties.

Towards the end of the novel, a mature Saru shuns extremes and takes a practical view of the circumstances. She is neither the typical Western liberated woman nor an orthodox Indian one. Shashi Deshpande does not let herself get overwhelmed by the Western feminism or its militant concept of emancipation. In the quest for the wholeness of identity, she does not advocate separation from the spouse but a tactful assertion of one's identity within marriage.

Shashi Deshpande wants to project that marital life is nothing but a queer combination of several forces acting upon two human beings in different capacities to fulfil the marital ambition and play a vital role in the society. The given roles of these two human beings do undergo a change both at the functional and psychological levels. This is precisely what happens to Saru when her economic independence is reinforced with the fact that she earns more than Manu. She still feels stripped of her independence by virtue of being assigned to the job of a housewife, i.e. bringing up children and subserving the interest of her husband. Tired of both the duties, indoors and outdoors, she wants to leave the latter one. But her husband does not want her to leave her job as they cannot maintain the same standard with his income.

Through the example of Saru, the novelist highlights the burden of double chores on working women. As a professional, she has to take care of her own profession. She faces all the challenges at the working place and at the same time she is supposed to manage the household affairs. This undue pressure, ultimately, inculcate feeling of frustration of disenchantment in her. With this growing feeling of disenchantment and imbalance, separation becomes inevitable.

We have seen that in the novel *The Dark Holds No Terrors*, gender issues have been given pivotal treatment instead of peripheral treatment given so far by other women novelists. In this novel, the novelist has successfully projected a situation in which a wife, who is also a successful professional, is unable to bear the sexual sadism of her husband. The novelist asserts the need for a woman to confront the reality and this opportunity is grabbed by the heroine in the present novel during her stay at her father's house.

The novelist wants to project that only financial independence can't prevent women from being subordinated. In this respect, Saru is at fault, when she visualizes financial independence as a means of freedom. The desire to achieve freedom inspires her to have financial independence. She gets highly self-willed and her problem ensues because of her outsized ego and innate love for power over others. This self-will motivates her to defy traditional codes. She defies her mother to become a doctor; she defies her caste to marry outside and she defies social convention by using Boozie to advance her career. Thus, we see that financial independence gives her courage to react against the shackles. Financial independence, certainly, frees one from being 'unwanted burden' but economic independence cannot provide insurance against subordination or suppression. The need to be independent financially eventually does become the need of inflated ego. Thus, the novelist wants to give the message that financial independence helps in contributing toward upliftment but it cannot prevent women from being subordinated. As a result, Saru could no longer admit the idea of being 'a small boat towed by a larger ship', but she is happy to be the larger ship herself.

This 'new woman' of today is not ready to sacrifice her social status, financial independence and professional success for the sake of her marital relation. This modern Indian has an inner desire to outshine others and to be a resounding success. She is ready to adopt any means to achieve her goal in life. She does not mind using 'god-father' as a means to achieve something significant in life. This so-called new woman has this realization that the disparity of achievement between them (husband and wife) is part of the domestic problem and the new woman is in no mood to undo what she has carefully built up. Earlier, when woman used to be successful in her career, she used to give credit to her husband even without his actual contribution. When wife is not a big success in life, her husband has no reservations about considering her as an equal and as a person. But when the success of the wife starts highlighting the failure of the husband, he degenerates. At this stage, we find a woman itching for domination who has nothing but indifference for the husband. Finally, she proceeds on a self-centred march to progress, nullifies her husband and his existence. She does not have any respect for weak-willed men like Padmakar Rao and Saru's father in the present novel.

Another issue that is highlighted by Shashi Deshpande is that if any thing goes wrong in the marital relation, it is the woman who is sensitive and reactive to the situation. When Saru goes away to her father's home, her husband writes to her and plans to come and take her back home as if nothing had gone wrong.

At this very juncture, Saru, the heroine tries to turn her back to the situation but it is her father who stops her from doing so and ultimately she overcomes her fears. The novelist offers the solution that the real solution lies not in running away from the situation but facing it boldly. Saru's father has been used as a mouthpiece for this purpose:

> Talk to him. Tell him what is wrong. (Shashi Deshpande 1990: 217)

According to the novelist, the solution lies in upholding what lies in your heart, instead of keeping it all piled up in your heart. Making use of dead persons like Dhruva, Saru's mother (who have been presented as cardboard characters) as symbols of old grudges and old differences, the novelist suggests to leave behind the old conflicts. She seems to suggest life should not come at a standstill because of her others. As Saru's father tells in the novel:

> ...they are dead. They can do nothing. Why do you torture yourself with others? Are you not sufficient for yourself? It is your life, isn't it? (Shashi Deshpande 1990: 217)

The novelist seems to suggest that every woman like Saru needs to feel that her life is her own and no one else has a right to interfere in that. But, at the same time, a woman should have courage to face the situation instead of turning her back to the circumstances. And, if a woman hopes that some charismatic person would emerge out of this mundane world and that person will be carrying the solution in his Pandoras box, then she is completely wrong. She will have to rescue herself. At one moment Saru is so much scared of facing the situation that she tells her father not to open the door when Manu comes to take her back:

> "Promise me" she said, promise me you won't open the door to him. Don't open the door when he comes. (Shashi Deshpande 1990: 218)

But, ultimately she comes to her own rescue and she realizes:

> Would it always be a failure, any attempt to reach out to another human being? Had she been chasing a chimera all her life, hoping for someone? Perhaps the only truth is that man is born to be cold and lonely and alone. (Shashi Deshpande 1990: 219)

Very soon she realizes that to her nothing matters except herself. She says:

> None of this matter. (Shashi Deshpande 1990: 217)

She is impressed by Madhav, a young boy, who declares very resolutely that nothing matters to him as his life is his own. And she decides to live life on her own terms. To quote:

> She had to go on. To blunder her way through this to some kind of a life that would seem right to her.
>
> Alright, so I am alone. But so is everyone else. Human beings...they are going to fail you. But because there is a just us, because, there is no one else, we have to go on trying. If we can't believe in ourselves, we are sunk. (Shashi Deshpande 1990: 220)

Shashi Deshpande seems to suggest that escapism is no permanent solution nor should one look to anything outside of oneself to provide the solution. Using Saru as her protagonist, the novelist suggests that there is no need to be scared of the darker aspects of life, one should take every thing positively. The novelist opines:

> the dark holds no terrors. That the terrors are inside us all the time. We carry them within us, and like traitors they spring out, when we least expect them, to scratch and maul. (Shashi Deshpande 1990: 74)

Rather than escaping from the dark or cursing the darkness, a woman needs to light within herself a candle and declare that dark holds no terrors. The novelist is of the view that a woman is as much responsible as a man is for the complex situation created in marital relationship. Escaping, according to the novelist, can never be a positive escape route towards resolving the tangled knots, exchanging old horrors to new ones. To come out of a situation, one has to confront a situation. Sarita finds Madhav leaving behind the problem of his brother's eloping away and setting on his studies. She resolutely puts behind all her tensions and decides to assert herself. She accepts her own limitations and ignores, at the same time what she finds unacceptable in others. The novelist writes:

> My life is my own...somehow she felt as if she had found it now, the connecting link. It means you are not just a strutting, grimacing puppet, standing futilely on the stage for a brief while between areas of darkness. If I have been a puppet it is because I made myself one. I have been clinging to the tenuous shadow of marriage whose substance has long since disintegrated because I have been afraid of proving my mother right. (Shashi Deshpande 1990: 220)

Saru has this realization that her brother, her mother or anyone else cannot bother her anymore.

When Ravi, a boy from neighbourhood, comes to call her as Sunita, his younger sister, is having fits, she immediately goes away little thinking about Manu who can arrive there at any moment. While rushing to Sunita's home, she tells to her *baba* that he should ask Manu to wait till she comes back. Her words 'tell him to wait' are indicative of her assertive nature. Now she is a woman with a firm and resolute attitude and she is not ready to give up her own cause for the sake of anyone else. Though the novelist has not provided with any clear-cut ending to the novel, yet we can say that the sentence spoken by Saru is a piece of advice to every woman. Indian women need to be assertive enough to win a fair deal in the battle of life and should accept their own limitations at the same time.

This way we have seen that Shashi Deshpande, who understands and lives within Indian socio-cultural milieu, has projected the feelings and emotions of Indian women in universal colours. The writer universalizes certain basic feelings irrespective of national characters. Deshpande makes it plain that a woman must develop the thinking that she is an individual who is capable enough of withstanding trials and tribulations in life all alone. The modern Indian woman is more than mere a mother, sister or daughter. In the present Indian context, what a woman needs is strong mind and will. Her identity is no longer seen in terms of identity of her male counterpart. This new woman passes through a process of transformation which signifies a change from bondage to freedom and self-assertion. As the novelist opines, the problem of loneliness and vacuum of feminine heart is indicative of inner disintegration. This disintegration is due to woman's ego and her will to dominate others. Economic freedom and education have ushered into their lives new set of values and these values are based on money, power and social status. The wholesomeness in women's lives is possible only if integration takes place. In other words, the new woman has to accept her children, her husband and duties of the lady of the house. In the end, Sarita arrives at a point of realization wherein nothing either becomes a problem or reveals any darkness. Her quest leads to uncover the strength in human beings which makes living a joyous possibility. Towards the end, we find her to be a human being throbbing with life with a reawakened individuality. That individuality is nothing but the reality which the individual has to face in order to overcome setback and set the things right. Once this realization comes, all other things that cause problems melt away because of the mental equilibrium attained through this realization. In a nutshell, we can say that it is the women's voice that is presented without any trace of sentimentalization or over dramatization of women's problems. Therefore, the novelist brings out emphatically the psychological, emotional problems faced by Indian working women and the solution offered by the novelist in-between the lines in the novel has also been presented by the novelist in the epigraph of the novel:

> You are your own refuge;
> There is no other refuge
> This refuge is hard to achieve. (*Dharampada*)

Works Cited

Das, Veena. "Reflection on Social Construction of Adulthood" in Sudhir Kakkar (ed.), *Identity and Adulthood*, New Delhi, OUP, 1992: 93.

Deshpande, Shashi. *The Dark Holds No Terrors*. Penguin Books, 1990.

Gray, John. *Men, Women and Relationship*. New York: HarperCollins, 1992.

Interview to Lakshmi Holmstrom in *Fiction of Shashi Deshpande* edited by R.S. Pathak; Creative Books, New Delhi, 1998: 249.

Jagger, Alison, M. *Feminist Politics and Human Nature*. NJ: Rowman and Allanheld, 1983.

Madan, T.N. "The Structural Implications of Marriage among Kashmiri Brahmins", contributions to *Indian Sociology*, Vol. 9.

Register, Cheri. "American Feminist Literary Criticism: A Bibliographical Introduction" in Josephine Donovan (ed.), *Feminist Literary Criticism*, The University of Kentucky Press, 1979.

Reddy, Y. Sunita. *A Feminist Perspective on the Novels of Shashi Deshpande.*

Sandhu, Sarabjit K. *Image of Women in the Novels of Shashi Deshpande.*

5

Economic and Emotional Independence: A Dominant Desire of Feminine Heart (*Roots and Shadows*)

Gender studies recognize the inadequacy of male-created ideologies and struggles for the spiritual, economic, social and racial equality of women who have been sexually colonized and biologically subjugated for a very long time. An expression of the mute and stifled female voice denied an equal freedom of self-expression, feminism is a concept emerging as a protest against male chauvinism and the marginalization of women. Sarah Grimke observes:

> Man has subjugated woman to his will, used her as a means to promote his selfish gratification, to minister to his sensual pleasure, to be instrumental in promoting his comfort; but never has he desired to elevate her to that rank she was created to fill. He has done all he could do to debase and enslave her mind.... (Sarah Grimke 1970: 10)

Feminism strives to undo this titled and distorted image of women whose cries for freedom and equality have gone unheard, and still go unheard in the patriarchal world. There are three phases related to gender issues. Shashi Deshpande's novels are directly related to all these three issues. In her novels, she explores and exposes long smothered wail of the incarcerated psyche of her female protagonists imprisoned within the four walls of domesticity and sandwiched between tradition and modernity, between illusion and reality and between the mask and the real face. These women, however, disown a ritual and tradition bound life in order to explore their true self. Concerned with quest for authentic selfhood and an understanding of existential problems of life, Shashi Deshpande's heroines are all agog to retain their individuality in the teeth of disintegrating and divisive forces that threaten their identity.

Roots and Shadows by Shashi Deshpande is a novel which explores the inner struggles of Indu, who represents a set of modern women who are educated and are very much in contact with the society, dealing with the critical gender issues like love, marriage, sex, settlement and individuality. As O.P. Bhatnagar says:

> The novel deals with a woman's attempt to assert her individuality and realize her freedom. It depicts how it brings her into confrontation with family, with the male world and the society in general. (O.P. Bhatnagar Unpublished Paper)

Roots and Shadows is the story of Indu, a middle-class young girl, brought up in an orthodox Brahmin family headed by Akka. The novel begins with the heroine's return to her ancestral house. The parental home initiates her into an understanding of the meaning of human life. It is here that she discovers what her roots are—as an independent woman and as a writer and what her shadows are—as a daughter, as a mother and as a commercial writer. She rebels against traditions of the society and she is used by the novelist as a mouthpiece to raise certain gender issues. In *Roots and Shadows*, Indu faces a crisis in her marital relationship and has to traverse the arduous and thorny road of self-exploration before she is at peace with herself.

First and foremost, the issue raised by Shashi Deshpande in the novel is that of biasedness in the society towards marital relationship. The need to take girl's consent for the marriage is never felt. Mini in *Roots and Shadows* is never consulted for knowing her choices and desires. She has not even seen the photograph of her would be husband, leave alone the question of meeting him before consummation of marriage. As the novelist observes:

> No, Mini was pre-eminently a realist. And had not the picture, not for Mini alone, but for most brides in this country, always been false? Behind the facade of romanticism, sentiment and tradition, what was marriage after all, but two people brought together after cold blooded bargaining to meet, mate and reproduce so that the generations might continue? (Shashi Deshpande 1983: 3)

It is not the case that only the arranged marriage has problems associated with it, it is also the love marriage which has its own share of problems, as it was in the case of Indu's parents. Her mother did not belong to their caste and ultimately she was not accepted by his family. Through the example of Indu's parents, the novelist wants to highlight the problems faced by women who marry out of their caste. Indu's mother was hated by the family members of her husband's family to such an extent that nobody mentions of her and Indu who had grown up as an orphan, comes to know of her mother from Naren who is an outsider. As written by the novelist:

> But I...no one had ever spoken of her, or ever mentioned her name. For me it had been a total blank. A blankness that had left its mark on me. And, incredible though it sounds, I had not even known of her existence, until Naren had said to me once, boastfully 'my mother drowned'. So did my father. How did your mother die? (Shashi Deshpande 1983: 43)

Indu's mother is hated by all the family members and later on she is remembered only by Atya who believes that Indu's father would have been happier if Indu's mother had remained alive. In that case, Indu's father would not have remained a wanderer.

Shashi Deshpande makes a caustic attack on the marriage system in Indian patriarchal society. The novelist makes use of character of Mini for this purpose. Although she is not actually married off in the novel, yet there are several indications as to the kind of man chosen for her. As the novelist highlights:

> He has passed his SSC. Went one year to college, I think and may be he didn't pass. What does this matter?

> He does not need a job. They have plenty. He can live in comfort like a lord on what they have. And what's the use of these degrees? Can they guarantee a job? Look at Naren.... (Shashi Deshpande 1983: 50)

Thus, instead of choosing a well-qualified boy like Naren, Mini's parents prefer a boy who himself is capable of nothing but boasts of his parental property. The novelist, here, wants to highlight the attitude of the Indian patriarchal parents who feel that there is no need for mental mapping and it is only the wealth which can buy happiness for a girl. When Indu objects to the suitability of the boy for Mini, Anant Kaka makes a deliberate effort to be angry and asks if the chosen boy does not have one head, two arms and two legs. This statement on the part of Anant Kaka symbolizes the traditional attitude of the parents who believe that any boy can be suitable for their daughter provided he has ample wealth. Parents in the patriarchal families take daughters as burden. Children learn about sex-roles in the pre-school years as the treatment meted out to them is role based. They learn to express their preferences according to the sex-roles assigned to them by the society. As a result, these girl-children adopt assigned sex-roles in such a deep-rooted manner that they are unable to shake them off even after they grow into adults.

The girls are told right from the beginning that they should behave in a particular manner because they have to grow into 'nice' and 'sophisticated' ladies, or because they have to go and stay with their in-laws, whereas the boys are supposed to grow into 'strong' men because they have to look after their families and become pillars of strength to be able to support them. This lays the foundation of the male and female roles. The message received, directly or indirectly, by the girls at an early age is that they are less important. They start distinguishing themselves from the boys, 'expressing' themselves with appropriate sex-role preferences and ultimately 'behaving' in accordance with the 'prescribed' sex-roles. The girl-child, thus, becomes a 'prisoner' of her gender. She is called the weaker sex. The Indian Constitution and the Charter give her equal rights but that does not make a big difference. This child of the weaker sex is, however, supposed to be strong enough to perform the more hazardous, unseen, unacknowledged, unaccounted domestic chores. If she goes to school, it is asked, who will look after the siblings? Who will help the mother go out and work to supplement the household income? What does the girl-child get in return? She gets a little food, just enough to keep her going, and an attitude of indifference from her parents. She is treated as a burden, destined to live in someone else's home. It is not considered worth sending her to school. It will be a sheer waste of money for their parents. Their marriage is also a kind of 'responsibility' to them. Such parents just want to get rid of their responsibilities. Anant Kaka, in the novel, says:

> Padmini is past twenty-four now. And there is her horoscope. And the problem of finding a family with a status comparable to ours. And when every thing clicks, there is the dowry hurdle. What am I to do? Let the girl stay unmarried? It is alright as long as I am alive. When I am gone, can you see her brothers looking after her? May be the boy is a little ugly, may be a little stupid...but every thing else is fine. The family is good it is known to us, they have money, she will be quite comfortable. (Shashi Deshpande 1983: 51)

Apart from the above-quoted dialogue, there are many hints in the novel which suggest that the boy is neither highly educated nor good looking. However, marriage with him does offer the prospect of security and a certain social status to Mini. Deshpande reveals the pragmatic aspects of arranged marriages by contrasting Mini with Indu who has both choice and freedom to shape her own life and who has had higher education and is economically independent. Mini, who has none of these advantages, has little option but to acquiesce to the marriage keeping in view the positive points of such an alliance.

Shashi Deshpande has dealt graphically with the problems that confront middle-class women in patriarchal Hindu society particularly in the context of domestic problems including that of marriage. She is not a strident or militant kind of feminist and does not believe man to be the cause of woman's all troubles. She deals with the psychic turmoil of women within the limiting and restricting confines of domesticity. One of the gender issues raised by Shashi Deshpande is the problems of the girls of the marriageable age who are not left with many choices in front of them. When Indu talks to Mini about her marriage plans, she has not given a thought to this plan and answers back that it is not one of the things to think about. Indu tells Mini that marriage is not a simple affair as she says:

> It means living with a man. You have to listen to him, endure his habits, his smell, his touch, his likes, his dislikes. You have to sleep with him, bear him children. Can you do all that with this man?
>
> ......
>
> (Mini) What choice do I have, Indu?
>
> ......
>
> Of course I am marrying him because there is nothing else I can do. I am no good at studies. I never was. I went to school because...I had to. And then to college because Akka said I must go. Boys prefer graduates these days, she said. So I went. But I failed and it was a relief to give it up. There is only one thing I am really good at...looking after a house. And to get a home, I have to get married. This is not my home, is it? (Shashi Deshpande 1983: 124-25)

In the above-cited lines, the novelist wants to raise the issue of aimlessness and purposelessness of young girls in the patriarchal Hindu families. Mini goes to college not with the purpose of getting education but she wants to be a graduate only for the reason that the most of the grooms want graduate for a wife. Here, the novelist highlights and makes a caustic attack on the present marriage system which compels a girl to get education as a passport to marriage. Middle-class girls are educated largely as a concession to a superficial social change. Given the new executive culture, a personable wife has become a necessary appendage. Matrimonial advertisements frequently mention at least a B.A. degree as one of the necessary assets of a would-be bride. Larger numbers of girl-women are now enrolling for degrees as a result, though many leave halfway if a 'good match' is procured. Those who persevere to the finish usually abandon all intellectual pursuits after marriage and settle down to the far more serious business of becoming good wives and mothers.

Shashi Deshpande also highlights another important issue: problems faced by young girls of marriageable age who have to parade before the families of suitable boys. The novelist emphasises on the point that it is an emotional harassment for a girl whose fate is decided in such a crude manner. In the words of Mini, who has been 'seen' by so many suitable boys and is fed up with this tradition:

> Yes, any man. Any man who says 'yes'. You do not know what it has been like. Watching Kaka and Hemant and even Madhava Kaka running around after eligible men. And then, sending the horoscope and having it comeback with the message that it does not match. And if the horoscope matched, there was the meeting to be arranged. And mother and Atya slogging in the kitchen the whole day. And all those people coming...and staring and asking all kinds of questions. And if we heard they were old fashioned people, I would dress up in an old fashioned manner and they would say 'she is not modern enough'. And if I dressed up well because some one said the boy wanted a smart wife, they would say 'she is too fashionable for us'. Or too short. Or too dark. Or something. (Shashi Deshpande 1983: 126)

The novelist, here, wants to bring on the surface the problems faced by parents in marrying off their daughters. Apparently, these parents are talking, laughing and smiling but in the core of their hearts they are anxious whether their proposal will be accepted or rejected. Usually, the boy party goes away and later send their answer in the form of rejection of the girl. Such a depressing treatment compels Mini to accept any boy. She says:

> He will look after me. And no one can say to me, 'How old are you? And not married yet! What a pity! I'm tired, Indu. I don't care what kind of a man he is. Once we are married and he becomes my husband none of his flaws will matter. (Shashi Deshpande 1983: 126)

Mini finds herself helpless amid her circumstances. In order to save her father from further complexities of her marriage, she poses a semblance of agreement and decides not to show her disagreement. Perhaps, the point raised by the novelist is that women, like Mini, who are always involved in fetishes (obsessive devotion) of traditions and household work, have no other option but to remain satisfied with the things provided. Women are also tuned or conditioned to merge their aspirations and desires with those of their families. Mini, too, absorbs the trend established by the elder women of her family. She has been prepared for looking after the house and Akka's desire to educate her is not because of desire to give Mini an independent identity but because it is felt that educated girls get good match. Vrinda Nabar comments:

> Moreover even if we concede, that the girl is an alien in her father's home, it is manmade laws and social strictures that make her so. Right from birth, a girl is made to feel like a bird of passage in her father's home. (Vrinda Nabar 1995: 160)

Mini's psyche was too fed with this idea. Her parents' growing concern to settle her marriage fills her with guilt...guilt for being a girl, guilt for remaining unmarried, guilt for being a burden on her family. She too feels humiliated when people reject her on the pretext of her physical appearance or the manner of her dressing.

Girls in the Indian patriarchal families perceive their husband's house as their final abode and their husband as oracle. The Indian women have been accepting their husbands with their flaws and trying to live up to their desires and demands by transforming and moulding themselves. Their predecessors act as archetypes for them. They absorb the trends set by these archetypes who dictate the feminine qualities to be displayed by these young women. Thus, Shashi Deshpande has given us the glimpse of the rigid system of marriage in India which is settled not on the basis of compatibility but on caste, religion and dowry. The novelist wants to hint at the problem of dowry in India which compels many parents to push their daughters in incompatible marriage because of their inability to give desired dowry. In the words of Shashi Deshpande, herself:

> [...] love leads to the certainty of marriage. But marriage invariably takes you back to the world of women, of trying to please, of the fear of not pleasing, of surrender, of self abnegation. (Shashi Deshpande 1983: 35)

In her march towards emancipation and selfhood, the contemporary Indian woman has to struggle against the insensitive fatality of options and indoctrination of centuries which silently yet persistently endeavours to fashion her into the mould of 'womanhood' as defined and defiled by the society. Simone de Beauvoir remarks that the present woman is an artificial product that the civilization makes. Thus, Shashi Deshpande reveals that in traditional Hindu joint families, these 'artificial products' (women) are merely puppets without any identity, voice or name. Marriage subjugates and enslaves women. It leads her to aimless days indefinitely repeated, life that slips away gently toward death without questioning its purpose. Women pay for their happiness at the cost of their own freedom. Such a sacrifice on the part of a woman is too high, for the kind of self-contentment and security that marriage offers a woman, drains her soul of its capacity for greatness. Indu plays the role of an ideal housewife but the role of a wife restricts rather circumscribes, her self-development—firstly, by taking away her freedom of thought and expression, and secondly, by denying her the scope of giving free play to her artistic potential. Regarding a woman's role playing, Rosemarie Tong observes:

> Sometimes women play their roles not so much because they want to, as because they have to in order to survive economically and/or psychologically. Virtually, all women engaged in feminine role playing. (Rosemarie Tong 1993: 208)

The events in Akka's life serve to focus upon several issues related to the treatment and position of women in Indian society. One such issue is the practice of child marriage (very common in some parts of India even today) and its impact on child-bride. Akka's traumatic girlhood is an example of the tragic consequences of child marriages. In the novel *Roots and Shadows* one can have glimpse of what kind of childhood a young girl of thirteen has when she gets married to a fully grown, uncaring man. At a tender age of thirteen, Akka has to submit to her husband's violent sexual advances. At an age when she barely understands the meaning of sex and love making, she is subjected to such a brutality that she begins to regard sex as a punishment. Akka tries to escape from her husband's house but to no avail. The novelist gives a very vivid description:

> She was just twelve when she got married. And he was well past thirty. I remember him. He was a tall bulky man with large, coarse features.... She was small and dainty, really pretty, with her round face, fair skin, straight nose and curly hair. Six months after her marriage, she 'grew up' and went to her husband's home. What she had to endure there, no one knows.... But I heard that twice she tried to run away.... A girl of thirteen. Her mother-in-law, I heard, whipped her for that and locked her up for three days. Starved her as well. And then, sent her back to her husband's room. The child (bride) they said, cried and clung to her mother-in-law saying, "lock me up again, lock me up". But there was no escape from a husband then. (Shashi Deshpande 1983: 70)

Even before she is out of her teens, Akka becomes pregnant. Her immature and underdeveloped body cannot give birth to a living child. This adds to her misfortunes, as she is branded inauspicious and evil because of her issuelessness. The novelist also raises the issue of the deeply ingrained sexist belief that a woman exists only for the purpose of satisfying a man's needs. In the patriarchal Hindu society, a woman is seen as a commodity useful for sex and for bearing children. She is discarded once her utility comes to an end. Akka's childlessness, therefore, results in an increased ill-treatment at the hands of her mother-in-law. The novelist, also, hints at the dual standard of patriarchal society which allows a man with wealth to have a mistress. As the novelist hints:

> Her husband.... You know how men were in those days, specially when there was a lot of money. He had a weakness

for women. How could a frightened child satisfy him? He always had mistresses. (Shashi Deshpande 1983: 70)

After the death of her mother-in-law and her husband's paralytic stroke, Akka could have grabbed all freedom but she is symbolic of a traditional girl, the product of patriarchal Hindu family, who has been trained since childhood to be the ideal and dutiful wife and thus she cannot desert the paralysed husband who has been nothing but an oppressor to her. The novelist makes a caustic attack on the traditional set of beliefs that a woman has to live in her husband's house till her death. Even the doors of her parental home are closed to her after marriage. Regarded as the property of her husband and his family, she is rarely extended support by her own family even in the face of proven oppression by her husband's family.

If M. Mani Meitei's opinion is to be taken into account, then Indian women can be divided into three groups: (1) those who follow tradition as a virtue; (2) those who are independent; and (3) those who realise what is good but still are unable to come out. To the first group belong the uneducated women who have been called female patriarchs. They bank upon age-old beliefs and superstitions, and it would be hard to change them. They are foolishly sentimental and egoistic. Narmada (Attya), Kaki, Sumitra, Kamla, Sunanda and Kaku are remarkably traditional in their manner and outlook. Although Akka has undergone great suffering at her husband's house, on her return to her father's house after her husband's death, she enforces a rigid code of conduct on women in the family. She insists a woman should never utter her husband's name, for it means not only disrespect towards him but also shortens his life-span. Caught in the matrix of age-old customs or traditions, she cannot break herself free from the clutches of tradition. She advises all 'women' in the family to circumambulate the *tulsi* plant to increase their husbands' life-span. These so-called female patriarchs, who themselves have faced the oppression, try to condition the younger generation to the drudgery of performing countless household chores, making their life miserable and when this goes unrecognised it makes their life more miserable. They make the task of male patriarchs easier by making women accept the disgusting sight of strewn plates and littered remnants lying about after the meal. These female patriarchs prepare wives to eat off the same dirty plates their husbands had eaten in earlier. The novelist makes use of these female patriarchs to show that the household chores are tiresome, boring and frustrating like the job of Sisyphus. As Simone de Beauvoir remarks:

> Few tasks are more like the torture of Sisyphus than housework, with its endless repetition; the clean becomes soiled, the soiled is made clean, over and over, day after day. The housewife wears herself out marking time. She makes nothing, simply perpetuates the present. (Simone de Beauvoir 1974: 470)

By depicting these female patriarchs, the novelist narrates about the prevailing injustice in society. These traditional women spare no efforts to indoctrinate young girls to play the role of meek and submissive daughter, wife and mother. These female thrust womanhood upon young girls in a graceless manner. When Indu's first menstrual cycle onsets, she is brutally told:

> You are a woman now.... You can have babies yourself. (Shashi Deshpande 1983: 87)

Indu is told that for four days she will be unclean and therefore she cannot touch any one or anything. This was how she has been introduced into the beautiful world of womanhood.

Akka, the representative of female patriarchs, does not let Saroja, the daughter of old uncle, learn music. She expects women to learn and to do the things which appease men. As the novelist comments:

> And of how she wanted to learn music and how Akka put her foot down. What—learn music from a strange man! Sit and sing in front of strangers! Like those women? Are we that kind of a family? Is not it enough for you to sing one or two devotional songs, one or two aarti songs? What more does a girl from a decent family need to know? (Shashi Deshpande 1983: 50)

When a girl decides to marry out of her own caste, she has to face the maximum protest from the ladies of the family. These patriarchal ladies not only dislike these out-of-caste marriages but also try their best to discourage the younger generation by their discouraging words. As Akka comments when she comes to know of Indu's marriage with Jayant:

> Such marriages never work. Different castes, different languages.... It is alright for a while. Then they realize.... (Shashi Deshpande 1983: 68)

For all these female patriarchs, no other achievement matters except her achievement to bear children. These women had their own standards for judging people. Academic distinctions, career, success and money would not impress these women. To get married, to bear children, to have sons and grandsons are some of the achievements for these traditional women. In one of her interviews with Geeta Gangadharan, Shashi Deshpande has commented:

> It is very difficult to explain. I have a very strong feeling that until very recently women in our society have been looked upon just as 'breeding animals'. They had no other role in life. I have a strong objection to treating any human being in that manner. Women have been so dispensable in my mother's family that one could see women dying and immediately the men getting married again. I could see that the female life had no value at all. The whole chronology of their life centres around childbirth. They would say, "this happened when my first child was born, this when I was pregnant..." and so on. It used to mystify me. Does nothing happen in your life other than having children?
>
> The stress laid on the feminine functions, at the cost of all your potentials as an individual, enraged me. I knew I was very intelligent person, but for a woman, intelligence is always a handicap. If you are intelligent, you keep asking 'why, why, why' and it becomes a burden. I was quite uncomfortable with my own intellect and at the same time, I was quite proud also. May be too much of thinking has made me express a sort of dislike for the physical aspects of feminine life, making it seem as if I am totally against all the feminine functions, which is not the truth at all. (R.S. Pathak 1998: 253)

Akka transforms a lot after she returns to her natal home after her husband's death. However, it is important to remember that there are limits to her transformation as she too is a product of patriarchy, having assimilated its power-based value system. As the elder of the family, she attempts to inculcate those very values (which she had acquired as a girl) among the girl children in the family, and succeeds with all save Indu. She is hard with the girls, preparing them for a life within patriarchy and saving 'all her softness for the boys'. In Akka's death one sees the end of 'patriarchy' and of a traditional way of life which nevertheless has its darker aspects. The majority of female patriarchs are neither educated nor do they have the freedom and independence. These women are traditional in their outlook and often, themselves, share patriarchal value system. Unwittingly, therefore, they even aid the oppression of other women. Deshpande relates this phenomenon, this deprivation, socialization and early conditioning of girls. She depicts both weakness and strength of women: weakness of women like Atya who are 'spending' their lives and strong women like Akka who give guidelines to other women who succumb to their dictatorial attitude.

It is unfortunate that in Indian society it is the male, rather than the female, who is taught to be progressive and creative. The girls are deprived of joys of love and tenderness in childhood by being rushed into the mother's role by the time they are able to stand and walk, whereas the boys are pampered. This is true of both the sexes throughout the world. Unpaid domestic work, everywhere, is regarded as women's work. Of course, it is important. Food has to be cooked, the children are to be fed, clothes have to be washed and mended, water and firewood have to be collected, the cattle have to be looked after...all these are time consuming activities. But the long hours and hard work that go into it are undervalued and unrecognized. And the situation of a working woman is still worse. Debby Taylor has correctly said:

> ...the chief injustice lies in the extra work women must do outside the home than in the assumption that it is their role—and their role alone—to do all the work inside it. (Debby Taylor 1985: 5)

By and large, they have become the victims of stereotype, traditional and rigid roles all over the world—and India is no exception! The qualities generally attributed to boys are independence, aggression, competitiveness, leadership, innovation, rationality, confidence and self-control, etc., whereas the girls are supposed to be dependent, passive, non-aggressive, non-competitive, weak and meek, yielding, emotional and nurturing by nature. The discrimination against women has gone a long way.

Simone de Beauvoir's classic observation, that a woman is defined and differentiated with reference to man, holds quite true in the context of Indian women though various laws and constitutional safeguards have been pronounced in her favour. She is still regarded as subordinate to him. There is, however, some change in the attitude of woman herself, who with access to education and exposure outside the family has begun to perceive herself as an individual in her own right. It is in this context that Shashi Deshpande depicts the anxiety of an educated, independent, middle-class Indian woman searching for a balance between her traditional role as a daughter, wife and mother in a predominantly patriarchal society and her new found sense of self and longing for freedom and personal space. Often, the role of provider is forced upon woman because of the rising cost of living and this compulsion is forcing them to leave aside their 'self-consciousness' and work for the financial interest of her husband's family. Initially when Indu takes up the job of writing for a women magazine, in which she writes about the dames of the city and showers them with adjectives, she enjoys her job. But later on she is amazed to know about the pretensions of these city dames. It is very frustrating for her to write appreciating articles about these so-called city dames, who are actually not worthy of it. The novelist makes a caustic attack on such women writers who take up writing as a profession not as a passion. As accepted by Indu when Naren asks her:

> I have read most of the things you have written. And now...interviewing society dames and showering them with adjectives. What do you do that for?
>
> Money, what else? It is my job.

> Money! He snorted. Does not your husband earn enough?
>
> Depends on what you mean by enough. (Shashi Deshpande 1983: 24).

Caught in the matrix of age-old customs and traditions, Indu cannot break herself free from the clutches of tradition. She painfully realizes that despite her education and exposure, she was no different from the women who circumambulate the *tulsi* plant to increase their husband's life-span. Even her husband, who is educated and apparently a modern man, is only a typical Indian husband for whom she has to remain passive and submissive. There are many instances which prove that many women in India have been playing the role of wife to perfection to keep their husbands satisfied. Despite her reluctance, she has to continue the frustrating job of writing for the magazine as she gets disillusioned by her experience with a so-called social worker, who has received an award for her social services. Indu was very much impressed by that sophisticated lady. As the novelist writes:

> I had finished my piece when someone had directed the little old man in the grimy *dhoti* and black cap to me. He had brought a piece too. About the same woman. Badly written though it was and full of spelling mistakes, I had read it to the end without a pause. Then incredulously, I had asked him, 'is this true?'
>
> ...
>
> And I had gone to my editor with two copies...his story and mine. He had read both and laughed.
>
> "Don't you believe it? I had asked angrily. He knew it was not my story I meant."
>
> "Of course I do. But...but...but".... (Shashi Deshpande 1983: 16)

And ultimately the worldly writer refuses to publish it. While agonising over the issue, like a typical middle-class husband, Jayant compels her to carry on. He has unrealistic expectations from her regarding her behaviour and her profession. He is ambitious and wishes to grow rich and prosperous at the earliest. He wants to reach a certain status where he can have a bungalow in the suburbs, a car and holidays abroad. To achieve this ambition, he wants Indu to go on writing even if it means compromising with the quality of her writing so that the money keeps flowing in. Indu resents the dishonesty but compromises because Jayant makes her believe that they need money. Jayant provides no psychological support to her. Rather he urges her to be practical like others. He says:

> What can one person do against the whole system! No point making yourself ridiculous with futile gestures. We need the money, don't we?... We have a long way to go.... (Shashi Deshpande 1983: 17)

This episode exemplify the fact that Indian woman is brought up to please her husband. No matter how unrealistic the targets and ideals set up by her husband, she strives to fulfil them.

Deshpande's concern with the patriarchal notion of subordination of women and that a woman must exist only in terms of her relationship with a man is very much explicitly in all her novels including *Roots and Shadows*. In patriarchy, woman is necessarily viewed as needing male control at all stages of her life. Her place as mother/sister/daughter-in-law is completely at the disposal of her male relatives, first by virtue of birth and second by marriage. Woman's role is rigidly defined by various males in her life. In Indian patriarchal family, the girl is considered as a thing to be given away. Marriage is the destiny of a woman; and to remain unmarried is suggestive of unnaturalness. It is considered as a matter of shame to woman's family. It is parents' social obligation and moral responsibility to get their daughter married before she passes the marriageable age. An unmarried man does not evoke the same response from the society. On the other hand, a woman is expected to live fulfilling the wishes and desires of others. For the sake of social approval and her parents' happiness, the girl has to go through the humiliating 'inspection' where she is examined by the boy's relatives as if she were a saleable commodity. Denied the freedom to choose or express herself, she is forced into marriage with him. The fact that she is also a human being with wants and needs of her own is ignored by everyone. Neither her parents nor the man ask what she wants. She is subordinated and subjugated in all the spheres. Even Indu in the novel, *Roots and Shadows*, who is an educated and professional woman, looks at herself from the perspective of her husband, Jayant. To quote the novelist:

> When I look in the mirror, I think of Jayant. When I dress, I think of Jayant. When I undress, I think of him. Always what he wants. What he would like. What would please him. I can't blame him. It is not he who has pressurised me into this. It is the way I want it to be. And one day I had thought...isn't there anything I want at all? Have I become fluid with no shape, no form of my own? (Shashi Deshpande 1983: 49)

These traditional women in patriarchal Hindu family end up their lives cooking food and cleaning strewn plates. The novelist raises the soul shaking questions if these women are to be treated as 'martyrs, heroines or just stupid fools'. These so-called 'martyrs, heroines or just stupid fools' are not allowed a share in the ancestral property, though there are constitutional provisions for it. All the males in Indu's family are shocked to hear that Akka has willed all her property in the name of Indu. Unable to get a share in the property all the male members try to convince her to gift the property to them for one or the other reason. Sunil, son of Madhav Kaka in the novel, is not able to control his emotions and bursts out his anger saying that:

> I think it is damned unfair. Why should all of Akka's money go to Indu?... She has no right at all, if you ask me. She isn't part of the family now, is she? (Shashi Deshpande: 1983: 93)

Here, the issue raised vehemently by the novelist is that why a girl is denied a share in the ancestral property and why a girl is not considered as the part of the family after the marriage.

The novelist also points out that an undercurrent of tension is ever present in joint family even during times of great rejoicing and excitement like marriage. Intrigues, groupism, jealousies, rivalries, barbed tongues and malicious words—all form a part of this family with everybody complaining against every one else.

There are so many diverse pulls and so many conflicting feelings that women would spoil the cooking to starve those they dislike, not caring if they starve themselves in the bargain. Amid these circumstances, Indu has seen women occupying secondary place and she has been a witness to this since her childhood. When she returns back to her ancestral home after a long time, she feels that though she considers herself a success in life, yet sending a cup of tea to her in her room is considered a breach of etiquette. When Anant Kaka asks the small child to get another cup of tea for Indu, she says:

> Sending up a cup of tea for woman whoever heard of it? Women, like children, were supposed to know their place. (Shashi Deshpande 1983: 48)

Indu, an orphan girl who lost her mother at a very tender age was brought up in a joint family and no chance was missed to acclimatize her to the patriarchal values. In the words of Indu:

> As a child, they had told me I must be obedient and unquestioning. As a girl, they had told me I must be meek and submissive. Why? I had asked. Because you are a female. You must accept every thing, even defeat, with grace because you are a girl, they had said. It is the only way, they said, for a female to live and survive. (Shashi Deshpande 1983: 58)

In the patriarchal family system, intelligence of a girl is considered as a burden. In Indu's ancestral home, the partition between male and female worlds is always very sharp. Women are not allowed to join important family discussions, not even Akka in her hey days. But Indu just thrust upon others when there is a discussion about how the *Big house* is to be maintained and how Akka's money is to be distributed. Although Indu is an educated and successful journalist, it is not without opposition that the male family members admit her to their discussion. To them she is just a woman more so a married woman and an outsider. They believe that she has no right to inherit either money or property because now she is a married woman. Among the uneducated women folk, she is a childless woman (although she and her husband opt out of getting children for personal and domestic reasons) no matter how educated she is and how successful she is in her profession. Here, Shashi Deshpande highlights gender-oriented views of these women folk. As long as the society remains patriarchal in its role allocation and division of labour, the culture of the second sex is bound to be eclipsed. When stereotyping of women in any form or any shape is noticed, Indu does not forget to remind all people around her that she has grown up and it implies that she cannot be treated at par with other women in the family. Deshpande believes that a woman's mind is shaped by constant hammering so that she is weak both physically and mentally and thus feels subordinate to man. To enforce subordination and subjugation of women in an effective manner, men in these traditional families don't want their women to 'think'. The day Indu 'grows up', the knowledge of her womanhood is gracelessly thrust on her with the cruel words that she should not forget her uncleanliness for four days. This seclusion during the four days is imposed upon Indu by the female patriarchs in the family who have no notion of their own identity and individuality. They identify themselves in terms of their relationships with others such as Kaka, Chacha, etc. They have even forgotten their own names. As the novelist comments:

> As if they have to be recognized by a relationship, because they have no independent identity of their own at all. And, in the process, their own names are forgotten. How does it feel not even to have a name of your own? There are women who are proud of having their names changed by their husbands during their wedding ceremonies. To surrender your name so lightly.... (Shashi Deshpande 1983: 117)

Kaki, in the novel, feels very happy to tell that she has not just one, but two good names. One name was given to her by her *father* when she was born, and the other by her *husband* when she got married.

Shashi Deshpande has compared the plight of women in patriarchal society with the plight of Sisyphus. It is said that for the crime of revealing the designs of the god, Sisyphus was meted out the following punishment: in the underworld he was compelled to roll a big stone up a steep hill, the stone always rolling down and Sisyphus had to begin all over again. This legend is also symbolic of the vain struggle of woman in the pursuit of identity of her own and of her fight against subordination in the patriarchal society. Many women in Indian family system share the same fate. Akki bursts out in Indu's presence as she says:

> Since I came into this house, my lot has been work, work and yet more work. As long as we live here, there will always be parasites. None of them even share the work. Am I every one's servant? And, after slogging for all of them, what do I get? (Shashi Deshpande 1983: 120)

Here, the novelist raises the issue of the frustrations piling up in the heart of a woman who is working incessantly and gets no credit for her work. Shashi Deshpande contemplates on the existence of inner strength in women of patriarchal families who have spent their whole lives slavishly without a word of appreciation for their services. Indu says:

> A woman's life, they had told me, contained no choices. And all my life, specially in this house, I had seen the truth of this. The women had no choices but to submit, to accept. And I had often wondered (...) have they been born without wills, or have their will atrophied through a lifetime of disuse? And yet Mini, who had no choice either, had accepted the reality, the finality with the grace and composure that spoke eloquently of that inner strength. (Shashi Deshpande 1983: 6)

The male characters in Deshpande's novel represent, in different degrees, the various facets of masculinity and patriarchy in Indian society. The majority of the husbands of the protagonists are patriarchal in their approach towards their wives. In her fiction, specially in *Roots and Shadows*, Shashi Deshpande has raised a number of questions about man-woman relationship in the Indian context. One of these issues is that of sexual sadism of husbands. The male characters who are flat characters in the novel are representative of certain attitudes prevalent in the society. The novelist exemplifies the fact that the Indian woman is brought up to please her husband. What is more disturbing to Indu is Jayant's rejection of her as an active partner in sex because traditionally a wife's role is only to fulfil her marital duty toward her husband. Indu, who is passionate by nature, feels thwarted and ashamed by the shock Jayant exhibits at her ardent behaviour:

> Jayant and I at the end of one of our moments of our love making. And I aghast at my total self-abandonment had cried out. 'It is not fair'. And Jayant, staring at me in bland astonishment, moving of me without asking me why I had said that and what it meant. (Shashi Deshpande 1983: 127)

When Indu, a passionate being, make an initiative in love-making, she is rejected by Jayant who says: 'no, not now'. As Indu tells to Naren:

> My response to him was so natural, so much beyond me and outside me.
>
> ......
>
> And now I know...it shocks him to find passion in a woman. It puts him off. When I am like that, he turns away from me. I have learnt my lesson now. And so I pretend. I am passive and unresponsive. I am still and dead. And now, when you tried to kiss me, I thought...this is Jayant. So that is all I am, Naren. Not a pure woman. Not a too faithful wife. But an anachronism. A woman who loves her husband too much. Too passionately. And is ashamed of it. (Shashi Deshpande 1983: 83)

Unable to discern why Jayant rejects her passion, Indu begins to conceal her real feelings from him and tailor her responses to meet his approval. Indu's predicament shows the differential equation of power between the two genders that remains unchanged whether the marriage is an arranged or one of their own choices. Gradually, Indu allows herself to enter into a passive and traditional relationship of submissive wife-dominating husband. She herself has so internalized the patriarchal value that a woman exists for the joy of a man and that she cannot conceive of herself as an independent being. It is only in the end of the novel, she makes a new beginning by deciding to assert herself.

Perhaps this view of Shashi Deshpande, it seems, is pointed by M. Alison Jaggar who comments:

> Superficially, women's sexual experiences differ widely from each other; some women are prostitutes, some are virgins; some are raped, while others are protected with obsessive care. Beneath the superficial variety, however, radical feminist assert the underline fact that men control women's sexuality for their purposes. Radical feminists believe that women, whether they recognize it or not, are the sexual slaves of men. (M. Alison Jaggar 1983: 260)

It is true to the core that Shashi Deshpande is not a propagandist novelist and she only aims at providing an intimate insight into the psyche of middle-class working women, oppressed due to their inferior social position and hemmed in by patriarchal socialization.

The novelist has also thrown light on certain traditional rituals which are nothing but efforts on the part of the male chauvinists to assert their dominance. In their effort to do so, they are helped by the so-called female patriarchs. Indu resents her womanhood as she is made conscious of her feminine by the elder women in the family. The novelist also focuses on the customs and rituals meant for women. They are expected to perform *vrat* and *pooja* to earn eternal wifehood as well as peace and harmony for their husbands. The novelist highlights that how women in Indian traditional families are involved in various rituals to ensure longevity of their husband's life and how a life without a husband is believed to be a curse. When Akka becomes ill and she is needed to be admitted to the hospital for the treatment, she denies going the hospital as she says that she is worried about the caste of the nurses working in the hospital and it is all because of her being an illiterate. She as a girl was denied the right kind of education as she belonged to the second sex. As told to Indu by Kaka:

> She would not let me. She did not want to go a hospital. She was worried about the kind of people she would come in contact with. 'God knows what caste the nurses are' she said. (Shashi Deshpande 1983: 21)

In the patriarchal society, widowhood is considered inauspicious. The novelist shows how a woman has to wear only white saree after the death of her husband and she has to get her head shaven off. When Narmada Atya becomes widow, Anant Kaka opposes her head being shaven off; ultimately, she is boycotted among the class of widows. Nobody eats the food cooked by her. As the novelist writes:

> And I understood why Kaka had, when Atya was widowed, so stoutly resisted the idea of her becoming a shaven widow. He had won, but at the cost of Atya's status. She was now a second class citizen in the kingdom of widows. The orthodox would not eat food cooked by her. (Shashi Deshpande 1983: 18)

Shashi Deshpande has depicted the plight of widows in the patriarchal society. In Indian society, a widow should remain celibate and forbearing till her death. She is graciously permitted to fast as much as she likes, is prescribed a vegetarian diet, and is warned against even mentioning another man's name. Chastity, restraint and life-long endurance are the other qualities she is expected to cultivate, but on no account can a 'virtuous woman' ever marry again. In contrast, a man is not merely permitted to take a second wife after he has performed the last rites of the first: he is actually exhorted to do so. The patriarchal society cautions him against neglecting his duties as a householder, and these duties require him to marry again. Another such discriminating practice is that of tonsuring of widows. It shows that men have created and perpetuated a whole new system of codes and practices started to humiliate women and keep them socially impotent. Whatever the reasons, therefore, for the origin of practices like the tonsuring of widows, they only accentuate the unequal basis of the male-female relationship. Other such strictures involve the restrictions on forms of food like meat. *Mangal-sutra, kumkum* and *alta* are gender-based symbols of matrimony and imply gender-discrimination. A woman, once widowed, is willy-nilly compelled to stop wearing them.

Like any educated and professional woman in the present Indian society, Indu is in paradoxical situation in which women find themselves enmeshed. Indu leads an ambivalent life. She cherishes within her heart deep and profound love but when the occasion comes to express it she retraces. This is because she is nourished and reared by a tradition ridden society in which she has been taught to be obedient, unquestioning, meek and submissive. The traditional society teaches a woman to accept every thing that comes her way in a graceful manner. As members of the subordinate sex, women are characterized by obedience and submission, and under male domination they have to develop a tendency to prevail by passive means. Indu surrenders to Jayant since she does not want to conflict. She clings tenaciously to Jayant and to her marriage not for the love alone but because she is afraid of failure of her marriage. She wants to show her family and to the world that her marriage is a success and so the traditional values she has been nourished with, compel her to put on the mask of an obedient and submissive wife. Such a 'relative identity' or rather the 'received role models', distort and problematize her self-perception. Such a world reduces women like Indu to a mere thing or mindless body for her feminine instinct for articulation is suppressed. Ever ready to please Jayant, Indu acquiesces to his desires. These traditional values make Indu realize that she does not exist for herself but for Jayant, who is the archetypal male, representative of imperialism and subjugation. The novelist asserts the idea that in a traditional society people exist in two groups—one the takers and the other the givers. In a traditional patriarchal society, the role of givers is assigned to women.

In the novel, *Roots and Shadows*, Shashi Deshpande talks of cruelty not even in middle-class society but also of the pitiable condition of women in lower class. Vithal's mother meets very unfair treatment at the hands of her husband who is a cook by profession and receives a beastly treatment from her husband. Ultimately, she runs away even without bothering about her son, Vithal. In the words of the novelist:

> Vithal's father had been a professional cook, hiring himself out for festivals, weddings and funerals. A dour, grim man who rarely spoke and never smiled, there was a streak of cruelty in him that came out in his relation with his meek silent wife. The boy, as a child, had been a frequent

> spectator of scenes in which the father had worked out his sadistic anger on the mother for the merest trifles. And then one day when the man was out on a job, the mother just disappeared. She had not even bothered to cook a meal for the child. When the man returned after a three-day job, he found the boy starving. The mother never returned. And neither the boy nor the father ever mentioned her name again. (Shashi Deshpande 1983: 138)

Similarly, in Indu's case her love marriage degenerates into a mere corporal affair that makes her feel as if she has abused her body's sanctity. She is having a marital relationship that suppresses her feminine demands. Her marriage has also denied fullness of her experience. Giving the example of Indu's married life, the novelist asserts that the Indian civilization is masculine civilization, a civilization that perpetuates myths created by male-oriented societies. Indu confesses the moral risks of a woman caught in the trap of a love-making with a traditional culture-created man of restrictive social code. Jayant destroys her respect for him by the callousness with which he takes her for granted and by this obliviousness to her human needs, he destroys her 'self-respect'. Thus, we see Shashi Deshpande's fictional world, like that of most of the other Indian women novelists, is marital relation centred. She concentrates on the theme of meaninglessness and sexual confusion suffered by women in tradition-oriented marriage institutions. For Indu, marriage is a serious conflicting situation. She suffers, questions and looks for the answers of the conflicts arising in her heart.

In Shashi Deshpande's *Roots and Shadows*, much critical controversy has been raised about the author's motive regarding the incestuous relation between Indu and her cousin Naren. It is Naren to whom she tells every little detail of her married life. Naren who is so open to her that easy compatibility develops between the two and ultimately she surrenders to him. She cherishes her momentary physical contact with Naren without any guilty consciousness. As she thinks:

> I can go back and lie on my bed. I thought, and it will be like erasing the intervening period and what happened between Naren and me. But, deliberately I went to my

> bed and began folding the covers. I don't need to erase anything I have done, I told myself in a fit of bravado. (Shashi Deshpande 1983: 168)

She resolves not to disclose this to Jayant as she thinks it had nothing to do with him. This is her first step toward her self-assertion. This assertion of has sparked off contradictory remark from the reviewers like O.P. Bhatnagar who laments:

> Indu's casual and matter of fact attitude to what she had done is shocking. Have our morals really gone so low that women commit this sin for nothing, just to prove that they do not lack courage? Is this really representative of modern Indian women? (O.P. Bhatnagar 1991: 129)

However, another critic, P. Ramamoorti does not view Indu's adultery some thing negative. To Indu it is an exercise of autonomy within marriage. As P. Ramamoorti says:

> This sheds a brilliant light on Indu's awareness of her autonomy and her realization that she is a being and not a dependent on Jayant. The novel gains its feminist stand in Indu's exploration into herself but it also moves beyond the boundaries of feminism into a perception of the very predicament of the human existence. (P. Ramamoorti 1991: 124)

Indu's affair with Naren becomes a metaphor for Indu's rebellion against Jayant's humiliation of her for being the initiator in their sexual relationship. The affair acts as a catharsis and frees her of self-imposed limits. Having purged herself of the feelings of guilt and shame towards Jayant, she decides that she will no longer try to deceive him in order to make herself more acceptable to him. Through this resolution, she learns to liberate herself of her complexes. She resolves to speak out and to stand up for herself. To quote her words:

> What kind of life can you build on a foundation of dishonesty? What kind of a home have I built? Now I would go back and see if that home can stand the scorching touch of honesty. (Shashi Deshpande 1983: 105)

Honesty requires one to have the courage to stand up for one self, one's values, one's needs, to possess the ability to assert.

She had passively accepted Jayant's values, his lifestyle and his ideas without thinking about her own choices. Her stay at the old house becomes that soul searching which results in her making the feminist decision of henceforth speaking out in the face of all oppression, overt and covert. A society wherein a man takes sexual liberties with impunity and a woman indulging in the same is looked upon with shock and horror and is branded as an adulterous or loose lady. Deshpande wants to shake the readers out of their complacency by thrusting in their face double standards being practiced in the patriarchal society. It also happens in the case of Akka whose husband has weakness for beautiful women. The issue, here, raised by the novelist is that how the Indian society does not disgrace a man for such a low act on his part whereas a woman is termed as a loose lady if she enjoys any illicit relation. Girls are not even allowed to interact with their boy-classmates. It is considered such a big offence which brings nothing but disgrace to the family. Akka in the novel objects to Indu's talking to a boy in the library. Indu is snubbed by Akka who says:

> That is enough of such talk. And even if you did nothing, it is bad enough being talked about. Why, three people have spoken to me about it since yesterday. And to your Kaka as well. No girls in our family has ever been talked about. (Shashi Deshpande 1983: 74)

Surprisingly, a boy is never snubbed or chided for this kind of act.

It has been observed that Shashi Deshpande has depicted many issues like subordination, subjugation, gender-biasedness, dowry-system, child-marriage, a woman being chided for any illicit relationship, etc. Not being a militant feminist, the novelist does not aim at giving any verdict; she simply puts the real life like situation before the reader; she herself does not draw any conclusion but lets her reader stress on his thinking and come out with his or her own conclusions. How to reconcile women's human demand for freedom with her need for love, and how to strike a balance between wifehood, career and spiritual fulfilment are some of the key issues raised by Shashi Deshpande in *Roots and Shadows*. Indu realizes that it is useless to 'hanker' after detachment which means freedom from all relationships as one cannot live in complete isolation. In the end, we find Indu equipped with 'quality of courage' which is necessary to face the challenge of identity-crisis. For a sensitive and intelligent Indu a woman should be autonomous self in a society that is largely conventional in its outlook, is a myth. She struggles to give shape and content to her individual existence in the sexist society and this struggle culminates in a crisis and ends in a compromise. In the end, Indu believes that there is no possible escape from relationships; only the old bonds are to be replaced by new bonds.

By taking the independent decision of financing Mini's marriage, Indu achieves her freedom. She does not let any one, neither Kaka nor Atya, come in the way of doing what she wants to do. She conquers her fears and achieves freedom in her life. She refuses to be influenced by Jayant, her husband, when he tries to make her change her decision of giving her job. He is bewildered in the beginning as if he has been cheated. Finally, he recognises her strength as well as her weakness which she had kept hidden from him so far. The ethos in the novel is neither of victory nor of defeat but of harmony and understanding between two opposing ideals and conflicting selves. Indu's predicament is representative of the larger predicament of women in contemporary Indian society where the new socio-economic forces have shaken old-cultural life. The break up of the joint family is the immediate result and visible symbol of imminent change.

The imminent change in the socio-cultural life has affected various relationships at various levels, especially husband-wife relationship. In the old family pattern, husband and the wife used to meet only briefly in the darkness of night. So there was hardly any occasion for conflict. But with husband and wife constantly thrown together in the present family pattern and with the wife sharing in many of the responsibilities which were earlier supposed to be only his, there have arisen the problems of incompatibility, maladjustment, expectation and despair. The Indian society continues to be male-dominated and attitudes towards women continue to be the same. Women, on their part, are becoming more and more conscious of the various emancipation moments. Hence, their predicament and their struggle to strike a balance have been well depicted by Shashi Deshpande in *Roots and Shadows*.

The novelist has very exquisitely and explicitly highlighted the inner struggle and suffering of the new class of Indian women through the character of Indu. She has raised many issues related to the educated, modern, sensitive women rooted in and shaped by the Indian customs, culture and traditions, on the one hand and, the new scientific knowledge from the West, on the other hand. When the Indian woman was uneducated and ignorant, she was hailed as *pativrata* or *sati*. Now this woman of today has started becoming aware of her own individuality and her place and role in the family and the society. Here, the writer has very rightly put forth the situation in which a young modern woman, who leaves behind the conventions and take the initiative to join the modernity, is entangled. According to Indu, who is the mouthpiece of Shashi Deshpande, one should listen to the dictates of one's own conscience and be true to oneself in speech as well as action. As O.P. Bhatnagar says:

> In the end, comes the realization that freedom lies in having the courage to do what one believes is the right thing to do and the determination and tenacity to adhere to it. That alone can bring harmony in life. (O.P. Bhatnagar 1991)

In this keen perusal of the novel *Roots and Shadows*, it has become quite apparent that Shashi Deshpande had dealt gender issues prevalent in Indian society, which is primarily patriarchal in nature. Apart from giving a true picture of problems related to gender issues, Shashi Deshpande moves from margin to the centre by giving a hint at the possible solution to the problem. Though the novelist who is neither a social worker nor a social activist, has sincerely depicted the true picture of condition of women in Indian patriarchal society using her pen as a brush. Using her novels as the canvass of her paintings, Shashi Deshpande depicts that the new education and awareness has awakened her to real self and as the 'awakened' self, she (modern woman) has started craving for independent and self-reliant status in life. The modern, educated protagonist, Indu questions the wilful unconcern for women's wishes. She has, already, shunned the long-preserved notions and taboos about women. She is the architect of her own fate and believes what Henric Ibsen has commented in *A Dools House*:

> ...I must take steps to educate myself. You are not the man to help me there. That is something I must do on my own. (Act III)

Works Cited

Beauvoir, Simone de. *The Second Sex*. Trans. H.M. Parshley. Harmondsworth: Penguin Books, 1974.

Bhatnagar, O.P. "Indian Womanhood: Fight for Freedom in *'Roots and Shadows'*". In *Indian Woman Novelists*, (ed.) R.K. Dhawan, New Delhi: Prestige Books, 1991. Set-I, Vol. V.

Deshpande, S. *Roots and Shadows*. New Delhi: Orient Longman Ltd., 1983.

Grimke, Sarah. *Letters on the Equality of the Sexes and the Condition of Woman*. New York: Burt Franklin, 1970.

Jaggar, M. Alison. *Feminist Politics and Human Nature*. New Jersey: Rowman and Allenheld Pub., 1983.

Nabar, Vrinda. *Caste as Woman*. New Delhi: Penguin Books, 1995.

Pathak, R.S. *The Fiction of Shashi Deshpande*. New Delhi: Creative Books, 1998.

Ramamoorti, P. "A Study of Shashi Deshpande's Women". In *Feminism and Recent Fiction in English*. Ed. by Sushila Singh. New Delhi: Prestige Books, 1991.

Taylor, Debby. *Women: A World Report, A New International Book*. London: Oxford, 1985.

Tong, Rosemarie. *Feminist Thought*. London: Routledge, 1993.

6

Inner Dilemma of Feminine Heart (*That Long Silence*)

It has been noticed that women writers mostly focus on women characters, on women's lives and gender issues in their writings. Books by women writers present detailed accounts of women's emotions, ideas and preoccupations. This, however, does not mean that their books are devoid of male characters. Perhaps, women's books have relatively few male characters or they occupy a less important place in the narrative. Being in the centre, women characters are visualized in terms of their relationship with men. These writers have written about all the aspects of love, marriage and sex. In a country like India where on the one hand, a woman is equated with man through the concept of *Ardhangini*, on the other hand, there are daily reports of bride-burning, dowry-harassment and rape. Therefore, a favourite theme with Indian women writers has been an analysis of women's position in the patriarchal society. A sensitive writer like Shashi Deshpande seems to grapple with the identity-crisis of the contemporary woman in her works. She employs her writings as a means to probe into women's lives and experiences. She bemoans the popular media-generated cultural climate which presents only "weeping women". This is a retrograde step.

That Long Silence, which won Shashi Deshpande the Sahitya Academy Award for 1990, tells the story of an Indian housewife, who maintains her silence throughout her life. The theme of the novel marks its presence very much in the epigraph of the novel which also alludes to British Feminist Manifesto as quoted in the epigraph:

> If I were a man and cared to know the world I lived in, I almost think it would make me a shade uneasy...the weight of that Long Silence of one half the world. (Shashi Deshpande 1989: Epigraph)

Thus, we can see that the novel is a protest against the limitation of women's lives. The force of Deshpande's depiction of women's plights lies in the way she is able to show their condition as endemic chiefly by drawing similarities among Jaya and variety of other female figures (Jaya, her mother, her grandmother, Jaya and her cousin Kusum, her widowed neighbour Mukta). All these women have been trained in maintaining silence in their lives. *That Long Silence* could be read as crystallization of memory and catharsis. It is an autobiographical narrative of Jaya. Her husband Mohan, suspected of business malpractice, has withdrawn with her to "her" small suburban flat in Bombay. This limbo of waiting allows Jaya to reflect on her life and to analyse her protean roles—as a daughter, sister, wife, mother, daughter-in-law, friend, mistress and a writer of general "feminine" newspaper pieces.

The married life of Jaya and Mohan is punctuated all along by "matrimonial silences". The estrangement between Jaya and Mohan reminds the reader of an ever-widening gap between a wife and her husband. This communication gap is felt throughout this novel. Jaya like Sarita in *Dark Holds No Terror* and Indu in *Roots and Shadows*, suffers from loneliness and this long episode of loneliness makes her deeply distressed.

That Long Silence, acclaimed masterpiece of feminist writing in Indo-Anglian fiction, raises the status of Shashi Deshpande among the writers of the present-day. The novel highlights the image of the middle-class woman sandwiched between tradition and modernity. Shashi Deshpande shows that a woman needs to go beyond the society-ordained roles of mother/sister/wife, etc. She has to find out who she is. The title of the novel also suggests the intention of the novelist to explore the female psyche during the quest of the protagonist for 'self'. *That Long Silence* is the period of self-introspection of a lonely woman.

During her stay at Dadar flat, Jaya introspects at her true identity. Deshpande's *That Long Silence* is an assertion of her belief that a woman is not an appendage, she is a 'being'; that too an autonomous being, and in the view of the writer, she has to find her own salvation. Deshpande never supports the radical view of "Amazon Utopias", female realms where men have been relegated to the secondary roles. The novelist moves a step ahead of the female psyche. The loneliness of a lady, according to the novelist, is no mental abnormality, but paves the way for the "New Woman's quest for self-discovery". The loneliness at Dadar flat gives Jaya space for self-interrogation. Traditionally, a woman has an identity only as 'husband's wife' or as father's daughter. Thus, the point, here, raised by the novelist is that a woman is always defined and redefined with reference to men only. The novelist writes:

> I was born. My father died when I was fifteen I got married to Mohan. I have two children and I did not let a third live. (Shashi Deshpande 1989: 2)

The real picture, the real 'you' never emerges. Looking for it is as bewildering as trying to know how you really look. Ten different mirrors show ten faces. The individuality of Jaya can't be defined. Indian woman is defined and her ideal image is conceptualized with reference to man in spite of legislations and many safeguards provided to her by the Indian constitution. Shashi Deshpande is aware of many constraints present in the Indian society and she defines freedom for Indian women from the point of view of the Indian socio-cultural milieu. Shashi Deshpande is not a militant or a radical feminist. Strong and rebellious female leadership is not Deshpande's choice.

Loss of identity of woman in the patriarchal Indian society is another important gender issue raised by the novelist in the present novel. Generally, a woman's identity is defined by others, in terms of her relationship with men, i.e. as a daughter, as a wife, as a mother, etc. The question "what a woman does" is never asked, but "who she belongs to" is always considered important. She doesn't have an identity of her own, even her name keeps on changing according to the wishes of others. A common Indian practice is to give a new name to the girl on her wedding day. This social practice seeks to supersede or supplant the identity of the woman. This gives the newly wed woman a new identity which is not even her true identity and is a pure product of patriarchal ethos. In *That Long Silence*, the writer has presented this phenomenon through the character of Jaya, who is named 'Suhasini' on her wedding day by her husband. Jaya, which means victory, is the name given to her by her father when she was born, and Suhasini meaning 'a soft, smiling, placid, motherly woman' is the name given by her husband. Both the names symbolize the traits in her personality as desired by two males in her life—her father and her husband. The former symbolizes revolt and the latter submission. The dreams of her childhood and desires to achieve her goals are shattered by the environment, the surrounding and above all by the society which imposes all sorts of restrictions on women. She is absolutely helpless and is unable to do anything to improve her situation. Ultimately, she tries to adapt herself to the main current. She longs to be called an ideal wife. She revolts in silence. She comments on a situation when her husband talks about women being treated very cruelly by their husbands and he calls women's silence as their strength.

Jaya forgets or rather pretends to forget her own identity, her own individuality. She builds an edifice of security around her husband and children and believes it to be a furrow into which she can crawl and can feel safe. She states in unequivocal terms that Mohan is her profession, career and means of livelihood. Unconsciously, she follows Vanita mami's advice, to treat her husband as a "sheltering tree". Like Sita who followed her husband into exile, she follows Mohan to Dadar flat. Like a faithful wife, she takes to wearing huge dark glasses, gets her eyebrows shaped and hair cut short to look exactly like the wife of an executive. In the process, she becomes dwarfed and annihilated as an individual but it all goes unnoticed even by herself. Her absorption into the family fold is so total that from a fiercely independent girl she gradually deteriorates into "stereotype of a woman: nervous, incompetent, needing male help and support".

Jaya has lost her identity to such an extent that she becomes over-dependent on Mohan and can't imagine life without him.

The thoughts of collapse of marriage, particularly those relating to the death of Mohan, keep constantly haunting her:

> I had lived in constant panic that he would die. I had clung to him at night, feeling with relief the warmth of his body, stroking his chest, letting my palms move with his even deep breaths. The thought of living without him had twisted my insides. His death had seemed to me the final catastrophe. The very idea of his dying had made me feel so bereft that tears had flowed effortlessly down my cheeks. If he had been a little late coming home, I had been sure he was dead. By the time he returned, I had, in my imagination, shaped my life to a desolate widowhood. (Shashi Deshpande 1989: 96-97)

The novelist takes the help of small details to imprint in reader's mind the secondary role of women in the Indian household. In Jaya's house, it was ordained that the girls clear up after the meals. Shashi Deshpande makes use of small dialogues to assert that how Indian girls are conditioned to take up the roles of 'would-be wives'. As the novelist writes:

> Cooking, clearing up had been exclusively female operations. Later, when only two of the girls, my cousins Veena and Sujata had been left at home, they had invariably quarrelled about whose turn it was to clear up. I remembered Sujata angrily bursting out one night when, for some reason, I had slept in Ajji's house, "why can't Jaya do it today?"
>
> "She is here for just tonight and you want her to do the work!" The Kaka had squashed her.
>
> "Then why can't the boys do it? Jaanu or Shridhar? Why does it have to be me and Veena?" (Shashi Deshpande 1989: 81)

Mocking face was the only answer to the question raised by a girl. The novelist propounds that in Indian patriarchal families not only men but also women participate in the process of preparing the girls for their roles of would be wives. Mohan, who is an educated and self-made man, is aghast when Jaya hints that he should cook during her confinement. Deshpande makes a point that if an educated man like Mohan is not ready to give a helping hand to his wife in the early state of pregnancy, as she feels sick because of the smell of spices and oil, then the plight of poor rural women can be well-imagined. One day, Jaya gets late returning home, Mohan shows his anxiety apparently, but does not care to prepare food in advance so that she can avoid the burden of cooking when she gets home. The novelist highlights that how domestic chores are considered woman's sole responsibility.

Another important issue raised by the novelist is that there is an ever-increasing desire to have sons and this desire is forced upon women not only by men but by women also. This desire to have a son as an heir is resulting in ever-decreasing gender ratio. Nayana, the sweeper, whispers to Jaya about her desire to have a son this time, though she has two daughters and has already lost two sons who died soon after their birth. She is quite optimistic that this time she is carrying a son in her womb. The novelist makes a point here that having a son is considered as a matter of pride in the patriarchal Indian society.

This love and preference for sons can be seen in the tradition of preparing family tree in which girls or daughters find no place. Jaya, the protagonist feels very surprised that the family tree which tells about the family history of over two hundred years has no place for daughters. To quote the novelist who depicts Ramu Kaka saying:

> I have been able to go back for nearly two hundred years. There are a few gaps of course, but I'll fill them up eventually. "Look, Jaya, this is our branch. This is our grandfather—your great-grandfather—and here's father, and then us—Laxman, Vasu and me. And here are the boys—Shridhar, Jannu, Dinkar, Ravi...."
>
> "But Ramukaka", I'd exclaimed. "I'm not here?"
>
> "You!" He had looked up, irritated by the interruption, impatient at my stupidity.
>
> "How can you be here? You don't belong to this family! You're married, you're now part of Mohan's family. You have no place here."

> ......
>
> Okay, I'd wanted to ask Ramukaka, if I don't belong to this family, what about the Kakis and Ai? They married into this family, didn't they, why are they not here? And what about Ajji, who single handedly kept the family together, why isn't she here? But I had said nothing to Ramukaka, not to Mohan. I had learnt it at last—no questions, no retorts. Only silence. (Shashi Deshpande 1989: 143)

Thus, novelist shows how a son is considered of much importance whereas a daughter is rejected in favour of son. The novelist, here, reveals that a woman has no identity of her own in the society except when she is somebody's wife, mother and daughter. The novelist also suggests at the beginning the custom of preserving the names of female ancestors just as the names of forefathers are preserved in the family trees. The episode in the novel affirms Deshpande's ideal that women must be re-instated to the equal position appropriated by men in a patriarchal society. Thus, Deshpande, not only tries to depict the thought-provoking instances of oppression, but also tries to provide an alternative world which is free of patriarchal oppression. So-called female patriarchs are also responsible for this kind of situation in the Indian patriarchal system. Ajji, Jaya's other grandmother has a great fondness for her jewels and Ai is optimistic that she will get the jewels one day but Ajji who can't give up her preference for boys, gifts away the jewel-set to her son and leaves something very meagre for her daughter. Jaya's Ai is also not able to rid herself of preference and love for sons and ultimately she gives her ultimate legacy to her daughter-in-law instead of her own daughter. Jaya speaks:

> I had not been in Ambegaon when other Ajji died, so I never had any idea of Ai's feelings when she had discovered that other Ajji had left nothing for her. All the jewels had been given to Chandu mama who had no children. But he was the Son. Perhaps the old woman had not been able to get away from the fact, finally. (Shashi Deshpande 1989: 112)

The novelist also gives another brilliant example of preference of women in the patriarchal society to have sons. Nayana is another woman in this tradition. She loves her daughters but she does not want them to live the kind of life she has lived. This uneducated working class woman has her own indigenous solution to counter patriarchal authority as she says:

> Why give birth to a girl, behanji, who'll only suffer because of men all her life? Look at me! My mother loved me very much, she wanted so much for me...a house with electricity and water, shining brass vessels, a silver waist chain, silver anklets...and what have I got? No, no, behanji, better to have a son. (Shashi Deshpande 1989: 28)

Apart from this, Nayana's husband threatens to throw her out in case if she delivers a girl third time again. Preference or love for boys can also be seen in the example of Mukta's mother-in-law. When Satish, Mukta's only brother-in-law wants to go abroad, his mother expresses her anger that who will cremate her as her other son (Mukta's husband) has already died and who left behind none but a daughter who according to Hindu rituals can't cremate her dead body. As the novelist writes:

> One son dead, the other running away, and not even a grandson; who will cremate us when we are dead? (Shashi Deshpande 1989: 183)

Thus, the novelist brings on the surface the gender-bias prevalent in the Indian society. Mukta's mother-in-law regrets not having a grandson.

Mohan's mother also suffers physical and emotional harassment at the hands of her husband. She always waits for him to come back, however late he is. He never tells her that by what time he will be back but at the same time expects her to serve him hot and fresh rice. She can't make children wait for long and therefore she serves them food and then she cooks fresh rice for him as he refuses to eat children's 'disgusting' leavings. One day she had just cooked rice and was waiting for him. In the words of writer:

> He came in and went straight to bathroom to wash. By the time he returned, she had his plate ready...and then he asked 'why is there no fresh chutney today'?

> She mumbled something. The next moment he picked up his heavy brass plate and threw it, not at her, but deliberately at the wall, which it hit with a dull clang. He stood up, and jerking his shirt off the peg walked out of house. (Shashi Deshpande 1989: 35)

Thus, we see Mohan's father walks out of home as if his rejection of the food is a punishment to his wife. Later, she sends him (Mohan) to a neighbour's house to get some chillies. The writer displays:

> When he went back his mother was lighting the fire blowing at it through brass blower to set the flames going. Her eyes were red but it could have been the smoke for the wood was always bad, it never burnt clean, and though they had got used to its pungent, acrid smell in the house, her eyes were always red with smoke. (Shashi Deshpande 1989: 36)

Mohan's reaction to this incident is very patriarchal as he comments about his mother that she was a tough lady as she bore everything very silently and this kind of 'toughness' is considered as a virtue by him. Thus, Deshpande points out that silence and surrender are considered as virtue of women in the patriarchal Indian society. Silence seems to be the common factor in the mode of suffering in the case of both Mohan's mother and Vimla, his sister. Vimla had an ovarian tumour with metastases in the lungs. She does not disclose it to anybody in the family. And ultimately she dies a silent death like her mother who died while trying to get her baby aborted with the help of the midwife. Vimla could not also come out with her feeling of not having any baby. Temperamentally, Mohan is an authoritarian. He is insensitive, particularly, towards the suffering of women. His mother had been a victim of his father's oppression and had keeled over when unable to endure his cruelty and the pressures of continuous child-bearing. Indifferent to her suffering, Mohan calls his mother "tough", though Jaya as a woman understands the desperation in her mother-in-law's life. Mohan's attitude, though surprising, is not unusual because sons of harsh fathers often tend to model themselves after them. Although he is not openly "authoritarian" with Jaya, Mohan is a typical patriarchal husband. To him, wife is exclusively husband's property and therefore can be used as a status symbol to be flaunted. His image of an ideal wife is a result of his observance of the submissive women that he has seen in his family during his growing years, and he expects Jaya to behave in a similar manner. The only difference is that he had wanted an educated wife to be able to live upto the standards set by his parents. He tries to use her education, etc. not for her development as an individual but for the furtherance of his own professional interests. Similarly, he values Jaya's ability as a writer, not as a mark of her personality, but as an asset to his social status.

We find that Mohan's mother is an exploited woman, who is exploited to the point of brutality by her husband. She keeps on suffering due to socially imposed reticence until she is not able to tolerate it any more. Ironically, her only act of rebellion—the abortion of her unwanted pregnancy—results in her death. The writer depicts the emotional struggle that Mohan's mother has to undergo to unburden herself from the burden of being only 'a breeding animal'. Though she has been depicted as an illiterate woman, yet finding herself pregnant again, she desperately tries to unburden herself from the burden of her biological role, i.e. her only role in marriage. This time she refuses to accept the patriarchal notion that the sole purpose of a woman's life is to breed and thus she opts for an abortion. Her decision to get her child aborted is a challenge to the popular patriarchal myth that womanhood and motherhood are the only possible synonyms. The novelist shows that a woman's body is her own and should not be used only as a reproductive machine. It should be solely upto the woman to decide what to do with it. In an interview, Deshpande has said:

> ...until very recently women in our society have been looked upon just as breeding animals. They had no other role in life. I have a strong objection to treating any human being in that manner. (Geeta Gangadharan 1994)

The reactions of Mohan and Jaya to her situation illustrate the different perceptions of men and women, of women's oppression. Mohan regards his mother's silent suffering as her "toughness", thereby revealing his internalization of the idea that a woman should bear her lot stoically. Her silence, to him, was a sign of her strength. Jaya, in comparison, feels a woman's sensitivity. In the dead woman's suicide (by getting her child aborted), Jaya sees:

> He saw strength in the woman sitting silently in front of the fire, but I saw despair. I saw a despair so great that it would not voice itself. I saw a struggle so bitter that silence was the only weapon. Silence and surrender.
>
> I'm a woman and I can understand her better; he is a man and he can't. (Shashi Deshpande 1989: 37)

Deshpande turns her head on the traditionally glorified virtue of suffering in silence which is ingrained in the Indian women, and she reveals the utter helplessness and lonely state of such a woman. The novelist also tells about the silent suffering of Jeeja, the maid-servant. The novelist writes:

> She knew what her purpose in life was—it was to go on living. Enduring was part of it and so she endured all that she had to.... There had been days when she had come to work bruised and hurt, rare days then had not come at all. But I had never heard her complain. (Shashi Deshpande 1989: 51)

Shashi Deshpande has raised another very important issue in the novel—the issue of the way the girls are married off in the Indian patriarchal society. The novelist highlights the qualities of a boy that are taken into consideration before selecting a boy for the girl and the qualities that are expected of a would-be bride. The novelist writes:

> And so I had been ready for Mohan who—he had told me this soon after we got married—had wanted to marry a girl 'who can speak good English'. That statement had amazed me as much as Dada's words, when had first told me about Mohan. "I believe", Dada had said, "that what he wants is an educated, cultured wife". He says he isn't bothered about dowry, money and all that. (Shashi Deshpande 1989: 90)

The novelist highlights the issue that a girl's consent is never needed. A boy is selected or rejected for a girl on the basis whether he has/hasn't good income.

The novelist shows that over the years, Jaya has moulded herself into the stereotype of an "ideal" wife and mother at the cost of her writing career. She sacrificed her writing career for the sake of her married life. The only aim in her life remains "what shall I make for breakfast/lunch/tea/dinner?" In the past, Jaya had written perceptively and sensitively about oppressed women, but gives it up because Mohan disapproves of such writing. He values Jaya's ability to write, not as a mark of her personality, but as an asset to his social status. As the writer writes:

> My wife is a writer—yes, that was something to be proud of, a respectable hobby, something that had set me (Jaya) apart from other women gave me a status that had added a bit to his, 'my wife is a writer', he had often introduced me.... (Shashi Deshpande 1989: 119)

Thus, the novelist wants to pinpoint here that how a husband views his wife as a status symbol to be flaunted among his peers but at the same time he interferes with her writings and persuades her to write in a manner that is fashionable even if unethical. Jaya has been a short story writer of moderate success. Although Mohan takes pride in the fact of being the husband of a writer, he strongly objects to her themes which he suspects to have strong autobiographical overtones. Once she writes a story about a couple, about a man who could not reach to his wife except through her body. Mohan thinks that people might think that the man in the story is none but him. To quote from the text:

> ...the day he had come back from carrying a magazine he had thrust at me, saying, 'your story is here'.
>
> 'My story?' Feverishly I had turned over the pages and stared at my name, entranced.
>
> Then I had turned to Mohan. 'Oh God, Mohan, I've won a prize, it's the story I sent for the contest, it's got a prize....'
>
> Mohan's face had finally silenced my bubble. 'Jaya' he had said dully, 'how could you have done it?'

> How could I have done what?
>
> "They will all know now, all those people who read this and know us, they will know that these two persons are us, they will think I am this man. How can I look anyone in the face again? And you, how could you write these things, how could you write such ugly things, how will you face people after this?
>
> ......
>
> "How can you reveal us, how can you reveal our lives to the world in this way?" (Shashi Deshpande 1989: 143-44)

Thus, the novelist shows that his wife's performance in her profession doesn't matter to Mohan, but how the society reacts to her performance is very important to him. To Mohan, Jaya is not a writer but an exhibitionist only. Jaya, on the other hand, relates her experience only after transmuting it into something entirely different. Thus, we have seen that through the character of Jaya, Shashi Deshpande presents a woman whose inner turmoils are so bitter that she is unable to speak them out and remains silent in order not to be frustrated and disappointed after the disapproval of her writings by her husband. She is unable to unfold the truth. She is like a bird who has got wings and knows that it can fly but somehow, does not. In the same way, Jaya is aware of her abilities and she knows that she can expose them openly, but she does not because of her fear of her husband's rejection. She always remains silent which indicates that the traditional roles of women still have primacy over all the newly-acquired professional roles. As Maria Mies points out:

> the career woman has not only to face the opposition of her surroundings and to struggle against many objective obstacles, but she is often divided in herself because she also often subscribes to the Indian idea of womanhood. Her problem arises, firstly, from the contradictions between this image and the demand of a new social situation and then from the discrepancy between new aspirations and lack of opportunity. (Maria Mies B5-145)

Shashi Deshpande has taken up another key-issue in the novel *That Long Silence*—the issue of the silence of the modern Indian housewife. Many woman writers tried their hand at expressing this 'long silence' that had turned women into non-entities, but those women writers could only provide psychological depths to their characters. They either created unreal sentimental romances or finally succumbed to the temptation of mouthing feminist ideology. But Shashi Deshpande's success lies in her psychological as well as emotional representation of silence of modern Indian wife. The novelist, herself, comments about:

> And then I wrote *That Long Silence*, almost entirely a woman's novel, nevertheless, a book about the silencing of one-half of humanity. A life-time of introspection went into this novel, the closest to me personally; the thinking and ideas in this are closest to my own. (Jasbir Jain 2000: 210).

Thus, Jaya represents the silence of half of the humanity and this novel attempts to break the silence imposed upon women and their experiences by an overpowering male-dominated Indian society. On the one hand, the silence expressed in the novel expresses the suppressed longings, emotions, aspirations and protests of women down the ages, on the other hand, it challenges the men to change and to give women their due position and rights. The kind of silence talked about by the novelist is not only silence of speech but also that of emotional silence. The novelist has given an example. Jaya likes to watch advertisements but Mohan always cracks jokes about advertisements and therefore she does not dare to watch the advertisements for the fear that she will be jibed at by him. As the novelist writes:

> 'There is no need to hurry', Mohan often said when we were getting ready to go to a movie. 'At the worst, we will miss the advertisements, and who wants to see them anyway?' I did, but I never dared to confess it to him. What if he too said, "what poor taste you have, Jaya!" Instead, I replied cravenly, 'yes, no need to hurry'.... (Shashi Deshpande 1989: 3)

Similarly, when Mohan and Jaya have shifted to their Dadar flat; Mohan is tensed because of some trouble in the office; he is not able to sleep at night and when he asks Jaya that if she could sleep soundly at night, she is not able to confess that she slept like a dog at night because she is afraid that she might be called insensitive. The novelist narrates another incidence in the novel in which a husband beats his wife fiercely who speaks nothing but moans only. Her silence is symbolic of lack of communication between a husband and a wife. As the novelist writes:

> "Talk", he was saying. "Where did you go today? Tell me. Open your mouth, why don't you open your mouth, you bloody whore? Open your mouth and speak the truth. Where did you go today? Can't you reply? Has someone cut out your tongue? Tell me quick or I'll give it to you. Talk. Fast. Say something."
>
> The sound of a blow. Soft moans.
>
> Another blow....
>
> Again the blows, and still the woman clinging desperately to her silence, abandoning it only to cry softly, "mother, mother, mother." (Shashi Deshpande 1989: 57)

Even when Mohan gets out of turn promotion, Jaya never asks him as to how he could manage that. She silently observes that they can send their children to good schools and could save enough to help Mohan's father which was not possible without extra income. Like Gandhari, an Indian patriarchal construct, Jaya ignores everything. Jaya is representative of an ideal wife in the patriarchal system who has to talk to her husband according to his mood. For instance, when Mohan complains of his brother and sister, Jaya is about to retaliate back but she keeps silent as she knows that his mood is better met with silence. As Cunningham says:

> You never find a woman criticising her husband, even playfully, in case it might damage the relationship. (Cunningham John 1988)

There is hardly any 'real' communication between Jaya and Mohan, neither verbal nor emotional. There is disheartening silence between husband and the wife. Deshpande presents here not a woman who has desire to revolt but one who 'silently' reconciles to her hapless lot.

Shashi Deshpande takes up the issue of transmutations a woman has to bring in her personality so as to make her marital relation work. The novelist shows that in the patriarchal Indian society a woman is never supposed to be angry. She can be neurotic or frustrated but not angry. There is only order and routine in her life and is always occupied with the thoughts like she has to change sheets on this day or has to scrub the bathrooms the day after. Simone de Beauvoir has also aptly pointed out the plight of woman in marital life and how marriage subjugates and enslaves women and it leads her to:

> aimless days indefinitely repeated, life that slips away gently toward death without questioning its purpose. (*Second Sex*, 1974: 500. Translated and ed. H.M. Parshley New York: Vintage Books, 1974)

Women pay for their happiness at the cost of their freedom and de Beauvoir emphasised that such a sacrifice on the part of a woman is too high for anyone because the kind of self-contentment, serenity and security that marriage offers drains woman's soul of its capacity for greatness. de Beauvoir says:

> She shuts behind her the doors of her new home, when she was a girl, the whole countryside was her homeland; the forests were hers. Now she is confined to a restricted space [...]. (*The Second Sex* 502)

The role of wife—particularly in Indian patriarchal society restricts rather circumscribes women's self-development. As Tong has also commented:

> Sometimes women play their roles not so much because they want to but because they have to in order to survive economically and/or psychologically. Virtually all women engage in the feminine role playing. (Rosemarie Tong: 1993)

It is against this encoded and pre-ordained role of a woman that Jaya revolts, though silently. She thinks that in this life itself there are so many cross-roads and so many choices but a married woman has a few or practically no choices left to her save what her husband wills and desires. But Jaya's is a life of instinct and urges. Unlike other married women, slavishly tagged to tradition, she has own say. In reminiscing about the past, Jaya succeeds in blotting out that long silence and making future life possible.

Jaya slips into passivity because she cannot envisage any other kind of life. Consequently, she has moulded her personality to suit her role as Mohan's wife and in this process she has suppressed and lost sight of her own values:

> I am Mohan's wife, I had thought and cut off the bits of me that had refused to be Mohan's wife. (Shashi Deshpande 1989: 191)

Jaya's review of her relationship with Mohan subverts the notion of marriage as the destiny of every Indian girl. To her, married life has become unendurable:

> I had to admit the truth to myself that I had often found family life unendurable. Worse than anything else had been the boredom of the unchanging pattern, the unending monotony. (Shashi Deshpande 1989: 4)

She thinks of herself and Mohan as a "pair of bullocks yoked together", living together because there was nothing better to do, creating "the illusion of happiness" as most couples do:

> We smiled, we laughed; I, the mother, served them with 'love and care'; Mohan, the head of the family, smiled indulgently, and the children were lively and playful. A visual-yes it had to be only that; for I could not find the words to match the picture. When I tried,...the scum of hostility floating to the top.... (Shashi Deshpande 1989: 4)

Deshpande here, appears to be a postmodernist who offers a glimpse into gender issues related to the falsely conceived idea of a happy family, and a critique of how it is created via the myth of the perfect wife and mother.

The novelist also tells about disenchantment in the married life of educated women like Jaya whose life superficially appears to be romantic. Jaya gets disenchanted and stops following instructions of women magazine which tells her (like all its readers) to make herself pleasing and attractive to her husband. Years later, she gives up all such exercises realising that he would sleep with her faithfully twice a week whether she creams her face or not. The relationship, thus, becomes dissatisfying to her—one devoid of meaning, since it exists too much on just one plane, i.e. the physical level. When Jaya looks back at her relationship with Mohan, she feels that she and Mohan do not make 'a really happy family'. They are just like 'a man and a woman married for seventeen years' but there are no bridges of understanding and love between them. They can't even decide upon a meal or a movie without trifle bickering. They live together but the novelist shows that there is emptiness in their relationship. Mohan accuses Jaya of indifference to him in the phase of crisis in his life but he forgets that she had also never mattered to him.

The feeling of disgust of living with a man who does not love the woman the way she expects him is a burning problem that the educated women face in our contemporary Indian society. The thought of desertion by the husband unnerves Jaya for she has not yet cast off the role of a traditional Indian woman. Through Jaya's character, Deshpande expresses an ambivalent attitude of contemporary educated independent-minded Indian women who can neither reconcile themselves to a situation when their husbands ignore them and crush their ambitions in life nor can they cast off their husbands, for the 'husband is like a sheltering tree' which they can't afford to live without. For instance, when Mohan gets the 'job of his choice', Jaya never questions the means by which he gets it. She asserts:

> If Gandhari, who bandaged her eyes to become blind like her husband, could be called an ideal wife too. I bandaged my eyes tightly. I did not want to know anything. It was enough for me that we moved to Bombay, that we could send Rahul and Rati to good schools, that I could have the things we needed...decent clothes, a fridge, a gas connection, travelling first class. And there was enough for Mohan to send home to his father—for Sudha's fees, Vasant's clothes and Sudha's marriage. (Shashi Deshpande 1989: 61-62)

Thus, the novel depicts the plight of an educated Indian wife of our time. The novelist shows that due to difference in attitude of the husband and the wife, their marital life grows shaky and gloomy. The marriage in such cases becomes more of a compromise than love. It is more based on social fear rather than on mutual need of each other. The cause may be rooted in their choices of a partner. Mohan marries Jaya for no other reason than that she can speak English fluently and Jaya gives her nod for marriage to Mohan for the reason that her mother was not in favour of her marriage with Mohan. Thus, the novelist wants to prove that a marital relation born out of such feelings and attitudes can have nothing but emptiness in it. This emptiness in the loveless marriage causes the wife and the husband to drift away from each other and ultimately results in total failure. Deshpande proves that in Indian patriarchal system, a woman can survive only by negating her own personality. And this negation of her own personality makes her completely powerless in the patriarchal order. Jaya in order to maintain her marriage as happy one, slowly transforms herself to and achieve this ideal of womanhood, where she learns to suppress her anger and always works up to please her husband. Jaya even transforms her appearance to suit her husband's idea of a modern woman. She ultimately gets so completely absorbed into the family fold that from a fiercely independent woman, she is transformed into the stereotype of a so-called ideal woman. Jaya desperately clings to her husband as if her life depends on him. Thus, we feel that Jaya's story, in the larger context, is the story of generations of Indian women. The novelist shows that how an Indian wife accepts the situation and her existence in relation to her family. She mars her own wish to look outside her family and 'wants' to be happy looking after her husband and children.

Female patriarchism is another key issue raised by Shashi Deshpande in her novels. By depicting these so-called female patriarchs, the novelist projects that these females have been conditioned by so-called Indian patriarchal society so as to execute male domination in a more effective manner. Deshpande's portrayal of female patriachism seems to be a reaction to the idealized depiction of the mother and motherhood in mythology and other Indian literature. The daughters in the traditional families are considered as the sole responsibilities of their mothers so that they prepare daughters for a harsher future as a part of the process of socialization. The patriarchy of the fathers remains hidden as these female patriarchs act on their behalf. According to Brown, the important reason underneath this female patriarchism is that the expression of aggression by women is always turned 'inwards'. This 'inward expression' is always towards theirs own sex and never against men, and it takes place in the non-public realm of the domestic household —the women's world. In Indian patriarchal families, numerous examples of this 'inwardness' occur. For example, Vanita mami in the novel has to face the 'inward aggression' of the two domineering women—Ai and other Ajji:

> Perhaps the truth was that Vanita mami had never known what it was to choose. Since the day she got married she, like the rest of Ai's family, was dominated and ruled by that ghoul, her mother-in-law, my other Ajji. Even Vanita mami's saris were chosen for her by the old woman. Later, there was Ai, who went back to her old home after Akka's death; there still is Ai. (Shashi Deshpande 1989: 45)

We see that Vanita mami is a victim of female patriarchism and 'aggression to self'. Numerous example of this kind of patriarchism can be seen in the example of relationships between mother-in-law and daughter-in-law. Once the mother-in-law gains in status through the marriage of her son, her suppressed aggression is turned against the daughter-in-law who is both inferior to her in status and a potential rival for her son's affection. Though there is big contrast between the personalities of Jaya, Ajji and 'other Ajji', yet there is a point of similarity between the two as both of them are the oppressors.

Acting on the same line of action, Vanita mami gives a piece of advice to Jaya on her wedding day. Vanita mami who herself is a victim of female patriarchism, gives patriarchal advice to Jaya. She tells Jaya:

> If your husband has a mistress or two, ignore it; take up a hobby instead—cats, may be, your sister's children.

So, we find that Vanita mami carries forward the legacy of giving patriarchal advice to the newly wed girl. She advises

Jaya that a husband is like a sheltering tree and without this tree (husband) a woman is unprotected and vulnerable. So, according to Vanita mami, a woman has to keep the tree alive and flourishing, even if she has to water it with deceit and lies. Acting on the same line of action as of her mother (other-Ajji), Ai (Jaya's mother) always takes favour of her son whenever there is something wrong between Ravi and Asha. Jaya predicts the patriarchal treatment for Asha, her sister-in-law by her own mother. As the novelist writes:

> She would rush to take her stance by Ravi. I knew it, she would say. "I always knew that girl was no good for my Ravi." She would believe it too forgetting how enthusiastic she had been about Asha at first. Ai's initial enthusiasm had been not for Asha's qualities, but for her good looks and her father's money. Both she and Vanita mami had made good looks and her father's money. Both she and Vanita mami had made a pet of Asha, fussing and cooing over her during the wedding, caressing and fondling her as if she had been a doll. They had hung over her as she sat decked in silks and jewels. Only her innate good nature had enabled Asha to stand all that rubbish, but I had enabled Asha to stand all that rubbish, but I had felt sorry for her, and indignant on her behalf. Until I had seen the pearls on her. (Shashi Deshpande 1989: 111)

Thus, the novelist shows how Jaya's mother will take side of her son whenever there is any controversy between her son and daughter-in-law. The novelist also highlights that only the old conventional ladies are not patriarchal in nature but well-educated women like Jaya can also be seen having patriarchal feelings. Jaya has sympathy with Asha who is meeting patriarchal treatment from her mother-in-law but she feels jealous of Asha when she finds her wearing ancestral jewels. When Ravi asks Jaya to convince Asha to come back to her matrimonial home, she, herself, makes a patriarchal statement to Asha:

> Go home like a good girl, Asha, I should say. Go back home and obey your husband. And never mind whatever it is he has done, he is your husband, after all, and a husband can do no wrong. (Shashi Deshpande 1989: 115)

At one point, Vimla (Jaya's sister-in-law) makes a statement that she is different from her own mother, but the novelist draws a parallel between mother and the daughter. Both the women died in silence. Mohan's mother died of repetitive pregnancies. She wanted the child in her womb to be aborted and in her efforts to do so she had lost her life. Similarly, Vimla developed cancer in her uterus and, therefore, she bled continuously but kept suffering silently and didn't tell anyone. Vimla's mother-in-law is also like any patriarchal figure, as the novelist writes:

> When Mohan and I had visited her—our normal routine visit during our annual stay in Saptagiri—her mother-in-law had shrugged heavily and said, "God knows what's wrong with her. She's been lying there on her bed for over a month now. Yes, take her away if you want to. I never heard of women going to hospitals and doctors for such a thing. As if other women don't have heavy periods! What a fun! But these women who've never had children are like that." (Shashi Deshpande 1989: 39)

Thus, we see that these so-called 'female patriarchs' have no sympathy with those of their own sex. Similarly, when Tara, Jeeja's daughter-in-law, curses and reviles her husband, Jeeja sternly shuts her up telling her the significance of living husband and the curse of widowhood. The novelist writes:

> Tara had none of Jeeja's reticence or stoicism. She cursed and reviled her husband and, sobbing loudly, moaned her fate. "So many drunkards die", she cried, "but this one won't. He'll torture us all to death instead." Jeeja sternly shuts her up. "Stop that! Don't forget, he keeps the '*kumkum*' on your forehead. What is a woman without that?" (Shashi Deshpande 1989: 53)

Hence, all these so-called 'female-patriarchs' are the guards of 'patriarchism' in the traditional Hindu family who take every care to keep women fettered in the chains of patriarchism and male chauvinism. The two Ajjis represent the power that a woman in a joint family could wield with the advancement of age and changing status. Their portrayal in the novel also draws attention to the strictures and social expectations in the traditional Indian family which can thwart individual growth and freedom.

In most of her fictional works, Shashi Deshpande has taken up the issue of the pitiable condition of widows in the traditional Indian families. As soon as a man becomes a widower, proposals for re-marriage usher in for him. But the life of widow is full of plightful conditions. Women in Indian families are taught that husband is like a sheltering tree without whom the existence of a wife is not possible. Kamlatai and Laxman kaka's wife in the novel, cannot imagine life after their husbands are gone. As Jaya observes:

> "How will I live without him, Jaya, how will I live?" she had cried out to me when I had gone to see her after Laxmankaka's death, her hands clutching mine in a painful grip. Jaanu had brought her from Saptagiri after his father's death and had, like a dutiful son, installed her in his house. Both he and his wife Medha had been kind, but Kamla kaki had wept unceasingly. Her face, which had been plump and jolly when she was just one of the '*kakis*', had been bewildered, like that of a boxer who's taken too many bad blows. "How will I live without him?". (Shashi Deshpande 1989: 138)

There is another story about the plightful condition of widows in Indian patriarchal system. This incidence was narrated to Jaya by her father:

> She was only a child, and they humiliated her, disgraced her in public because she hadn't her head shaved off. They called her a whore, a daughter of a whore—I remember Akka saying that. (Shashi Deshpande 1989: 147)

The novelist shows how Indian wife obeys the rituals of *pujas* and fasts so as to avoid the curse of widowhood. For this, Indian wives can be seen ritually circumambulating *tulsi* and *peepal* tree. Apart from these, there are certain other rituals like a widow can't put on the certain pieces of jewellery like 'mangal sutra' or 'maang-tika' and can't be the part of any family celebration. While depicting the character of Ajji, Deshpande offers us a glimpse of the kind of life a widow leads in a traditional patriarchal family:

> Ajji, a shaven widow, had denuded herself of all those things that make-up a woman's life. She had no possessions, absolutely none, apart from the two saris she wore. Her room was bare, except for the large bed on which my grandfather had slept, a bed which, ever since I knew it, was unburdened by a mattress. There were also two chains in her room, large wooden chairs with arms, the hardeners of their slatted seats unredeemed by the cushions, augmented, in fact, by sharp nails that seemed to sprout from the most unexpected places. As if the carpenter had driven in, generously and at random, nails that sprang out to punish your skin, your clothes, your hair. Ajji herself sat on the bare ground and slept on a straw mat at night. The bed was a memorial to grandfather, and the chairs meant for any male who, wearing trousers, could not sit comfortably on the ground. (Shashi Deshpande 1989: 126)

Thus, Deshpande gives a very vivid account of status of widow in Indian patriarchal families and she makes her reader aware that how widow in Indian patriarchal society are forbidden from participating in festivals, wearing new clothes, etc. so that their sexuality may remain unexpressed rather suppressed.

Many critics criticise Deshpande's protagonists for having an illicit or so to say extra-marital relation. But this seems to be a misinterpretation as a careful reading of the text reveals that Jaya never forgets her married status and does not succumb to desire in her friendly relationship with Kamat. Shashi Deshpande herself remarked in an interview:

> [...] I did bring in Kamat to serve a purpose: to show Jaya the kind of relationship that she could achieve with a man. She gets a kind of companionship with Kamat that she never gets from her husband. Yet that is marriage and that isn't. (Lakshmi Holmstrom 1998: 247)

Thus, Kamat is brought in the novel so as to show that any intimacy between a man and a woman is not looked upon with respect in the patriarchal society. Jaya is drawn to him only for this reason that he treats her as his equal and offers constructive criticism to her on her writings. He even receives her mail at his address to help her avoid any confrontation with Mohan as he disapproves of her writings. The novelist presents him as a male feminist as he does not have any aversion to cooking and such other domestic chores meant to be performed by women exclusively. She feels so much at ease in his company that her womanly inhibitions wither and she opens up her problems to him. Sometimes, his behaviour is father like which on occasions turns into lover-like. On the physical level, she remains passive, as she does not want to endanger her marriage. The incident is proof enough of the fettered selves of so-called educated middle-class people who do not accept any relation between a man and a woman even if the relation may be only on the emotional level.

Despite the fact that Jaya married Mohan and subsequently becomes a mother of two children, she feels lonely at heart. Her husband can't understand her feelings, as a result of which she is torn from within. Shashi Deshpande uses a beautiful image to describe Jaya's married life and her emotional loneliness:

> a pair of bullock yoked together...a clever phrase, but can it substitute for the reality? A man and a woman married for seventeen years. A couple with children. A family somewhat like the one caught and preserved for posterity by the advertising visuals I so loved. But the reality was only this. We were two persons. A man. A woman. (Shashi Deshpande 1989: 8)

To an Indian reader the image of a pair of bullock yoked together suggests a world of meanings. It means that the bullocks so yoked share the burden between themselves but no one knows whether they love each other or not. The image of the beasts performing the duty mechanically undermines the husband-wife relationship, who are supposed to be united in marriage for love and not for leading a mechanical life terminating in mutual hatred and distrust. Social conformity has always been more obligatory for a woman than a man and this social conformity lead her to an emotively lonely and secluded life. Due to her sensitive nature, Jaya is very particular about moulding her tastes in order to suit her husband even if her superior intellect is not satisfied. In the very beginning of the novel, we see that she tries to reason out with her father as to why she should not listen to the songs broadcasted on the radio, but ultimately she keeps silent, suppressing her desire to listen broadcasted songs.

Shashi Deshpande has presented the theme of loneliness through the theme of lack of communication. As she herself declares:

> The themes of lack of communication may be over-familiar in western fiction, but in extrovert India it is not much analyzed. (John Cunningham 1988)

In the present novel under study, Shashi Deshpande presents the theme of emotional loneliness of women through the theme of silence of feminine heart.

> You learn a lot of tricks to get by in a relationship. Silence is one of them. ...you never find a woman criticizing her husband, even playfully, in case it might damage the relationship. (*Ibid.*)

Jaya, suppresses her emotions at every stage of her life and compromises to conform to the note of an ideal Indian woman. In order to become an ideal wife, she has to snip off those bits of her that had effused to be Mohan's wife. She feels that she will 'break down', that she can't go on, and 'can't cope' but does not give expression to these feelings because of her fear of hurting Mohan and jeopardizing her marriage. In the Indian context, marriage is absolutely a sacrosanct contract and the images of the devoted wife and husband conformity to the concept of *ardhanarishwara* have been held up as the imminent reality of the relation between the sexes. Discussing gender, Catherine Stimpson says:

> Cultural laws of gender demand that feminine and masculine must play off against each other in the great drama of binary opposition. They must struggle against each other, or complement each other, or collapse into each other in the momentary illusory relief of the androgynous embrace. In patriarchal cultures, the struggle must end in the victor of the masculine; complementality must arrange

> itself hierarchically: androgyny must be a mythification. (Catherine R. Stimpson 1986: 1)

Jaya, more or less, feels in the same way when she says:

> Man and woman—it was then that I realised the deep chasm between the two. They are separated for ever, never more than at the moment of total physical togetherness. (Shashi Deshpande 1989: 98)

Marriages in India 'never end, they cannot—they are in a state of being'. This is mainly because of the necessity of conforming to cultural ethics. This necessity leads to emotional loneliness. The image of the pair of bullocks yoked together suggests that yoked bullocks should share the burden between themselves, but no one knows whether they love each other or not. The image of the beasts performing their assigned duties mechanically undermines the relationship of husband and wife, who get united in marriage for love, not for leading a mechanical life.

Apart from taking up certain key issues like silence and loneliness of feminine heart, gender-based discrimination and oppression, female patriarchism, marital discord, extra-marital affair, etc., Shashi Deshpande has written about her women characters' plightful condition in isolation. Shashi Deshpande has depicted Mohan's mother on the one hand who revolts, though in silence, and portrays Kusum's mother on the other hand, who has accepted her role as 'breeding animal'. It seems as if she has lost her purpose of life. The novelist seems to suggest how a woman, who is burdened by repetitive pregnancies and child-birth, is not able to fulfil her other responsibilities of motherhood. To quote from the text:

> [...] she looked at her own children, Dilip, Kusum, Shaila and the others, in the same way, as if she wondered who they were and why they were there. The only reality for her was the baby who lay on her outstretched legs. Its funny, now that I think of it, how her babies were always there, never on her lap, as if she was preparing them for life by denying them the softness of her lap, giving them, instead, the hardness of her shins. (Shashi Deshpande 1989: 23)

Shashi Deshpande also talks about female infanticide. Though the novelist mentions that this custom was more prevalent a century back fact, yet baby-killing has been noticed in certain parts of India even today. Although, with the advancement of technology, nowadays, female infanticide has taken the ugly shape of female foeticide. To quote the novelist:

> Where was it I had read an account of how baby girls were done to death a century or so back? They were, I had read in horror, buried alive, crushed to death in the room they were born in; and immediately after that, a fire was lit on the spot—to purify the place, they said. Perhaps it was to ensure death. (Shashi Deshpande 1989: 53)

When Vanita mami is diagnosed with a tumour in her ovary, Ravi instead of sympathising with her, makes fun of her saying that:

> In fact, he [the doctor] suggested she get operated immediately, but Vanita mami refused. She is scared. Or, may be, he sniggered, "she is holding on to her uterus hoping even now she'll get a kid." (Shashi Deshpande 1989: 107)

Shashi Deshpande here brings home the idea that a man can't understand women. Men can't and should not deny the link between woman and her womb. Only a woman can understand the significance of painful spasms in the middle of each cycle and those massive driving-on-to-madness contracting pains of child-birth.

Most of the women characters in Shashi Deshpande's novels are middle-class and well-educated women. But it does not point to the assumption that the novelist talks about the plight of only middle-class heroines. The novelist also talks about the plights of the poor and downtrodden women like Jeeja, Nayana and Tara. Jeeja is an issueless woman and her husband has married another woman. Jeeja does not blame her husband and rather thinks herself responsible for that as she is not able to give children to her husband. Jeeja's endurance increases when her husband and 'the other woman' die leaving behind their three children, and she brings them up showing her loyalty to her dead husband. To quote the novelist:

> And I was wrong when I thought that Jeeja's life had changed because her husband was dead and she had cast off those auspicious symbols of her wifehood. The son had stepped into his father's shoes, the son of that man Jeeja's husband had married because Jeeja had been unable to give him a son;
>
> ......
>
> This son, Rajaram, now drank and beat up his wife, Tara, so that Tara and her three children had become Jeeja's responsibility. I remembered Tara as a bride, a plump, round-faced girl,...she had occasionally accompanied Jeeja on her rounds. After three years...her face skeletally hollow, the clavicles more prominent than her breasts at which her baby suckled with a kind of desperation. (Shashi Deshpande 1989: 52)

One of the most structured patterns of the Indian society is the role assigned to man and to woman—woman is the follower, man the leader. Woman is the sufferer, man the ordainer. The husband expects wife to follow silently the path trodden by him. But when a woman decides not to follow the same trodden path, there is hostility between the two. Dr K. Madhavi Menon observes:

> When woman asserts her right to take a different path and ceases to be the silent sufferer, there is hostility. ("The Crisis of Feminine: Shashi Deshpande's *The Long Silence*", *Commonwealth Quarterly*, Vol. 18, No. 46, December-March 1993: 30)

Man's inflated ego is not able to bear the silent revolt by woman as he expects her to be a cushion to his inflated ego. As Indira Bhatt opines:

> (Mohan) wishes to use his wife as buffer, an opiate to soften the impact of the forces he has set into motion against himself. (Indira Bhatt in R.K. Dhawan 1991: 153)

The soft and cosy shell of matrimony which most Indian women snugly fit into can break any day and leave the couple exposed as prey to horror and trauma. Mohan takes it for granted that Jaya is going to follow his decision. When he gets involved in malpractice, he makes his wife and children responsible for it and shows that he cares for them so much that he goes out of his way to get the things done. Though Mohan explains to assure Jaya's company with him, he never looks into her demands and neither does she communicate anything directly to Mohan and hence, there always remains a gap between husband and wife and silence prevails in the house.

Towards the end of the novel, Jaya emerges as a determined strong-willed modern woman, who is prepared to face life, accept her responsibilities squarely and tries not to escape from or avoid them. Jaya observes that meaningful co-existence of man and woman can come only through understanding, respect and compassion not through domination or subjugation. Choice is the right of both man and woman. The only thing to remember is that choice is relevant only when there is knowledge. In the same way, freedom is relevant only when there is responsibility —responsibility to oneself. Freedom is to survive 'as a whole' within the system, and Jaya ultimately feels that it is possible. Usha Thambe remarks:

> The confused and clumsy Jaya appears a contrast to the smiling, efficient housewife Suhasini. But, finally she comes to grips with herself and realises that her total personality will have to co-ordinate both of them and that fragmentation of self is not possible. (Usha Thambe in Barucha and Sarang 1994: 127)

Finally, Jaya realizes that it is the fear of insecurity on the part of women that has allowed the subjugation of women to continue. The novelist sends out the signal that women need not succumb and assume the roles cast upon them. Sarla Parker remarks very significantly:

> The important insight that Shashi Deshpande imparts to us through Jaya is that women should accept their own responsibility for what they are, see how much they have contributed to their victimisation instead of putting the

> blame on everybody except themselves. (Sarla Parker in R.K. Dhawan 1991: 169)

Jaya finally understands that she also has contributed to her victimisation and that she has to fight her own battle and work out her own solution. Accordingly, she feels the necessity to break the silence, articulate her predicament, establish her identity. She knows that there is always room for discussion and compromise. It is not the fault of men alone that has caused the feminine discontent. A patriarchal order can be subverted if only women take their status on the basis of intelligence and individuality. Jaya feels, as P. Rama Moorthy affirms:

> ...it is possible for a woman to live in the world where men also live. (P. Ramamoorthy in R.K. Dhawan 1991: 169)

Jaya decides that now onwards, she will live without sacrificing her identity and individuality. She will make adjustment but it will not be a servile one. Her decision to give up writing for the newspaper column "Sita" symbolises her rejection of traditional role-model of wife. Now she decides to write what she wants to write and will not look up at Mohan's face for an answer she wants. This makes her voyage of discovery complete. Very appropriately, Sumitra Kukreti remarks thus:

> The realization that she can have her won way—*yathecchasi thatha kuru*—gives a new confidence to Jaya. This is her emancipation. (Sumitra Kukreti 1998: 30)

While the heroines of Nimbkar or Shobhaa De walk out of marriage or refuse to re-enter it, those of McCarthy or Mukherjee tend to accept it as a challenge, in spite of its severe drawbacks. Shashi Deshpande, with her innate pragmatism as well as her traditional middle-class background, does not take rebellion against male-dominated world to the bitter end. Marriage, according to her, may not offer the best of all possible worlds to a man and a woman. Yet in the present set up, it is more or less essential and must be made to work, for neither a man nor a woman is complete in himself or herself. Both biologically and emotionally they need each other and if they can develop a measure of harmony in their relations, so much the better. Even Jaya begins to realize this and anxiously awaits the return of Mohan. She even visits their former Churchgate bungalow, ostensibly to pick up the mail, but more pertinently to re-think herself about her past with its bitter-sweet memories.

Jaya makes us hope that a slightly transformed Jaya will return to Churchgate bungalow. Jaya affirms with confidence:

> I'm not afraid anymore. The panic has gone. (Shashi Deshpande 1989: 191)

She finally decides to do as she desires. This implies that she will, henceforth, be more objective, ready to take the blame where it is due rather than finding convenient scapegoats, whether in the form of Mohan or someone else. She knows that her journey, henceforth, is not going to be easy: it would be a highly challenging one. Self-transformation is never easy to accomplish. "We don't change overnight", she concedes. And it is possible that we may not change even over long periods of time. To quote from the text:

> But it is no longer possible for me. If I have to plug that 'hole in the heart', I will have to speak, to listen, I will have to erase the silence between us. While studying Sanskrit drama, I'd learnt with a sense of outrage that its rigid rules did not permit women character to speak Sanskrit. They had to use Prakrit—a language that had sounded to my ears like a baby's lisp. The anger I'd felt then comes back to me when I realise what I've been doing all these years. I have been speaking Prakrit myself.... Why do I presume that the understanding is mine alone? Isn't it possible that Mohan too means something more by 'all well' than going back to where we were? People don't change, Mukta said. It is true. We don't change overnight. It is possible that we may not change even over long periods of time. But we can always hope. Without that, life would be impossible. And if there is anything I know now it is this: life has always to made possible. (Shashi Deshpande 1989: 192-93)

Forgetting the patriarchal maxim that 'a husband is like a sheltering tree', Jaya realizes that a sheltering tree also deprives the plant growing under it of sunlight. She has even convinced herself earlier that she has no wants, no desires of her own. In her bold self-examination, she now sees herself as not a mere travesty of the great Gandhari. The exile at Dadar flat serves to show to Jaya that she has distanced herself from her 'inner self' because she has hitherto defined herself only with reference to others, forgetting that she is an individual, too, requiring a self-definition in her own right. But now she knows that if she wishes to correct the situation, then she would have to take steps herself. John Gray, the author of the best-seller, "Men are from Mars, Women are from Venus", writes that women find it more difficult to assert themselves than men because:

> Setting limits (i.e. asserting) and receiving (in response to their needs) are very scary for a woman. [A woman] is commonly afraid of needing too much and then being rejected, judged or abandoned. Rejection, judgement and abandonment are most painful because deep inside her unconscious, she holds the incorrect belief that she is unworthy of receiving more. This belief was formed and reinforced in childhood every time she had to suppress her feelings, needs or wishes. (John Gray 1992: 52-53)

For the first time in the narrative, Jaya now moves towards "setting limits". Even though it may not seem very radical or militant, the very act of taking such a decision is a feminist one. She steps out of the passive existence that she has created for herself and resolves to speak out to rebel against the silence imposed upon her by social conditioning. However, she also knows that 'life has to be made possible'. She hopes to make Mohan understand her viewpoint and thus she hopes of achieving new possibilities.

The best part of Shashi Deshpande's writings is that her protagonists are no heroines with extra-ordinary qualities. They are recognizable as the 'women-next-door'. Their lives are without adventure, punctuated and relieved by births, weddings and deaths. The problems depicted by the novelist are those of any real life woman—a marriage that has become dull and monotonous, an unwanted pregnancy or, at the most, an extra-marital relationship. The motif of enclosure and confinement recurs in Shashi Deshpande's novels including *That Long Silence.* This motif is employed, both to signify the lack of freedom and the circumscribed existence of the middle-class woman as well as to reflect the alienation and loneliness that often sets into marriage. Jaya has a dream in which she finds herself:

> [W]alking between rows of hours, so close to one another that is a sense of claustrophobia. (Shashi Deshpande 1989: 85)

Another key message that is sent out by the novelist in the very opening lines of the novel that to achieve anything, to become anything one has to be hard and ruthless. In one of her interviews to Geeta Gangadharan, the novelist also subscribes to this philosophy:

> Yes, very much so. Unless you are ruthless, you really can't achieve much in life. Take any achiever and you see that the ladder is usually made up of other people. It takes a very hard person to do that but there are people who have done that. The lack of women achievers is because of our incapacity to be ruthless. Women are more sensitive and do not give on individual human needs and pulls easily. It is more important for us to be loved and liked as individuals with the family. My own writing can be given as an example. Even writing requires a certain amount of ruthlessness. If everything I write, I start doubting whether this would hurt somebody or other, I will never be able to write. But to achieve anything in life, one has to learn to get over these sensitive aspects and, to some extent, I have been able to do that. (Geeta Gangadharan 1994: 254)

Deshpande has portrayed the feel and tone of Indian life, of ordinary problems in everyday life. A life of complete inwardness, of a subjective indulgence, according to novelist, is not for Jaya. Complete conforming and total draining out of individuality is also not the proper way out of the dilemma. One can't live in fragments; the absolute self and the relatedness must join hands and hope for the fuller enjoyment of life. The protagonist accepts the reality of the situation, her existence in relation to her family. She shifts from past to present like sand in an hour-glass. She tries to fathom her real role in life. Her awareness of her individuality is essentially healthy, though she becomes physically ill. Of course, this makes her feel entrapped and she desires to be free. On the other hand, it makes her visualize her life bereft of her man. The emotional atmosphere permeates the whole novel. The personal past, the experiences of Kusum, her own mother and aunts, Mohan's mother and his sister and their silence in life pressurise her and mould her responses to the present situation. The idea of existence in an unrelated meaningless world, in a void is not acceptable to her. She seeks a reorientation of her relationship to her husband. Deshpande's use of the myths of Sita, Gandhari and Maitreyee sharply focuses the plight of the 'existence' of Indian wife, at the same time revealing the Indian wife's awareness of this existence and her acceptance not of Seeta-role and Gandhari-role but of Arjuna's way of facing life.

Works Cited

Cunningham, John. Indian Writer's Block, *The Indian Post.* March 6, 1988.

Deshpande, Shashi. *Roots and Shadows*. New Delhi: Orient Longman Ltd., 1983.

Beauvoir, Simone de. *Second Sex*. Translated and Ed. H.M. Parshley, New York: Vintage Books, 1974.

Holmstrom, Lakshmi. "Shashi Deshpande Talks to Lakshmi Holmstrom". *The Fiction of Shashi Deshpande*. Ed. R.S. Pathak. New Delhi, Prestige Books, 1998: 247.

Interview with Geeta Gangadaharan, "Denying the Otherness", Indian Communication. *Sunday Magazine* (20 Nov. 1994): II-III.

Jain, Jasbir (ed.). *Creative Theory: Writer on Writing*. Delhi: Pencraft International, 2000.

Kukreti, Sumitra. "Female Protagonist in Shashi Deshpande's Novels". *The Fiction of Shashi Deshpande*. Ed. R.S. Pathak. New Delhi: Creative Books, 1998: 30.

Palkar, Sarla. "Breaking the Silence: Shashi Deshpande's *That Long Silence*". *Indian Women Novelist*. Ed. R.K. Dhawan. New Delhi: Prestige Books, 1991: 169. Set-1, Vol. V.

Ramamoorthy, P. "My Life is My Own: A Study of Shashi Deshpande's Women". *Indian Women Novelist*. Ed. R.K. Dhawan. New Delhi: Prestige Books, 1991: 160. Set-1, Vol. V.

"Shashi Deshpande as a Feminist and Novelist", *Indian English Fiction, 1980-90: An Assessment* (Ed.) Nilufer E. Barucha and Vilas Sarang. New Delhi: B.R. Publications, 1994: 127.

Stimpson, Catherine, R. "Gertrude Stein and the Transportation of Gender". *The Poetics of Gender*. Ed. Nany K. Miller, New York: Columbia Univ. Press, 1986: 1.

Tong, Rosemarie. *Feminist Thought*. London: Routledge, 1993.

"The Crisis of Feminine: Shashi Deshpande's *That Long Silence*", *Commonwealth Quarterly*. Vol. 18, No. 46, December-March 1993: 30.

7

'New Woman': A Ray of Light (*A Matter of Time*)

Shashi Deshpande is a leading Indian English writer, championing the cause of women, who have suffered the age-old masculine yoke. Woman, intimate yet underlying in human relationships, has often been at the receiving end in the male-dominated world. Stifled by the precast-moulds and pre-defined roles in the native context, she could hardly demur against the patriarchal notion a couple of decades ago. Women writers like Shashi Deshpande have probed into the suffocated psyche of women to highlight their suppressed desires, to lay bare their ambitions and frustrations, soothe their aches and pains and activize their slumberous feminine 'I'. As a writer of gender issues, Shashi Deshpande has put on blinders as she is quite focused in her writings.

Like a naturalist slum photographer who would refuse to waste his plate on anything that is not sordid, she stays at most of the time away from what is bright and happy in a woman's life. There are families and situations where a woman plays a pivotal role but in the novel after novel Shashi Deshpande has dwelt on the native cultural scenes and presented a faithful picture of familial, marital and filial bonds in the Indian society. Love between married couples of different higher and lower categories, love among themselves, love between children and parents, relationships of grandfathers and grandmothers, the family of the typical Hindu society, family under traditional feudal days and modern times, corporate solidarity of different Hindu families as one integrated family, inalienable joint participation in the woe and weal of an individual and family by all close relatives, observance of different religious, social and familial ceremonies and practices, sharing of joys of dinners, feasts and parties and the sorrows of disease and death, and pre-dominance of committed filial and familial bonds over isolation and alienation provides her novels traditional anchorage. Amid all this, in all her novels including *A Matter of Time*, she talks about issues like marital discord, the biasedness in upbringing of a girl child, emotional and physical exploitation of wife, etc. Talking about the origin of the novel, it is quite appropriate to quote Amrita Bhalla:

> The idea of the novel came to her significantly when she saw an old stone house with a garden, a relic of its past glory, in Malleswaran, a locality still exuding an old world charm in Banglore, now the computer capital of India. Deshpande says that in her mind she saw the figures of three women going into this house: in this combined with the real-life experience of a friend's mother who, after forty years of marriage, was abandoned by her husband, she found the story of *A Matter of Time*. (Amrita Bhalla 2006: 63-64)

Shashi Deshpande's novels generally centre on family relationships. According to her, everybody has to live within relationships, for there is no other way. In one of her interviews to Vanamala Viswanatha, she has mentioned that in patriarchal society a woman has to live within relationships but rigid rules governing these should not be rigid as it makes a woman unhappy. A woman should not be only defined within relationships and this idea is again and again conveyed in her novels. Deshpande informed another interviewer even in more precise terms:

> Human relationship is what a writer is involved with. Person to person and person to society—these are two primary concerns of a creative writer and, to me, the former is of immense importance. Pre-occupation is with interpersonal relationships and human emotions. (Geeta Gangadharan 1994)

She agrees with C.D. Narasimhaiah who is of view that gender issue in patriarchal society is a theme on which epics after epics has been and can be written. In one of her interviews, she has revealed that family relationships and gender issues associated with them are the most mystifying things in Indian context and she will continue to write about it. Thus, gender issues are of prime concern in the fictional world of Shashi Deshpande. She has asserted in her novels what Yasano Akiko has expressed in her poem:

> The Day for moving mountains is coming,
> You don't think so?
> It is coming: for a while the mountain sleeps,
> But in other times,
> Mountains all moved in fire. If you don't believe that,
> Oh man, this at least believe:
> All sleeping women
> Will awake now and move. (Yasano Akiko 2003: 107)

The bonds that bind human life help individuals in continuing their lives despite the betrayals and cruelties associated with human survival, every woman has a life of one's own to live. So is also for Sumi in *A Matter of Time*, who is dauntless even in the time of adversity. She is different from Indu, Saru, Jaya and Urmila—the women protagonists of Shashi Deshpande's earlier novels. Sumi evolves herself from the utter desolation and bitterness linked up with invisible chains of patriarchal pressure and other family responsibilities. She is seen gradually emancipating herself as a new and independent woman. Gopal's desertion makes her experience the trauma of a deserted wife and the anguish of an isolated partner. All the agonies of life come to her at the age of forty and make her stand alone and helpless along with her teenaged daughters: Aru, Charu and Seema. Generally, on being deserted, a woman seems to be emotionally shattered. But Sumi is not emotionally broken. Like any responsible mother, Sumi helps her children to get on with their lives as before. *A Matter of Time* deals with the three women representing three generations of the same family. As usual Deshpande has given expression to the pains of these women of three generations.

One common thread that runs through all the novels of Shashi Deshpande is the depiction of biased upbringing of girl-child in the patriarchal society. In a family dominantly governed by patriarchal values, a girl is considered as a burdensome debt needed to be paid off. Right from the day of her birth, she is looked upon as someone's '*amanat*'. As she grows up, she is made aware that her father's house is not her permanent abode. She is considered as her mother's prime concern and her father has no sense of emotional responsibility towards her. Sumi and Premi, in the present novel, could never enjoy a healthy relation with their father who never bothered to talk to them. As Premi tells to Anil, her husband, after her marriage to him:

> "My father never spoke to me until I was ten", she had told Anil after their marriage and he had not believed her. Just as she wouldn't have believed, if she had not seen it herself, that there could be families like Anil's. At first it had been like watching a movie—it was pleasing, interesting pretty, but it could not possibly be true. People did not touch and use words of endearment so casually. No, it was a false picture. The truth was a father who stayed in his room, who never came out, never spoke to you, a mother who put her hand on your mouth so that you did not cry out.... (Shashi Deshpande 1996: 18)

This communication gap between father and the daughter continues even after her marriage with Anil. Whenever she visits her parents after her marriage, visiting to her father's room is like an ordeal for her as he does not talk to her as a daughter but as an acquaintance. Like a typical patriarchal father, he does not enquire about her (Premi) but prefers to talk about Nikhil (her son), Anil (her husband) and her father-in-law. This behaviour on his part is indicative of the patriarchal attitude of males in the Indian society.

The novelist also reveals the kind of hardships a girl has to undertake to pursue her aim of education in life. Sumi and Premi, both the sisters, have their own versions of their childhood deprivations. Sumi complains of lack of books during her school days as she admits that she used to steal books. As she says:

> I would borrow them and if the girls didn't ask for them back after a time, I would tear off the first page, write my own name on them and keep them. After all, if they didn't miss them, why shouldn't I have them? (Shashi Deshpande 1996: 133)

Sumi's confessional statement reveals that if an educated man like Shripati, who is a lawyer, does not pay heed to the educational needs of his own daughters then the plight of daughters in the lower strata can be well-imagined. The memories of deprivation and fear during childhood find more bitter expression in Premi's feelings and her personality as well. After her marriage to Anil, she does not want to give up a single chance to show that finally, she has been able to overcome her childhood deprivations. To quote the novelist:

> ...Premi's memories, even the few she can speak of, are only of deprivations and fear. Looking at Premi, the picture of Bombay chic' as Charu calls her, in her expensive cotton saree, her beautifully groomed hair, her simple but expensive jewellery, Gopal has always felt that she is constantly reminding herself of how far she has got away from the child Premi. (Shashi Deshpande 1996: 133)

As a child, Premi has very strong impression about the uniqueness of her family in the sense that all the four members don't enjoy normal relationships. Fear of father marked a much dented impression on her childhood psyche. As a child she never brings any of her friends to her house. She has fears that if any of her friends asks about her father or any other question like why he does not interact with her or her mother or why does he ring the bell from his own room whenever he needs anything.

Even Goda, Sumi's *maushi*, has to lead a childhood full of miseries. She loses her mother at the time of her birth; her father remarries immediately thus making her an orphan in effect. Later, her father sends her to his brother's house to live on his mercy. Soon, he forgets the very existence of his motherless child. Another character that draws our attention is Manorama, whose schooling was something which could come in way of her marriage prospects.

Along with the repressive power of paternal love, the institution of marriage is the site of the most insidious form of sexual politics. It is within the private hell of maladjusted marriages that we have the most moving explorations in fiction of the repressive forces of patriarchal attitudes. In the novel under perusal—*A Matter of Time*—there is a sustained presentation of failed marriages posing instated questions regarding the functioning of marriage within the patriarchal structures of the Indian families. In the sophisticated upper middle-class ethos generally depicted by Indian women writers in English, severe economic deprivation or physical brutalization is largely absent; what is foregrounded is the psychological repression created through a male supremacist ideology which consumes any possibility of mutual love and concern, corroding the woman's self-esteem and devouring her sense of identity and self-hood. In these fictional representations of reality, marriage becomes an institutionalized form of the domination of women by men within the most personal of relationships. Deshpande's forte is her handling of maladjusted marriages. Sarita, Indu, Jaya, Kalyani and Sumi—are all women of deep emotions and fine sensitivities who are entrapped in marriages with men who are never outrightly cruel, who carry out their husbandly obligations assiduously but are impervious to their wives' pleas for understanding, communication and respect for their individuality. Such emotionally incomplete relationships have a fatal effect on the female psyche and Deshpande's women find themselves tortured by a painful sense of alienation and excruciating loneliness of the spirit.

Marriage system and marital relations form an integral part of the plot and structure of Deshpande's most of the novels including *A Matter of Time*. She has presented all the three aspects of marriage in this novel: traditional marriage (Kalyani-Shripati marriage), love marriage (Sumi-Gopal marriage) and arranged marriage (Anil-Premi marriage). While analyzing a literary work of a liberal feminist like Shashi Deshpande, one has to take into consideration many factors like—religion, caste, class, language—which are specific. Indian sociologists also echo similar sentiments. According to Seema Chitnis, the historical circumstances and values render the difference to women's issues in India. Women in India gained equal status directly with the drawing up of the constitution, while in the West women had to wage a long war. Again, in India the institution of marriage and family is still considered necessary because of the security and social status it gives to both men and women, who find it difficult and traumatic to break away. So what makes gender issues in context of India, different from issues in West is that the gender studies in India highlight their voice against the social injustice and oppression of women rather than her freedom from the institution of marriage in India. One major issue related to marriage system in India is child-marriage. Although child marriage is on decline in India, yet it has not effaced completely from the face of Indian society. Kalyani, in the present novel, is married off to Shripati at a tender age. She is a bright student who aspires to become an engineer but her aspirations are crushed by her own mother. Manorama couldn't give a male heir to Vithalrao, her husband. Vithalrao's uncle pressurizes him to adopt his own grandson. But Vithalrao, a modern man in the real sense of the word, rejects the idea. Few other relatives suggest him for the second marriage. Manorama is terrified of the idea of the re-marriage of her husband to such an extent that she takes Kalyani off the school and gets her married to her own younger brother, Shripati so as to prevent the family property from going out of the family. To quote the novelist:

> To add to her security, that main crutch, the one most women depended on, a son, was denied to her. All that she had was a daughter Kalyani, who would get married and become part of another family.
>
> "I was a clever girl", Kalyani said once. "I was very good at Maths like my father. He wanted me to become an engineer—can you believe that? You will be the first woman engineer in the country, he used to say."
>
> And yet Kalyani was not allowed to complete her schooling. She was taken out of school and married off by Manorama to her own brother Shripati. Perhaps, after this, Manorama felt secure. The property would remain in the family now. (Shashi Deshpande 1996: 128-29)

Thus, the novelist reveals that how a girl child is used as an instrument in family feuds. Opinion of Kamla Bhasin in this regard is worth considering. She comments:

> In India, the 'existence' of separate personal laws based on different religions also affects gender relation.... And all religious laws favour men in matters relating to property rights and inheritance. (Kamla Bhasin 2000: 30)

Goda's father's remarriage immediately after her mother's death also highlights that a society which does not accept woman's second marriage or remarriage easily, prompts a man to take another bride in marriage so easily.

Indian society is patriarchal in nature and the institution of marriage has not remained untouched by its patriarchal nature. Right from the day one, girls are told and retold that they do not belong to the family they are born in. They are considered as birds who will fly away, ultimately to their own nests. As commented by Aru's Amma, who makes Aru realize that she (Aru) does not belong to the place:

> "You shouldn't pamper an old woman like this, Aru!"
>
> "Why not?"
>
> "What will I do when you go away?"
>
> "I'm not going anywhere, Amma."
>
> "Of course you will. Daughters don't belong. All three of you birds will fly away to your own nests." (Shashi Deshpande 1996: 198)

Thus, daughters, other's, *amanats* have to go to their 'own homes' where they are told that they don't have any right at this place, too. Thus, a woman spends her entire life having no 'home' of her own. She is also conditioned right from the beginning that she has to live in subordinate position to the males in her whole life. A would-be bride is taught by the female patriarch to like what is liked by her husband and to reject what is disliked by her spouse. She is supposed to be less qualified, smaller in height and status to her husband. Even Manorama, who is taller than her husband, hates her height as the patriarchal society has conditioned her to think that a husband should be taller than the wife. To quote the novelist:

> [Goda says] I have never seen anyone as beautiful as Mami. She was as fair as milk. And so tall—she was like a queen, wasn't she, Kalyani asked?
>
> "But she didn't like that. She hated her height."
>
> "I know. I remember Mama teasing her, saying that if they'd known how tall she would grow, his father would never have chosen her."
>
> "She cried when he said that...". (Shashi Deshpande 1996: 117-18)

When we move to the next generation, we find the situation of to-be-married girls no better. Even Premi, who is a doctor professionally, is not consulted before her marriage is fixed with Anil, the son of Shripati's former colleague. Even Kalyani, Premi's mother, is not taken into confidence in this regard and Premi's opinion is not considered needed at all. As Premi tells Anil after marriage:

> The first time he really talked to her was when she had completed her medical finals; he had called her up to his room then, summoned her actually, to tell her she would be marrying Anil. (Shashi Deshpande 1996: 18)

Another example of emotional sacrifice in marriage can be seen in the case of Sudha (Gopal's sister). After the death of their parents, Sudha gets ready to marry P.K. so that Gopal, her younger brother can find a safe and normal home. As the novelist writes:

> And I know this too now, that she did it for me. It was this, and her almost immediate marriage to P.K. that helped the quick transformation of a house of mourning into a normal home in which a family lived. (Shashi Deshpande 1996: 42)

A careful perusal of marriage system in India shows that daughter is like a debt to be paid off. Many sociologists are of the opinion that dowry is partly responsible for the tendency among Indian parents to consider daughter as a burden. Sons, on the other hand, are considered as cheques to be cashed in. When Sumi along with her three young daughters goes to her father's place, the biggest worry for Kalyani is the marriage of Sumi's three daughters. Sumi becomes an object of pity for everyone. Ramesh, son of Sudha and P.K. takes pity on her and gets ready to help Sumi financially and he deposits money in her account which, as he tells her, she may use for the marriage of her daughters:

> "Look, Sumi, don't think too much about it. I'll deposit the money in your account, may be we'll make it a joint account with Aru. Let it be there, you can use it in times of need—perhaps for the girls' wedding?" "Weddings! Now you're talking like Amma." Sumi laughs, but the topic of her daughter's marriage is one she can't really ignore. Kalyani and Goda won't let her forget it. It's always on their minds, in their conversation, something which seems to them both a problem. Sumi, like Aru, is amazed by Kalyani. How can she, of all people, think of marriage with enthusiasm? She is angry, too. Gopal and I never thought of our's daughter's marriage, never as a problem anyway. May be we should have taken out marriage policies in their names like so many parents do, may be we should have.... (Shashi Deshpande 1996: 124)

Therefore, we see that Goda and Kalyani, the female patriarchs in the novel, who never enjoyed a very happy married life, are ready to push the young girls in the same kiln. Goda is a dedicated matchmaker who takes a creative pleasure in arranging marriages. She comes to Kalyani with a proposal about a boy from U.S. who wants to get married before going back. The novelist, here, makes a caustic attack on people who believe marrying to be like shopping which is to be finished or accomplished within fixed time. The novelist also makes a comment on habitual matchmakers like Goda who poke their nose into other's affairs. She like a patriarch woman rejects the head-on handling of the situation by Charu, who jokingly proposes to get married to the boy whose proposal has come for Aru. Most commentaries on the marriage have focused on their temperamental incompatibility as the root of their tragedy. As Gopala and Sumi have different temperaments they drift apart through the very process of their living together. There is an impassable gulf between Gopala and Sumi. Gopala is an existentialist who is searching for the meaning of life and Sumi is a matter of fact kind of lady who is occupied with the worldly affairs. The same kind of incompatibility is visible in the relationship of Kalyani and Shripati. Shripati is a prominent lawyer whereas Kalyani is a young girl whose career is cut short by her mother. The mismatching of temperaments becomes an insurmountable barrier because it is aggravated by Shripati's inability to respect and treat Kalyani as an equal human being with the precious right to think on her own terms. It is in this context that we find a clear working of patriarchal attitude in the private world of two individuals. Shripati's attitude (his rejection of his wife) is a concomitant effect of the male supremacist ideology which serves as the bastion of patriarchal social structures.

Another important issue that is highlighted by Shashi Deshpande in this novel is the emotional suffocation for a married woman on account of lack of communication between husband and the wife. Marriage unites two bodies but this unison is incomplete if there is no unison of two souls also. Shashi Deshpande has also talked about the same kind of vacuum in women's lives in one of her interviews to Sue Dickman:

> All these years men have been telling the world in their writings that women, not men, are mysterious, women are fascinating, women are strange.... So, now women are also telling and talking to the world that men are strange, men are mysterious.... So, many of their things we do not understand. You may be close to your friend or husband or lover or whatever but at the same time there is always that element of the unknown. (Sue Dickman 2000: 134)

This issue can be prominently seen in the case of Shridhar-Akka and Gopal-Sumi relationship. Gopal does not give any reason for his separation from Sumi, but he does not feel like continuing in this relationship. There comes a stage in their relationship when he feels that ultimately the body shrinks from annihilation. Sumi and Gopal are no longer able to sustain the excitement of the relationship and are unable to go on in this relationship. Marriage needs a commitment of lifetime but they feel unable to fulfil the demand of this relationship. Sumi has the realization that they can't move on together. As the novelist writes:

> We can never be together again. All these days I have been thinking of him as if he has been suspended in space, in nothingness, since he left us. But he has gone on living, his life has moved on, it will go on without me. So has mine. Our lives have diverged, they now move separately two different streams. (Shashi Deshpande 1996: 85)

Gopal walks out of the relationship without thinking about the various kind of problems to be faced by Sumi and her daughters. When Charu, like a mutinous child asks her mother (Sumi) to take back Gopal, Sumi realizes that a point has been reached in their relationship where there is no scope of convergence. As Sumi speaks to Charu:

> High and mighty? No, I can never be that. But taking him back—I don't know, Charu that sounds odd to me. As if he's a pet dog who's strayed away or some thing. No Charu, I'm not trying to be funny. The truth is, as I told Aru, I'm not a good hater. I can never keep it up for long. But even if he comes back, things can never be the way they were, you know that, don't you? (Shashi Deshpande 1996: 194)

It is the same kind of lack of communication and suffocation that pervades the relationship of Akka and Baba. At the first place, it was a forced marriage for both, Shridhar and Kalyani, and to add fuel to the fire, Kalyani loses their only son and Shridhar blames her entirely for it and stops communicating with her. He lives all alone in his upstairs room and never comes down. He doesn't have his meals with the rest of the family members and never speaks to Kalyani. They don't enjoy a normal relationship that exists between a husband and a wife. Kalyani always remains frightened of him. He rings the bell and she responds as if she is an animal in circus not a wife. When Aru comes to know of the reason of the ever widening gap between her grandfather and grandmother, she is surprised to know that for a well-educated man like Shridhar, who is a lawyer by profession, a mentally imbalanced son is more important than his wife to whom he has not talked for the last thirty years. Ultimately, he cuts off himself completely from his wife. There is nothing between them but silence. Referring to the theme of 'silence' in her novels, Shama Futehally states:

> Silence whether forced or voluntary, whether imprisoning or freeing, lasting days or years, has been a recurring theme which Shashi Deshpande, one of those which make her work a united whole. (Shama Futehally 1997)

Kalyani, who has been facing her husband's rejection for more than thirty years, knows how it feels when one is cut off from one's spouse. She does not want the same kind of rejection and bitterness in the life of her daughter. This is the reason why she goes to see Gopal. She says to Gopal:

> "What have you done to my daughter, Gopala, don't do this, and don't let it happen to my daughter, what happened to me."
>
> ......
>
> "When Sumi married you, she was too young; but I was not anxious for her, you were older, you were sensible and you cared for her, yes, you did. I can still remember how you scolded me for being angry with her when she refused to nurse Seema.... How can you change so much, Gopala?" She goes on, moving from surmise to surmise. Has anyone poisoned his mind against Sumi? Has she done some thing wrong? Can't he forgive her? She knows—and she says this placatingly, so humbly that it hurts—he is a generous man. And Sumi too—he shouldn't think that her friendliness with others means anything.
>
> ......
>
> "But, Gopala", and now she hesitates, "how could she have known what being a good wife means when she never saw her mother being one? I taught her nothing, it's all my fault, Gopala, forgive me and don't punish her for it."
>
> ......

> "Look at me, Gopala", she says when she can speak. "My father died worrying about me, my mother couldn't die in peace, she held on to life though she was suffering—she suffered terribly—because of me, she didn't want to leave me and go." (Shashi Deshpande 1996: 46-47)

Thus, Kalyani, a helpless mother, pleads to her son-in-law not to leave his wife. She pleads as if she is seeking forgiveness for her daughter's faults, though she has not done anything wrong.

Loneliness of a feminine heart is another important issue that has been highlighted by the novelist. A woman, according to the novelist, may be in the company of other people, but is all alone in the emotional sphere. Sumi and Gopala started their life as a couple in love. After spending many years together, Sumi feels a vacuum and loneliness in their relationship. When they start living apart, finally, she has to shoulder the entire responsibility all alone. The novelist says that as a woman needs time to get adjusted to somebody's presence, in the same way it is a traumatic experience to get accustomed to silence and loneliness of being 'alone'. When Sumi comes to settle down at her father's place, she chooses to live in her grandfather's room. Her mother asks:

> Why do you want to be alone? She had asked. Not to lose sight of my loneliness, not to let empty sound of it be muffed by the voices of other humans during the day,... It takes time to get used to sharing your life with another person, now I have to get used to being alone. (Shashi Deshpande 1996: 23)

This sense of loneliness, isolation at times, compels the woman to take on all kinds of responsibility upon her shoulders. Sumi's daughter, Aru, is like a typical Ray's heroine and moves away from a child like playfulness to sombre gravity. She takes on many chores at home. Playing the role of the eldest, Aru leaves Charu free for her studies. She insists on accompanying her mother to the dentist and everywhere else. Aru tries to play the role of Gopal, and thus, fills the vacuum left by Gopal in their lives. Aru, here, is representative of the 'new woman' who tries to steer her mother and sisters through the stormy passage of change. However, Sumi's emptiness has been well expressed by the novelist:

> But Gopala never went to the dentist with me, he didn't do so many of these things Aru is now doing. And yet his absence has left such a vast emptiness that I can't find my bearings, there are no markings any more to show me which way I should go. (Shashi Deshpande 1996: 36)

After settling down in her father's home, Sumi realizes that she needs to have a separate house for herself and her daughters. She, all alone, has to undertake the task of searching a house for herself. At one moment, she wants to talk to Gopal, when she meets him, about this problem. But, observing the indifferent attitude of Gopal, Sumi resists the idea and starts discussing about Shankar and his family and Gopal's work in the press.

The novelist has also depicted this sense of loneliness and isolation of women through the character of Sudha. She had been a vigorous, healthy and confident girl who was ever, cheerful, even after the death of her parents. With marriage and motherhood, she blossoms and becomes an attractive woman. However, after her husband's death, she starts looking 'empty' as if everything is over for her. She looks as if she has been betrayed by her husband as he had departed (died) earlier. As Gopala narrates:

> And then she underwent surgery for her tumour. She came to us to convalesce after that, and this was yet another woman—a peevish self-centred invalid, constantly complaining of her pains. But I, who knew her so well, realized what she was doing. She was diverting us, cleverly drawing our attention away from her real pain. It was not her illness, not the depletion of her physical self with surgery and post-radiation sickness, not even P.K.'s sudden death or the fact that he died first, when she had, with the knowledge of her cancer, expected to go before him—no, I knew it was something more than all these things that made her the way she was. She had retreated from us; none of us, not her own children, nor I, her brother, nor my children whom she dearly loved so, could reach

> her. And she was frightened of this world of loneliness she suddenly found herself in. (Shashi Deshpande 1996: 51)

Thus, the novelist has realistically depicted the loneliness in the life of a widow woman who had never felt so lonely or purposeless in her life as after the death of her husband. It is the kind of loneliness that occupies the heart and soul of a woman who is a widow. The novelist, on the other hand, highlights the loneliness of a 'single' woman who chooses to live alone. She has to face the sarcasm of the society for staying away from her husband. Shankar's mother, representative of female patriarchs advises Sumi not to desert her husband. She tells her that husband's home is a woman's real home and she shouldn't mind his wrong doings if he has done any. To quote the novelist:

> When are you going back to your husband?, the old woman asks abruptly. You should be with him. Look at his state! It's all right to stay with your parents for a while, but that's not your home. When my daughters come home, I don't let them stay long. Go back to your husband, he is a good man. If you've done wrong, he'll forgive you. And if he has—women shouldn't have any pride. (Shashi Deshpande 1996: 161)

In most of her novels, Shashi Deshpande has depicted the issue of widowhood being regarded as a curse in the Indian patriarchal society, and *A Matter of Time* is no exception in this regard. This novel does not present Akkis and tais as widows as in her earlier novels, but the novelist unfolds the psyche of Indians regarding widowhood. Kalyani narrates the story of Goda and Vidyapati. Vidyapati falls in love with Goda and proposes to marry her. Manorama, Goda's mami rejects the proposal and, ultimately, Vidyapati dies as he catches galloping TB. When this episode is being narrated by Kalyani, Goda's countenance and her reaction speaks enough about the fear of widowhood being embedded in the Indian female psyche. It will be worthwhile to quote from the text:

> Sumi notices Goda's involuntary shudder, the way the colour drains from her face, her hands clench into tight fists, as if she feels the dreadful flap of the wings of

> widowhood brush past her. And Sumi wonders, is this what has helped Kalyani to endure everything, the fact that she is a wife and not a widow? The fact that she has the right to all the privileges of the wife of a living husband? Sumi remembers the tray of Kumkum, paan-supari and coconut Manju brought her, she thinks of the old woman's words, "what is a woman without her husband?" (Shashi Deshpande 1996: 167)

The novelist, here, makes a sarcastic point how widowhood is regarded as a curse even if a married woman has to undergo mental harassment in the name of marriage. The example of Kalyani is the biggest illustration in this regard. Her husband has not talked to her for the last thirty years and they do not have a normal relationship like any other normal couple. She is deprived of her husband's love. In the words of novelist:

> It is enough to have a husband, and never mind the fact that he has not looked at your face for years, never mind the fact that he has not spoken to you for decades? Does this wifehood make up for everything, for the deprivation of a man's love, for the feel of his body against yours, the warmth of his breath on your face, the touch of his lips on yours, his hands on your face, the touch of his lips on yours, his hands on your breast? Kalyani lost all this (had she ever had them?) but her kumkum is intact and she can move in the company of women with the pride of a wife. (Shashi Deshpande 1996: 167)

Thus, the novelist reveals how a woman in the patriarchal society is conditioned to regard the status of a married woman as the status of supreme importance. To prove this point, the novelist reveals the ritual of inviting a prostitute to thread a bride's black beads. The underlying reason behind this ritual may be that a prostitute not being a married woman does not face the danger of becoming a widow. We have observed that Shashi Deshpande has dextrously depicted that in a patriarchal society widowhood is looked upon as a curse and to have a living husband is 'boon', however obnoxious he may be.

The novelist raises the issue of problems faced by a woman who is planning to get divorce. Aru, is who is militant feminist in her viewpoint, wants Sumi to sue Gopal in the court. But Sumi has the realization that even law is not capable enough to compel Gopal to bear the responsibility of the family. Sumi laughs away Aru's idea as she knows that nothing can compel Gopala to pay maintenance to her or stay with them. They can seek maintenance from him only in the case he earns. The novelist depicts the helplessness of women in such a situation. To quote the novelist:

> "I think you should see a lawyer", she says to her mother.
>
> "You mean because of Gopal? Devi's been saying that to me, to, she wants me to meet Murthy's cousin who is a lawyer. But I don't see the point of it."
>
> "The point? The point is you've got to do something."
>
> "What? Get a divorce? I'm not interested."
>
> "But he owes you, he owes all of us, yes, you especially, he owes you—lamely something. He can't get away like this! He has to give us maintenance."
>
> Sumi laughs, she seems genuinely amused. Gopala has outsmarted the law. He's given us all that he had. And he has nothing now, not even a proper job. I don't think he is getting more than a bare subsistence from Shankar's press—so Ramesh tells me. So what can the law make him do? (Shashi Deshpande 1996: 60-61)

When Sumi goes to search for a house for herself and her daughters, she is advised not to reveal her marital status of being a 'single mother'. The novelist suggests that the patriarchal society does not accept easily such women. Whenever Nagraj takes her to any landlord he advises her not to reveal her single status as it will, in his opinion, mar her chances of getting a house on rent. He tells her to tell a lie about the whereabouts of her husband. As he says:

> "Don't tell people your husband is not living with you", he suggests when she has explained her household to a prospective landlord. "People think wrongly, sometimes take advantage of you."

Something she realizes, he has never done. In fact, it is only now that he reveals his knowledge of the fact that she will be living alone.

> "What do I say? Do I tell a lie?"
>
> "Say he has been transferred. That he is working to be placed abroad—America or Dubai or something." (Shashi Deshpande 1996: 77)

Here the novelist also highlights about the problem of insecurity faced by women living alone in the patriarchal society. Sumi can't afford to stay somewhere else as she has three young daughters of marriageable age. Nagraj, who helps Sumi in searching a house for her, is a representative of patriarchal society who makes a statement which is completely patriarchal in tone:

> That is a very good decision, madam, a very wise decision. Safer for you and your daughters to be with your parents. The world is not a good place for women to be on their own. (Shashi Deshpande 1996: 195)

Thus, the novelist tells about the despair of a woman who has severe problems before her including a house for herself and her daughters; education of girls and maintenance of household. The novelist also means to highlight the need and importance of financial self-reliance for women. Had Sumi been employed or professionally qualified at least, she would not have found maintaining her daughters so difficult. The novelist has not left the issue of emotional vaccum untouched in the novel. A woman really gets so stressed in such a condition of despair that she finds it very difficult to overcome the most difficult time in her life. When Devaki, her younger cousin, expresses her grief at the breakdown of her relationship, Sumi tells her about her own emotional despair. Devaki, initially, believes that it is a small domestic 'tiff' which will get resolved in due course of time but later she feels very heart broken to see the love of Gopala and Sumi break into pieces—the love which she used to consider as a touchstone for all the lovers. Sumi's real plight is that she is not even able to express her remorse, anger or despair at the situation. She tells Devaki:

> I've never been able to cry easily, you know that. And what do I say, Devi? That my husband has left me and I don't know why and may be he doesn't really know, either? And that I'm angry and humiliated and confused...? Let that be, we won't go into it now. (Shashi Deshpande 1996: 107).

Thus, we find that the novelist has truthfully depicted the emotional humiliation a woman has to undergo during a tough time like separation. Sumi is representative of the 'New Woman' who is not as weak as to break down in front of anybody but she is not able to control her feelings when she is alone. Tears, she had controlled in Devaki's house suddenly claim her and she breaks down and it reveals the hidden pain in her heart.

Preference for the son in the patriarchal society is another important issue that has been depicted by Shashi Deshpande in most of her novels including *A Matter of Time*. The Indian patriarchal society has a natural inclination for sons who are always preferred to daughters. The condition of women who have given birth to daughters is really deplorable, though it has been a scientifically established fact that a woman is not responsible for the gender of a child. She is given a red-carpet treatment if she gives birth to a son and is not cared at all, if she gives birth to a daughter. The attitudinal issue has been depicted by the novelist:

> And yet Kalyani is right in playing down everything but her mother's disappointment in her, for it was that which played the biggest role in her life. Manorama wanted a son; instead there was Kalyani. Not an unloved child, no, never that. But for Manorama, she became the visible symbol of their failure to have a son. And then she fulfilled none of the dreams Manorama had for her daughter. Her daughter, she had thought, would be beautiful, accomplished, she would make a brilliant marriage that would be Manorama's triumph, that would show them, the family, all those women who had treated Manorama, the daughter of a poor man from a village, with such contempt. Instead there was Kalyani, who could do nothing that please her mother.

> Except once, when she gave birth to a son. There was great rejoicing then. Vithalrao, joking had called a red-carpet lying-in. It was literally that, for there was a beautiful red carpet by Kalyani's bedside for her to put her feet on, the moment she got out of bed. And the fire under the huge copper pot burned all day, so that Kalyani had hot water to wash even her little finger. The naming ceremony was the occasion of a lifetime. The house was full of guests, fragrant with flowers, gleaming with silverware. The poor were fed and the dustbin in the street was overflowing with used banana-leaf plates for two whole days. (Shashi Deshpande 1996: 150-51)

Thus, the Indian patriarchal society gives the best treatment to a woman giving birth to a son but at the same time rejects her when she either gives birth to a daughter or something untoward happens to the son because of any fault of hers, as it happened with Kalyani. She was married at a very young age and became a mother quite early. Thus, she was unable to handle the small children. While going to Bangalore, she lost their only son who was mentally retarded and she was literally punished by her husband for it. She was left all alone at the station along with her two daughters. To quote the novelist:

> Amma was coming home to Bangalore for the holidays when it happened. It happened at V.T. station—she lost him there!
>
> "Lost?" Aru repeats the word. "Lost?" "You mean, really lost? Not dead?"
>
> "No, not dead, not then at least."
>
> "Oh my God!"
>
> "Baba had gone to check the reservations, leaving Amma with—with children. When he returned, the boy wasn't there!" Aru waits for more. It comes grudgingly. "He was never found."
>
> "At night.... She was still there, sitting on the platform, her luggage and children about her, waiting for Baba."
>
> "Where was he?"

> "They didn't see him for nearly two months. He was searching, he went about the city like a mad man, they found this out later, searching the streets, railway platform, beaches, even hospitals and mortuaries. He never found him."
>
> ......
>
> Baba had not spoken to her since the day it happened. (Shashi Deshpande 1996: 139-40)

The novelist projects the probable reason behind the biased treatment of parents to a son. It may be, according to the novelist, due to the probability of acquiring a male heir to the property. Even if a property is in the name of the female only, it is used by males only. For example, Manorama gets her only daughter married off to her own brother so that the property may remain within the family. Though Manorama and Vithalrao could have given their whole property to Kalyani, yet this is the patriarchal value that compels Manorama to gift her property to Shripati instead of Kalyani. It may be the possible reason behind the celebration of the birth of a son in the patriarchal society. To quote the novelist:

> A son is born to me, dear friend, a son is born to me.
>
> It was Goda who sang the song at Nikhil's naming ceremony, a song full of joy, a woman sharing her joy in the birth of her son with her friends.
>
> Nine months I bore the pain and now my house is filled with light.
>
> Sumi saw it then, the adoration of the male child. It must have been this way in the stable in Bethlehem, in Nanda's house on the banks of Yamuna in Gokul. (Shashi Deshpande 1996: 71)

A Matter of Time is certainly a development over her earlier novels in the sense that in this novel, the novelist has strongly depicted the self-assertive 'New Woman'; this 'New Woman' is no longer in mood to bear silently. She knows that no body will ever come to her rescue and she herself is her own refuge. Sumi and her daughters are representative of 'New Women' who are self-assertive and decision-makers. Aru tries to assume the role of the head of the family and she becomes the caretaker of the family. She is a bit militant in her attitude. She wants that Shripati should realize his mistake and he should compensate for the wrongdoings done to Kalyani. She explains Kalyani's silence on the matter. To quote the novelist:

> She must have been scared. You know how Baba is, even I find myself tongue-tied sometimes.
>
> To Aru that is no excuse. It is important to her that you speak out, state the truth, that you stand up and defend yourself, that you refuse to be misjudged. Aru is at the moment reading Erica Jong and the words 'to name oneself is the first act of both the poet and the revolutionary' have filled her mind, keep resounding in it. (Shashi Deshpande 1996: 143)

Aru has her own plans not only about suing her father, or making her grandfather realize his mistake but also plans for herself. When her mother, Sumi, suggests to her to take a holiday and go to Premi mausi's house, she blatantly refuses. She wants to support her family financially and for this purpose, she intends to join computer classes. Apart from the computer classes, she wants to join a women activists' group. Devaki happens to see her standing in a group of silent demonstrators standing in a public place and trying to attract the curious stares of passer-by. When Devaki tells Sumi about it, Sumi gets startled and wants Aru to take a holiday. But Aru has finally, a clear vision of her life and she can't bear anybody's objection towards fulfilment of her own vision.

Shashi Deshpande's *A Matter of Time* depicts the conceptualize version of writer's vision of 'a new woman'. Aru is symbolic of this concept of 'New Woman'. As a new woman she is determined to speak out what lies in her heart. Aru is unlike the traditional woman who keeps her mouth shut but she prefers to unfold her ideas.

The story takes shape after Sumi along with her three daughters shifts to the parental home. The four females, baffled, angry, indifferent and mute, each according to her reaction to the reality, try to adjust to the situation and during this period of adjustment—both physically and psychologically—they encounter the past, layer after layer. Aru, the eldest daughter, is more observant, angry and restless. She is the focal point of the novel. She has a legion of questions—why is her grandmother (Kalyani) so oppressively silent? Why is there no communication between grandparents? Why has their father left? What will the future hold on for them? And so on. Slowly, the mystery is unfolded. Her grandfather Shripati has shut himself up ever since his only son was lost at the age of four on the Bombay Railway Station. He blames his wife for the loss. He and Kalyani have led two separate lives for the last thirty-five years. This and many other revelations explain the suffering of Kalyani, the real mistress of the Big House. As Sumi tries to gather the threads of her shattered life, she and her father are killed in an accident. Aru becomes the beacon of light to her grandmother and Gopala leave for Alkananda, on his 'endless wanderings'.

The novel does more than just narrate a tear-soaked tale of suffering and endurance of women. First, it subtly shows the difference between the value ascribed to stereotypical male and female traits in which man's needs take precedence over woman's needs. Second, it depicts the many faces of female resistance that make survival possible. To take up the first issue, let us have a look at the two male characters—Shripati and Gopala. Both leave the domestic sphere because they can't cope with life's commitments. Gopala has an unexplained existence drive and he leaves everything behind, including a happy family. Shripati locks himself up against all the communication because of frustration, anger and despair. For him nursing his suffering self is far more significant than caring for his wife and daughters. He forgets or rather does not wish to recognize that the grief of having lost a son is not his alone; it is Kalyani's as well. By severing all his ties with Kalyani, he tortures her doubly. Thus, by running away from the battlefield of life, the two men try to escape their duty and responsibility towards their families. The reality of Sumi—Gopala's life is also very stark. Gopala leaves his family in the mid-current; his daughters are in their teens (a difficult period for growing up adolescents); his wife is not employed and is not economically equipped to meet the day-to-day requirements; his in-laws are economically sound but they have their own problems. Social disgrace and psychological displacement add to their worries. At one juncture, Aru admits that they feel embarrassed by the sense of shame and disgrace caused due to desertion of her father. Gopala does not give thought to these social concerns and like an escapist runs away turning his back to life's challenges. His simple answer that marriage makes demands and that it is not possible for him to tolerate a life of commitment, does not satisfy Aru. She voices her resistance more vociferously than the others. Her father's desertion brings with it social stigma and myriad unanswerable questions. She is piqued with her mother for not taking a legal stand against Gopala. In Aru's resistance, there is the restlessness of younger generation to obtain justice.

Not only Aru's mother Sumi but also her grandmother comes under the scathing censure of girls. Aru and her sisters can't take in their grandmother's placid attitude and refusal to explain the circumstances under which her son was lost. Sometimes, they have an eerie suspicion that Kalyani may have let him get lost because he was mentally handicapped. For Aru, it is important to stand up and defend oneself. As against Sumi's controlled approach, Kalyani's strategy of defiance is far more formidable in its impenetrable silence. She is the victim of power game and she has endured the anguish of rejection. First, Manorama, her mother, rejected her emotionally for being born a girl-child; in addition, Kalyani somehow failed her mother on every count—she was neither beautiful nor intelligent and not even healthy. Kalyani had adopted the strategy of resisting her mother's dominance by her stoic silence. Her silence is as hard as a rock. Manorama, fretfully, devices a plan to keep the property in the family. She forces her brother, Shripati, to marry Kalyani. Both Kalyani and Shripati bear the burden of this forced relationship and they remain unhappy. After Shripati ceases all communication with her, Kalyani does not react with show of emotions. She resists him by building her own cocoon, having her sister and her daughters around her. It is Shripati who is confined to an accused loneliness, not Kalyani. This does not, however, mean that Kalyani does not suffer. We can read the suffering self of the one who knows the hurt of desertion by her husband and who has experienced the anguish of rejection. But by and large, she maintains a stoic silence. According to the novelist, silence can be powerful tool of resistance. Kalyani's resistance is so hard that even the author remarks in one of her interviews that Kalyani appears to Aru not "as a victim but as woman who comes out of all that victimization intact" (Ramarao 1998: 256-59). When silence becomes deliberate, it acts as a barrier to the penetration of the soul by a perceiver; it works as an operation of power rather than powerlessness. As it withholds communication, it produces a kind of awe and becomes a potent tool of resistance. Deshpande valourises Kalyani's individualistic, dogged resolve to resist her emotional harassment and survive on her own terms.

Though the three women are victims of patriarchal dominance, they reclaim their identity by their acts of resistance. Aru tries to re-position her lost situation by angry protests; Sumi regains her identity when her merit as an individual is recognized as her 'drama' wins acclaim; and Kalyani feels empowered when Shripati's will, referring to her as Vithalrao and Manorama's daughter and not as his wife, is read out to her. She does not feel the sting of having been robbed of her marital status. To quote the novelist:

> On the contrary, it is as if the words have given her something more than the house, restored something she had lost; they seem to have strengthened her. (Shashi Deshpande 1996: 245).

Ultimately, she finds her identity and her individuality.

If *Binding Vine* is a story that is built on the ironies around the issue of rape, *A Matter of Time* deals with the dilemma of wife-desertion. The liberal feminist approach of Deshpande, even as it tries to subvert and undermine mechanism of patriarchy, explores the issue of consolidation of the female identity in the larger context of modern society. Female bonding and resistance are central issues in *A Matter of Time*. The novel, we have seen, underlines wife-desertion as yet another dimension of betrayal and cruelty to women. Gopala's desertion of Sumi and their three daughters, Aru, Charu and Seema, results in a swift dismemberment of the family leaving despair-filled hearts behind. It is like a death in the family, 'a death without a body'. In Sumi, a deserted wife, there is no outward distress but there is a silence about her that is like the cry of despair. Sumi's apparent stoicism throws others into confusion and they treat her like an invalid. Gopala's desertion is not only a emotional tragedy to the family but also a disgrace as the disgrace clings not so much to the man who walks out on his family but to the wife who is deserted. The impact of the shock is traced mainly in two characters, who assume the central position in the novel: Sumi and her eighteen years old daughter, Aru, 'charting her inner space'. Their reactions are different as one is mature enough and the other stands at the beginning of the journey of her life. In *A Matter of Time*, for the first time, there is a liberal attempt to understand the male psychology and Gopala who deserts his wife and children, is not condemned without a hearing. Although Sumi reasons out that the metaphysical question of the ultimate truth of human life and the persistent human search for meaning in existence is Gopala's reason of her desertion, yet she questions that why they should bear the result of his spiritual unrest. But she will not coerce him into coming back to her and here she explores ways of coming to terms with the painful reality and going on with her life. She tries to get a job and learns to ride a scooter and above all, discovers the writing talent within her and produces a play for her school children. On the other hand, Aru is filled with anger and resentment against her father and thinks that he should not be allowed to go scot free, and explores possibilities of bringing legal action against him.

The aim of Shashi Deshpande is not merely to document female resistance to patriarchal ideologies, but also to focus on the strategies of readjustments her female protagonists undertake in order to forge an identity of their own. Her women characters struggle to learn to become "one's own refuge" and value the fellowship of other women. She recreates sensitively the female world and through modes of women's experience, she gives it mainstream position. In her fictional works, she consciously creates feminine sensibility and specificity. In *A Matter of Time*,

Shashi Deshpande, successfully, weaves an intricate pattern of relationships within an extended family spanning across generations. Manorama, Kalyani, Sumi and Aru belong to four generations of the same family, each representing a specific mode of experience. Manorama is the typical product of patriarchal value system, for she resented the birth of Kalyani, her daughter, as she wanted a son. She forces a marriage between two unwilling partners, her daughter Kalyani and her younger brother Shripati and she even holds Kalyani responsible for all the sorrows and calls her an enemy. But it is Kalyani who represents the survival power of women which prepares her to bear her own mother's ill-treatment and her husband's rejection. As the novelist observes:

> They don't seem to realize that the real miracle is Kalyani herself, Kalyani who has survived intact, in spite of what Shripati did to her, Kalyani who has survived Manorama's myriad acts of cruelty.
>
> Manorama died unforgiving, she never relented in her anger towards her daughter. There was more to it than the disgrace of her coming back home, a rejected wife. Manorama's treatment of her daughter led to a breach between Vithalrao and Manorama, the first since their marriage. Vithalrao was a changed man after Kalyani's return home. To everyone's surprise, the man of science turned to astrology and a different astrologer came home every few days. It was as if Vitharao was searching for someone who would tell him, "your daughters will soon be reunited with her husband, they will live happily together".
>
> ......
>
> Vithalrao had a stroke soon after and for this, too, Manorama held her daughter responsible. She would have liked to punish her by keeping her away from her father, but that was not possible. (Shashi Deshpande 1996: 151-52)

There is a transition from Manorama to Kalyani as Kalyani's attitude towards daughters is different from her own mother and it is evident when Kalyani says to Aru:

> My mother didn't care for my children either. Daughters again, she said.... I'm luckier than my mother. She is the one unlucky who didn't know how to enjoy her children and grandchildren. (Shashi Deshpande 1996: 226)

When Gopala walks out on Sumi, it appears to Kalyani like a re-enactment of her own life, but unlike her mother, she gives emotional support to her daughter. In Sumi, we see the struggle to learn to live alone and assert oneself against the tides of tragedy. If Sumi is trying to work out a strategy to withstand the shock and the emptiness left behind by Gopala and creates a life for herself and her daughters, Aru is full of the sense of injustice and protest against her father. If Sumi is trying to retain self-identity, Aru fights for the rights of women.

Thus, we have observed that in the post-independence era, India can boast of some of the most advanced legislation protecting the rights and status of women. The constitution granted Indian women citizen status—something for which women in the West had to agitate for more than a century. Yet, political enfranchisement has been inefficient in real social terms. There have been labour legislation, the Hindu Code Bill, the Prohibition of Dowry Act, the suppression of Immoral Traffic Act, bills legalising abortion but the actuality is that these laws remain, by and large, "paper tigers" when it comes to the reality of the individual women's existence. The implementation of these laws is hindered by the harsh reality that a woman's subordination remains embedded in the personal psyche of people in the Indian patriarchal society. Legal changes are thus difficult to enforce.

Shashi Deshpande's *A Matter of Time* is the assertion of the belief that the male-supremacist ideology is experienced in its most acute form within the domain of the family, subtly subverting the most personal of human relationships. Millet has asserted that patriarchy's chief institution is the family. It is both a mirror of and a connection with the larger society; a patriarchal unit within a patriarchal whole. Within the clearly marked hierarchal structures, the man controls women's sexuality, labour of production, reproduction and mobility. The psycho-social conditioning within the family imparts the earliest lessons in gender discrimination and differential valorisation of male/female experience. This novel explores the writer's awareness of the subtle expressions of male power and domination in the family, often concealed under an overt show of love. Underneath all these explorations, Shashi Deshpande wants to assert what she has stated in 'No (Hu)man is an Island':

> I believe that women are neither inferior nor subordinate human beings but one half of the human race. I believe that women (and men as well) should not be straitjacketed into roles that warp their personalities, but should have options available to them. I believe that Nature, when conferring its gifts on humans did not differentiate between males and females, except for the single purpose of procreation. I believe that motherhood does not bar everything else, but is a bonus, an extra that women are privileged to have. (Shashi Deshpande 1992)

Works Cited

Akiko, Yasano. "Woman in the Novels of Shashi Deshpande: A Study". Ed. Dr. S. Prasanna Sree, New Delhi: Sarup and Sons, 2003: 107.

Bhalla, Amrita. *Shashi Deshpande*. Devon, UK: Northcote House Pub., 2006.

Bhasin, Kamla. *Understanding Gender*. New Delhi: Kali for Women, 2000.

Deshpande, Shashi. *A Matter of Time*. New Delhi: Penguin, 1996.

Deshpande, Shashi. "No (Hu)man is an Island." In *Times of India*, 23 April 1992.

Deshpande, Shashi. In an interview with Sue Dickman in *Post Independence Voices in South Asian Writings*. Eds. Malashri Lal, Alamgir Hashmi and Victor J. Ramraj. New Delhi: Doaba House, 2000.

Shama, Futehally. Review of *A Matter of Time*. *The Hindu*, 19 June 1997.

Conclusion

After a detailed and analyzed perusal of each of Shashi Deshpande's novels, we can conclude that she is essentially a novelist of gender issues. She has touched upon almost all the issues which are normally of great concern to all the feminists, Indian feminists in particular. Perusive readings of her fictional corpus make us convinced that gender issues can and should cut across class and language differences in order to lead towards feminist frames for Indian literature. In her fictional works, she writes about the 'marginalized' community of women in India and expresses her concern for women's disadvantaged condition within patriarchy. The protagonist of Anamika's poem "Without a Place" tells us in a nutshell about the gender issues discussed by Shashi Deshpande in her novels. Anamika writes:

> When hair, women and nails,
> fall from their place
> they remain no where....
> so our Sanskrit teacher
> would analyse a verse
> and panic would freeze
> us girls
> in our places.
>
> Place? What is a place?
> This we had learned
> In our very first class!
> We remembered every moment
> Of our first classes...
> Ram, go to school!
> Radha, cook a meal!

Ram, come, have a sugar-cake!
Radha, sweep the house!
Your brother will sleep now,
go and make his bed!
Wonderful! A new home!
Ram, look, this is your room!
'And mine?'
'Silly girl,
Girls are air, sunshine, earth,
they don't have a home!'
Those who have no home
What place can they have? (Malashri Lal 2008)

The experience of women cannot be uniform, though feminists talk of global sisterhood. Recent psychologists carrying out their research at the Stone centre, USA have recognized the importance of women's inner strength.

Shashi Deshpande has shown in her fictional works those intrinsic values in women which have been devalued by a patriarchal society and she tries to raise her protagonist's consciousness by highlighting the centrality of the feminine experience. She probes how care, nurturing, empathy and other allied values, central to the female experience, go unrecognized in favour of the so-called male virtues of power, success and career. She brings to the light that the practice of these patriarchal notions leads to women's devaluation and the devaluation, in its turn, leads to women's enslavement and society's degeneration.

Being the 'liberal' feminist, Shashi Deshpande highlights that 'self-assertion' is a positive quality, but when self-assertion is practiced at the cost of negation of care for others and other positive feminine values, it creates ultimate discontent. For example, Saru (in *The Dark Holds No Terrors*) negates her family, asserts her independence, refuses to identify with her mother but suffers when the basic demands of her own 'self' clash with the dominant social values.

Shashi Deshpande believes that care and nurturing are natural to the female psyche. If allowed to blossom, these qualities lead women to self-actualization but unfortunately, these qualities are 'imposed' upon women as female attributes that must be adhered to and any deviation is seen as threatening. Conditioned by the so-called patriarchal society, women follow these norms and the values of care, empathy, tolerance and nurturing, which are the fountainhead of strength and empowerment, but ultimately, they become a source of suffering. When women care for others out of a fearful need to please others, they loose their own sense of 'self'.

Deshpande depicts that female friendship is significant for woman's healthy self-image. Those who are successful in developing female bonding (as for Mira in *The Binding Vine*) grow as stronger characters whereas those who fail in developing a bond with others suffer in isolation. A good example of female bonding is displayed in a situation, wherein women fall back on other women. But the problem arises when elderly women play the power game of patriarchy and behave as female patriarchs.

In Shashi Deshpande's opinion, there is a difference in the male and female models of independence. Women want to live in relationship and yet desire to remain 'whole', which is not acceptable to patriarchy in India. On the other hand, the male model of a completely independent person is one of absolute autonomy and since this does not conform to the female model, the result is either women's invisibility or silence. The sexist bias of society hinders the freedom required to validate one's self in case of women. The community grants enough freedom to men to develop their sense of 'self', but women have to juggle multiple responsibilities to prove themselves. The present study depicts how various women characters—Indu, Saru, Jaya, Urmi and Sumi—are compelled, in the name of upholding the values and ideals of the traditional patriarchal society in India, to repress their urge to act according to their own will. The study reveals that there is a need to overhaul the present steely social system (which is chiefly patriarchal in nature) to make way for a humane social order. Shashi Deshpande makes a suggestive use of her epigraph taken from *The Dharmapada*. The epigraph in *The Dark Holds No Terrors* suggests that for a woman there is no refuge other than her own 'self'. The epigraph reads:

> You are your own refuge;
> there is no other refuge.
> This refuge is hard to achieve. (*Dharmapada*)

These lines show the significance of drawing sustenance from 'within' and her protagonists reach that stage of drawing strength from their inner 'self' after much conflict. The most important concern of feminist agenda is that women should be 'visible' and their voices must be 'audible' in the society and this concern gets a proper place in Shashi Deshpande's fictional works. By taking the gynocritical stand, the novelist tries to locate women's voices within the patriarchal discourse.

The central theme in her novels is not the facile one of opposing tradition with modernity or westernization with Indian culture. Her characters grapple with their struggle which drags them through innocence and experience, ignorance and knowledge, girlhood and adulthood, repression and submission, and joy and sorrow to the achievement of that 'self'. To Deshpande, life as a girl is an integral part of an adult life. In her novels, she recognizes childhood influences on the growth of a girl, and in the time of crisis, her characters turn back to the past to search for reasons of biasedness within and outside the family. Her fiction is an example of the ways in which a girl child's position in the family, social reality and psychological growth determine her personality. She argues that it would be psychologically unrealistic to imagine that awareness of childhood influences within the woman emerges suddenly, that she becomes a 'person' with the onset of adolescence. The role of early life experiences, the role of education, closeness to parents, sibling relationships are some very crucial elements that go a long way in creating a woman's personality. Thus, Shashi Deshpande traces the pattern of socialization and internalization of patriarchal norms and values.

Shashi Deshpande has also talked about the plight of wives, both, housewives as well as professionals. Money is an important factor in the lives of her middle-class characters. Hence, the wife who brings money is 'kept' as a hen that lays golden eggs. The man is the dominant factor in the Indian family set up. He exercises his superiority, not by trying to earn more than his wife but by inflicting physical abuse and having brutal sex with her whom, he believes to be his slave. She may be a big person in the society; she may be famous; she may even earn more than he does, yet, within the four walls, he makes it very clear that he is the real master of the house. The woman stoops only to avoid the difficult situation within the family. She does not try to conquer or override the man. She does not use her potential to defy the man or the society. The role of woman in the society has not been explored by Shashi Deshpande. She only excels in individual analysis within the Indian patriarchal set up. In most of the novels analyzed, we do not see the existence of true love between husband and wife, though there is a natural inclination among women for altruistic love. The woman seems to be bearing the yoke more with resignation and not with dedication and love. This may be so because there is no expression of true love and affection from her counterpart, the husband.

Shashi Deshpande is always in quest of creating 'new woman' out of her protagonists who belong to different cultural, religious and linguistic backgrounds. The novelist is against the patriarchal establishments, which cripple the innate creativity of women. The protagonists of Shashi Deshpande enter into marriage with the hope that the marriage would provide them respect, security and status in the society but, unfortunately, they get disappointed and subsequently disillusioned. Deshpande celebrates the major explorations of her heroines by transcending the boundaries of the female gender; she creates initial revolters who finally compromise like Jaya in *That Long Silence*. Her characters experience the gravitational pull of patriarchy and tradition which they negate in an assertive manner.

The concept of 'new woman', according to Shashi Deshpande, is an attitudinal transformation which every woman has to experience so that a radical social change is effected throughout the world. To a 'new woman', the stifling and oppressive system of sex roles should give way to undistorted gender equality. A 'new woman' is a feminist who is in search for the means to overcome oppression, develop her own powers and abilities for personal growth as an individual and self-actualization.

Shashi Deshpande is more a novelist of human relationships and human situations. Amid these relationships and situations, she raises gender issues which are of interest to any feminist in

India. Detailed analysis of texts of her novels make one believe that to forge healthy man-woman relationship, the morality of care centred on the maxim of not hurting others should be universal and not restricted to women, otherwise they will rebel and negate it, which, in turn would evoke a cold and unsympathetic feminine world. This problem can be tackled only in conjunction with men. They should help each other to build a society based on mutual care, cooperation and compassion. There should be redistribution of responsibilities so that:

> We do not give femaleness and maleness all the meaning we presently give them. There is no reason that serving others has to be threat to maleness. This, like many other notions, is culturally imposed. (Jean Baker Miller 1976: 167)

Shashi Deshpande believes that the concept of womanhood and image of women need to undergo a positive change. According to her belief, no society can ever progress without an active participation of women, who are an integral part of human civilization, in its overall development. She attempts to interpret and record the reverberations of gender issues as revealed in her fictional works. She evinces keen interest in the empowerment of women in the multi-faceted aspects of life. The women of Shashi Deshpande face formidable challenges to gain their rightful place in the society. They are culture specific traditional. The major problems faced by Shashi Deshpande's women characters are the psychological conditioning and the gender discrimination which determine the adult personality of the female child. This feminist consciousness is achieved by her educated middle-class women.

Shashi Deshpande suggests Indian women to have quest for identity and to exercise 'certain' autonomy within marriage. The novelist desires the transformation of the society and she highlights the necessity for women's education and economic independence which can eradicate feminine financial dependence. She is more concerned about self-fulfilment and self-actualization of women.

Shashi Deshpande's women question the existing traditions and customs and critically examine the patriarchal values of the

Indian society. But each of these women arrives at a concept of feminism which is a step towards revolution of social reality of women's subordination. In *That Long Silence*, Shashi Deshpande speaks of the problems of unwanted pregnancies of women in India. She depicts how women in India (like Vimla in the aforementioned novel) continue to bear in silence a series of unwanted pregnancies. Unsafe conditions of abortion carried out by untrained quacks unleash a whole range of problems for the Indian women. This so-called 'new woman' Vimla, despite the obstacles of poverty and the denial of formal education, identifies her rights and uses her own potential to take her decisions successfully. In the same manner, Shashi Deshpande allows one of her woman characters, Jaya, to exercise her reproductive right by aborting unwanted foetus. These new women think and feel differently from traditional Indian women and use their potentials in a new perspective. The novelist makes a caustic attack on 'supposed' duties of a devoted wife, *pativrata*, and raises the issues of women's inner struggle to revolt against emotional slavery. But her women come to the point of compromise and avoid all open verbal fights. They practice non-violence and advocate that people should learn to negotiate disagreements and problems without fighting. This is observed in the ending of *That Long Silence* where the woman protagonist, Jaya, decides to clarify the matter with her husband, on his return from his self-imposed exile. Shashi Deshpande wants women to move in a positive direction to maximize their potential. Neither Shashi Deshpande nor her creations (her characters) advocate Western feminism. Still they are feminists—Indians, in all respect, rooted to their conservative culture. They subsist on compromise in life.

The theme of marriage and sexuality as traced in Deshpande's novels shows a development from tradition to revolt to affirmation. Her women rebel and marry the men of their choice but, ultimately, succumb to tradition and expectations of their husbands. The novelist unveils the social fact that Indian men often carry the old traditional image of a woman. Therefore, they fail to understand the feelings and aspirations of their wives. The intelligent and educated protagonists soon begin to feel restricted in the traditional claustrophobic existence. But the balanced and practical approach of her middle-class heroines towards life makes them realize the importance of marriage and family. Instead of walking out of matrimony, her women strive to make changes within marriage. These women realize the importance of matrimony but they are also aware of importance of their own individuality. Suma Chitnis also says:

> ...the historical circumstances and values render the women's issues difference in India. ...again, in India the institution of marriage and family is still considered necessary because of the security and social status it gives to both men and women, who find it difficult and traumatic to break away. So what makes Indian women 'feminists' different is the fact that they raise their voice against the social injustice and oppression of women rather than ask for her freedom from the institution of marriage and family. (Suma Chitnis 1998: 84)

Therefore, we see that whereas Anita Desai's heroines succumb to their weakness and find solution in homicide or suicide, Nayantara Sahgal's women defy traditional norms in search of emancipation, Shashi Deshpande's heroines are willing to take their share of the blame of their suffering and they bravely face the situation.

Shashi Deshpande does not make moral judgements while unfolding the extramarital relationships in her novels. In this context, Dieter Riemenschneider in his essay "Indian Women Writing in English: The Short Story" has observed:

> (Indian women writers) are neither concerned with an analysis of their heroines' past tribulations, nor anxious to justify their heroines' decision to be free.... Rather they confine themselves to portraying a woman's deliberate step to liberate herself from the shackles of traditional roles. The act itself...is the essential point...(the writers) ignore question...of morality, an astounding development considering the emphasis on respectability in Indian society. (Dieter Riemenschneider 1985: 314)

Shashi Deshpande's refusal to take a moral stance on adultery ought not to be misconstrued as her inability to take a stand on question of morality. Rather, it reflects her defiance and rejection of the prevailing social norms. Extramarital relationships of Saru-Boozie (*The Dark Holds No Terrors*), Indu-Naren (*Roots and Shadows*), Jaya-Kamat (*That Long Silence*) and Urmi-Bhaskar (*The Binding Vine*) are used by the novelist as a metaphor for women to liberate themselves from the chains of socially ordained moral codes. However, in most of her novels, her 'militancy' remains at the level of technique mainly as she does not allow her protagonists (with the exception of Indu) to actually consummate their relationship with their male friends. It is almost as if Shashi Deshpande wishes to 'liberate' her protagonists in the radical sense but prefers to keep them faithful in accordance with their socio-cultural context as it renders the portrayal more realistic in the Indian context.

Through her portrayal of Saru, Indu, Jaya, Urmi and Sumi and their situations, Shashi Deshpande not only presents a feminist insight into patriarchal values, but also prescribes a balance between tradition and modernity as a working philosophy for the contemporary Indian women. By tradition she means those values of security and harmony that symbolize the Indian way of life, while modernity essentially refers to the assertion of the independent and individual 'self'. Her protagonists, at the beginning of their quest, find that they have passively accepted their socially ordained roles. Shashi Deshpande advocates that to realize her own 'self', a woman must be true to her self. The novelist proves by subjugation and subordination of her women that the sacrifice and nobility that is expected of a woman is a stereotype that only bogs down the woman in a mire of negation and suppression. The woman needs to venture out of the familial framework, to discover her potential as an individual and give expression to her inner space and self. At the same time, she need not repudiate her marriage or family. All her protagonists take a break from their 'routine'; ponder over the crisis in their lives and successfully come out of the chaos. Most of her heroines experience a major crisis in life and they leave home. Urmi in *The Binding Vine* and Saru in *The Dark Holds No Terror*, leave home with the hope of finding their 'identity' in their natal homes where they live in their husbands' absence. The protagonists then subject their past to a close scrutiny and search themselves for answers to their problems. In the process of delving into past, they grow from anxious, unhappy and unassertive women which they are at the beginning of the narrative, into mature, awakened and assertive women who understand and perceive the gender politics of socialization and the need to break its shackles. They also recognize the need to make their choices as free women and as independent human beings. Through these portraits of educated middle-class women trying to realize their 'self', Shashi Deshpande offers feminist critiques of the patriarchal Indian society.

Feminism for Shashi Deshpande (and in the Indian context) does not mean taking the militant anti-men and anti-marriage stance. It means, instead, concerted action by men and women towards making of a more egalitarian, balance and mature gender relationship. Every relationship has its own share of problems; and there can be no generalized solution to these problems. Each of her protagonists realizes that she has to work out her own strategy to overcome her problems. At present, the woman bears the onus of making the effort to free herself of the oppressive patriarchal stereotypes that society has imposed on her. However, an egalitarian society will emerge only when everybody realizes that she is an independent human being. Shashi Deshpande believes that a woman should do what Virginia Woolf has held:

> ...no need to hurry; no need to sparkle, no need to be anybody but oneself. (Virginia Woolf 1977: 17)

Thus the novelist depicts her protagonists asserting their own 'self'. She suggests that women must not succumb to the pressures of patriarchy, particularly in the domestic arena.

Through her portrayal of the older women and their values and contrasting them with the modern protagonists, Shashi Deshpande depicts that the older generation of women had little freedom and choice. Subsequently, they turn oppressors themselves (as did the *Ajjis* in *That Long Silence*, Saru's mother in *The Dark Holds no Terror* and Akka in *The Binding Vine*). Shashi Deshpande holds their conditioning and socialization responsible for their patriarchal attitudes. She values the traditional ideals of family and responsibility, but is also critical of their potential to limit a woman's identity, individuality and freedom. The patriarchal women had neither the education nor the financial independence of the protagonists to stand up against oppressive situations. Lack of a supportive social structure had further prevented them from breaking shackles of patriarchy. Without the family that provided them the security they would have been rendered homeless. So, partly out of fear and partly out of lack of means, they had tried to adjust or compromise with their circumstances. The multiple stories of these women and their oppression enable the reader to generalize about the universal inferior position of Indian women.

A realistic depiction of gender issues is one of the chief concerns of Shashi Deshpande as a writer of human emotions and relationships. Her fictional works are religiously focused on this theme, bringing about social awareness unravelling the changes in the social sphere and the effect on it of several subterranean forces. Though Shashi Deshpande depicts multiple relationships that exist in a family, yet man-woman dyad is the most central to her writings. The most healthy man-woman relationship, according to the novelist is the one which vouchsafes mutual growth. Mutual understanding, trust, compassion and support lead to authenticity in a relationship and, thus, concretize it. Problems arise when they are one-sided and it diminishes and destroys a relationship. Viewing these man-woman relationships in the societal context which determines the different codes of behaviour for males and females, one finds that for men, the development of the sense of self is based on individuation, autonomy and separation and for a woman it is in the 'relational' context:

> ...women not only define themselves in a context of human relationships, but also judge themselves in terms of their ability to care. Woman's place in a man's cycle has been that of a nurturer, a caretaker and helpmate, the weaver of those networks of relationships on which she, in turn, relies. But while women have thus taken care of men, men

> have in their psychological development tended to assume or devalue that care. (Carol Gilliagan 1982: 17)

The absence of reciprocity of care thus generate feelings of worthlessness, lack of zest, isolation, depression and inertness, further leading to neglect, lack of communication, alienation, conflict and identity crisis among women.

In the Indian culture, marriage is a sacred institution where the wife is the half of man, *ardhangini,* but ironically she submits *completely* to the husband for he is *pati-parmeshwar*, an earthly substitute for God, around whom her whole being revolves. Though Indian women have attained emancipation from the stereotype-roles to some extent, they still lead contradictory lives. A woman in the patriarchal Indian society, according to Shashi Deshpande, is expected to submerge her whole being in doing her duty to her husband (as Kaki does in *Roots and Shadows*), irrespective of what he is. This often leads to tension in the lives of women. Many women (most of the minor women characters in the novels of Shashi Deshpande) continue in the battering relationships and some (her protagonists) rebel to attain 'individuation'. The first category of women represents the battered and exploited Indian women, whereas the second category represents the desired roles to be played by women.

The characters of Saru, Indu, Jaya, Urmi and Sumi show how disillusionment, springing from the absence of healthy communication and reciprocal care in the family, results in the estrangement of individuals and creates bad marriages, which leads to depression in the women. But Indian women have a tendency to see themselves in relation to others (men). Therefore, they stay with, build on and develop in a context of attachment and affiliation with others' and eventually for many women:

> ...the threat of disruption of an affiliation is perceived not just as a loss of a relationship, but as something closer to a total loss of self. (Carol Gilligan 1982: 69)

Women, in order to continue and save relationships from disruption, suffer compromise. They adapt even to battering relationships without raising their voices. Tara in *That Long Silence*; Sulu in *The Binding Vine*; Vithal's mother in *Roots and*

Shadows; Madhav's mother in *The Dark Holds No Terrors* and Kalyani in *A Matter of Time* are Shashi Deshpande's portrayals in this regard. All of them undergo suffering caused by physical and psychological violence in marriage. It is their conditioning to the Indian ideal of womanhood that they don't give voice to their grievances. They suffer at the hands of brutal male members (who are none but husbands, fathers, brothers and sons to them) mutely, for the Indian tradition, idealizing the myths of Sita and Savitri expects and emphasizes passivity in women. They efface their very 'being' to serve their 'masters'. Miller puts it more explicitly:

> The woman is not encouraged to take her own needs seriously, to explore them, to try to act on them as a separate individual. She is enjoined from engaging all of her resources and thereby prevented from developing some valid and reliable sense of her own worth. Instead, the woman is encouraged to concentrate on the needs and development of men. (Miller 1976: 18)

Most of the Indian women mutely embrace their lot without voicing their discontent.

Shashi Deshpande has also touched upon the issue of temperamental incompatibility in marriage (for example in the relationship of Jaya and Mohan). Right in the beginning of their relationship, a wife is not able to conform to her husband's demands. She feels unhappy and discontented and finally converts herself into her husband's serf, obliterating her 'self', thinking that this would win her his devotion also. Miller, again, puts it more explicitly:

> Some women come to believe that others will love them (and become permanently devoted to them) because they are serving these others so much and so well. The tragedy here is that people don't usually love others for this reason. They become dependent on their services, but that is different from real love and interest. (Miller 1976: 64-65)

Thus, Shashi Deshpande has depicted successfully how Indian woman fasts twice a week for the well-being of her husband;

wears what her husband likes; eats what her husband finds delicious; works outside if her husband allows and stays back at home as a housewife if her husband prefers so.

Being the pro-family feminist, Shashi Deshpande affirms gender differentiation but at the same time celebrates traditional feminine qualities, particularly associated with mothering, which had been discarded by the early advocates (Western) of feminism. The stereotyped masculine image is not accepted as a yardstick of excellence or virtue by Shashi Deshpande. She aims at a society where a woman is not forced to be feminine and rejects the male-female polarity and stereotypes. She holds firmly that there is no 'masculine' quality such as strength, dominance or fearlessness or 'feminine' quality such as caring, nurturing, love or obedience, etc. All of these are human qualities and are not/ should not be specific to either to men or women. Just because a girl is born a girl, her feminine destiny should not be loaded on her. Femininity is the result of gendering, which is a matter of culture which refers to social classification of men and women into 'masculine' and 'feminine'. If mothering, sacrifice, tolerance and care are most essential virtues, it is surprising that men don't like to practise them but devalue them in favour of power, success and dominance. She holds that both men and women should share the positive masculine qualities and that everyone should be gentle, caring, nurturing, strong, rational, emotional and individualistic.

While depicting female patriarchism in her novels, Shashi Deshpande argues that the development of motherly attitude that is the development of the ability to care and nurture, is cyclical for women as mothers produce daughters with mothering capacities. By contrast, women as mothers produce sons whose nurturing capacities and needs have been systematically curtailed and repressed. Thus, due to their patriarchal conditioning, girls and boys inhabit different emotional environments. Gillian, in her *In a Different Voice*, argues:

> Women's deference is rooted not only in their social subordination but also in the substance of their moral concern, sensitivity to the needs of the others and the assumption of the responsibility for taking care lead

> women to attend to voices other than their own and to include in their judgement others' point of view. (Gillian 1982: 17)

In Indian culture, the segregation of the sexes is customary. The masculine and feminine codes of behaviour prescribed in the religious texts are literally revered and to liberate the mind from the shackles of these accepted prejudices is not easy, for it is deeply fabricated in the Indian ethos. Our culture idealizes female martyrdom and self-denying women are extolled in the various myths that constitute a part of the Indian cultural legacy. There is a separate religion and caste for women, i.e. the *stridharma* and *strijati*. Women are conditioned and brought up through the examples of timeless feminine symbols of Indian womanhood like Sita and Savitri. It is very saddening that woman's innate strength is hardly given any recognition in the patriarchal Indian society and men devalue their virtue in favour of their own success, power and careerism. Shashi Deshpande depicts in her novels how the feminine virtues are devalued by the patriarchal Indian society. Though women try to be good, they feel bad internally for their intrinsic goodness is not only overlooked, but also becomes a tool of their exploitation.

Thus, we have seen the gender issues discussed by Shashi Deshpande are very much prevalent in the Indian patriarchal society and these issues have been given ample space and examples in her fictional writings by the novelist. All the gender issues including rape, marital-emotional suffocation, biasedness in upbringing of a girl child, preference for a son, problems of widowhood, financial dependence on men and subordination of women have been given enough space within the pages of her fictional writings. In each of her fictional pieces, one or the other gender issue finds subtle treatment or depiction.

Shashi Deshpande's *The Dark Holds No Terrors* shows woman's subjugation in the patriarchal society along with depicting the biased attitude of parents towards the upbringing of the daughters. Sarita undergoes great humiliation and neglect not only on the account of special treatment given to her brother by her parents but also on the account of their indifference towards her. The novelist highlights the issue of pitiable condition of girls in their own parental homes and discloses at the same time domestic-chores' burden on the shoulders of the young girls in the patriarchal Indian homes. At the age when they should be occupied with playing, they are given the responsibility of taking care of their younger siblings. It is not the case that Shashi Deshpande wants to depict physical exploitation as the only possible aspect of marriage in the Indian society; she wants to project that marriage has been used rather misused as a licence by Indian men to assert their superiority and the subordination of women. Shashi Deshpande has highlighted in *The Dark Holds No Terrors* that an urban working woman belonging to the middle class is oppressed at all the levels including domestic, professional and marital and she seems to have lost her control over her own life.

In *Roots and Shadows*, Shashi Deshpande has asserted the importance of economic and emotional independence for women. Deshpande's concern with the patriarchal notion of subordination of women and that a woman must exist only in terms of her relationship with a man is very much explicit in all her novels including *Roots and Shadows*. In patriarchy, woman is necessarily viewed as needing male control at all stages of her life. Her place as mother/sister/daughter-in-law is completely at the disposal of her male relatives, first by virtue of birth and second by marriage. Woman's role is rigidly defined by various males in her life. In Indian patriarchal family, the girl is considered as a thing to be given away. Marriage is the destiny of a woman; and to remain unmarried is suggestive of some unnaturalness. It is considered as a matter of shame to woman's family. It is parents' social obligation and moral responsibility to get their daughter married before she passes the marriageable age. An unmarried man does not evoke the same response from the society. On the other hand, a woman is expected to live fulfilling the wishes and desires of others. For the sake of social approval and her parents' happiness the girl has to go through the humiliating 'inspection' where she is examined by the boy's relatives as if she were a saleable commodity. Indu leads an ambivalent life. She cherishes within her heart deep and profound love but when the occasion comes to express it she retraces. This is because she is nourished and reared by a tradition ridden society in which she has been taught to be obedient, unquestioning, meek and submissive. The traditional society teaches a woman to accept everything that comes her way in a graceful manner. As members of the subordinate sex, women are characterized by obedience and submission, and under male domination they have to develop a tendency to prevail by passive means. Indu surrenders to Jayant since she does not want conflict. She clings tenaciously to Jayant and to her marriage not for love alone but because she is afraid of failure of her marriage. She wants to show her family and to the world that her marriage is a success and so the traditional values she has been nourished with, compel her to put on the mask of an obedient and submissive wife. In the end, Indu believes that there is no possible escape from relationships; and they need to be lived in with emotional and financial independence. That is why in the end she decides to resign from her job and takes to full-fledged writing. By taking the independent decision of financing Mini's marriage, Indu, achieves her freedom. She does not let any one, neither Kaka nor Atya, come in the way of doing what she wants to do. She conquers her fears and achieves freedom in her life.

Shashi Deshpande's *That Long Silence* is a psychological novel that expresses the loneliness that occupies a feminine heart. The novelist shows that in spite of being surrounded by father, brothers, husband and children, a woman feels lonely and is unable to give expression to her feelings. For example, the married life of Jaya and Mohan is punctuated all along by "matrimonial silences". Deshpande's *That Long Silence* is an assertion of her belief that a woman is not an appendage, she is a 'being'; that too an autonomous being, and in the view of the writer, she has to find her own salvation. Another important issue raised by the novelist is that there is an ever-increasing desire among Indians to have sons and this desire is forced upon women not only by men but by women also. Thus, Deshpande points out that silence and surrender are considered as virtue of women in the patriarchal Indian society. Shashi Deshpande has raised another very important issue in the novel—the issue of the way the girls are married off in the Indian patriarchal society.

The novelist highlights the qualities of a boy that are taken into consideration before selecting a boy for the girl and the qualities that are expected of a would-be bride. Shashi Deshpande has taken up another key-issue in the novel *That Long Silence*—the issue of the silence of the modern Indian housewife. On the one hand, the silence expressed in the novel expresses the suppressed longings, emotions, aspirations and protests of women down the ages, on the other hand, it challenges the men to change and to give women their due position and rights. This emptiness in the loveless marriage causes the wife and the husband to drift away from each other and ultimately results in total failure. Deshpande proves that in Indian patriarchal system, a woman can survive only by negating her own personality. Social conformity has always been more obligatory for a woman than a man and this social conformity leads her to an emotively lonely and secluded life. In the end of the novel, Jaya emerges as a determined strong-willed modern woman, who is prepared to face life, accept her responsibilities squarely and tries not to escape from or avoid them. Jaya observes that meaningful co-existence of man and woman can come only through understanding, respect and compassion not through domination or subjugation.

In *Binding Vine*, Shashi Deshpande shows that sisterhood is certainly a comfort but not a complete solution to the problems of women. The concept of sisterhood, i.e. female bonding challenges the male-centred interpretation of female psychological development and offers new paradigms to contextualize female friendships. Sisterhood or the female bonding provides comfort to women only to the extent as Urmi's patient hearing of Shaku *tai*'s plight but Urmi can't do anything to solve Shaku *tai*'s problems. Shashi Deshpande has shown that considering the woman as weak and dependent, the Indian tradition empowers the male members to take control of her life. It is socially accepted that in marriage a husband has a right over his wife's body and it is the duty of the wife to satisfy the physical needs of her husband. This traditional negation of a woman's right over her body and her own sexuality also forms the theme of Shashi Deshpande's novels. The novelist also examines the response of society to the situation. Through the character of Vanaa, Shashi Deshpande presents the selfless life of women who live a life of servitude because tradition has taught them to do so. Vanaa submits to Harish so as to keep her marriage intact.

In the light of changing social reality, the novelist shows that the utmost need of the hour is a reassessment of what exactly the Indian woman wants. Her so-called 'new woman' chooses to opt out of the purposive control of man over her. She elects to exercise control over her own life and her own body. At the same time, she wants the grace and tenderness associated traditionally with femininity. In other words, she wants to have it all, the best of both the worlds! Shashi Deshpande's *A Matter of Time* depicts the conceptualized version of writer's vision of 'a new woman'. Aru is symbolic of this concept of the 'New Woman'. Though the new woman is a victim of patriarchal dominance, she reclaims her identity by her acts of resistance. Her 'New Women' struggle to learn to become "one's own refuge" and value the fellowship of other women.

Thus, we have observed that Deshpande explores the problems faced by modern Indian women. She portrays her female protagonists trying to juggle domesticity, love, children, career and emotional fulfilment and ending up exhausted, on the verge of mental crisis. All her women characters focus attention on the tensions involved in contemporary living and the inevitable concomitance of loneliness that force every woman to draw upon her inner resources eventually. After spending sometime in loneliness, these women emerge as 'New Women' and realize that there is absolute need for sufficient courage and power to stand their ground.

A few critics are of the opinion that the new Indian woman does not don the victim's role or they make use of sexual play to succeed in life. They are the strong women who can express themselves, do things, travel and live with the partner of their choice with or without marriage. Shashi Deshpande does not reject this fair side of the picture. But she only means to suggest through her writings that such women are in minority in India and they, too, are suffering from the inner dilemmas. In India, as portrayed by the novelist, the dependency needs of woman are so prevalent that the woman is caught between the narrow worlds of non-choice and immobility. Marriage being a sacrament in the Indian context, every Indian woman looks upon it as the only suitable career open to her. Amidst all the paraphernalia of modesty and chastity, she trains herself to be a fit object for her man's pleasure. Dependency needs at the economic and emotional level pulls her down. Thus, Shashi Deshpande portrays that the Indian woman has a long way to go before she reaches self-sufficiency. The novelist successfully makes a caustic attack on the norm of legal equality which exists only on papers. Social menaces like bigamy and dowry are still observed around. Like a naturalist slum photographer who would refuse to waste his plate on anything that is not sordid, Shashi Deshpande stays most of the time away from what is bright and happy in a woman's life and truthfully depicts the gender issues prevalent in the patriarchal Indian society. Though she does not offer any fixed solution to women's problems in India, yet her only hope lies in Indian women emerging as 'New Women' who challenge the traditional patriarchs as also done by Saeeda Gazdar, who has written:

> You snatch from me the status of a human being.
> I refuse to give birth to you. (Saeeda Gazdar 1994)

Works Cited

Chitnis, Suma. *Women in Indian Society: A Reader*. Ed. Rehana Ghadially. New Delhi: Sage Publication, 1998.

Gilliagan, Carol. *In a Different Voice*. Harvard: HUP, 1982.

Lál, Malashri. *Women, Literature and Culture in India: Perspectives*. New Delhi: JMI, 2008.

Miller, Jean Baker. *Towards a New Psychology of Women*. Boston: Beacon Press, 1976.

Riemenschneider, Dieter. "Indian Women Writing in English: The Short Story". *WLWE* (25:2): 1985.

Woolf, Virginia (1925). *A Room of One's Own*, rpt. London: Granada, 1977.

Bibliography

Books

Akiko, Yasano. *Woman in the Novels of Shashi Deshpande: A Study*. Ed. Dr. S. Prasanna Sree, New Delhi: Sarup and Sons, 2003: 107.

Bala, Suman (Ed). *Women in the Novels of Shashi Deshpande*. New Delhi: Khosla Publishing House, 2001.

Beauvoir, Simone de. *The Second Sex*. trans. H.M. Parshley. New York: Alfred Knopf, 1952; rpt. Vintage Books, 1989.

Bhasin and Khan. *Some Questions on Feminism and it's Relevance in South Asia*. New Delhi: Kali for Women, 2003.

Bhatnagar, O.P. "Indian Womanhood: Fight for Freedom in *Roots and Shadows*." In *Indian Woman Novelists* (Ed.). R.K. Dhawan, New Delhi: Prestige Books, 1991. Set I, Vol. V.

Brown, Penelope. "Universal and Particulars in the Position of Women." *Women in Society: Interdisciplinary Essays, The Cambridge Women's Studies Group*. London: Virago, 1981, rpt. 1985.

Chitnis, Sunita. *Women in Indian Society: A Reader*. Ed. Rehana Ghadially. New Delhi: Sage Publication. 1998.

Das, Veena. "Reflection on Social Construction of Adulthood" in Sudhir Kakkar (Ed.) *Identity and Adulthood*. New Delhi: OUP, 1992: 93.

———. "The Body as Metaphor: Socialisation of Women in Punjabi Urban Families". *Manushi*, 28.

Deshpande, Shashi. *Roots and Shadows*. New Delhi: Orient Longman Ltd., 1983.

———. *That Long Silence*. New Delhi: Penguin, 1989.

———. *The Dark Holds No Terrors*. Penguin Books, 1990.

———. *The Binding Vine*. New Delhi: Penguin, 1993.

———. *A Matter of Time*. New Delhi: Penguin, 1996.

Dhawan, R.K. (Ed.). *Indian Women Novelists*, Vol. 5. New Delhi: Prestige, 1991.

Desai, Anita. *Cry, The Peacock*. New Delhi: Orient Paperbacks, 1963.

———. *Fire on the Mountain*. New Delhi: Orient Paperbacks, 1971.

———. *Voices in the City*. New Delhi: Orient Paperbacks, 2006.

Eagleton, Mary (Ed.). *Feminist Literary Criticism: A Reader*. Oxford: Blackwell, 1992.

Friedan, Betty. *The Feminine Mystique*. Harmondsworth: Penguin, 1971.

Ghadially, Rehana. *Women in Indian Society: A Reader*. New Delhi: Sage Publications, 1988.

Gilliagan, Carol. *In a Different Voice*. Harvard: HUP, 1982.

Gray, John. *Men, Women and Relationship*. New York: HarperCollins, 1992.

Grimke, Sarah. *Letters on the Equality of the Sexes and the Condition of Woman*. New York: Burt Franklin, 1970.

Iyengar, Srinivasa K.R. *Indian Writing in English*. New Delhi: Sterling Publisher, 1993.

Jaggar, M. Alison. *Feminist Politics and Human Nature*. New Jersey: Rowman and Allenheld Pub., 1983.

Jain, Jasbir. *Gendered Realities, Human Spaces*. Rawat Publications.

Jain, Jasbir and Avdesh Singh. *Indian Feminism*. New Delhi: Creative Books, 2001.

Jain, Jasbir (Ed.). *Creative Theory: Writer on Writing*. Delhi: Pencraft International, 2000.

Jaisingh, Indrani. "Survivors: Changing Attitude to Divorce among Women in India". *Uncertain Liaisons*. (Ed.) Khushwant Singh and Shobhaa Dey. New Delhi, 1993.

Jung, Anis. *Unveiling India: A Woman's Journey*. New Delhi: Penguin Books, 1990.

Jhabvala, R.P. *To Whom She Will*. London: George Allen and Unwin Ltd., 1955.

Kakkar, Sudhir. "Feminine Identity in India" (Ed.). In *Women in Indian Society: A Reader*. New Delhi: Sage Publications, 1998.

Kane, P.V. *History of Dharamshastra*. Pune: Bhandarkar Oriental Research Inst. Pub., 1941.

Kapur, P. *Love, Marriage and Sex*. New Delhi: Vikas Publishing House, 1973.

Kirpal, Viney (Ed.). *The New Indian English Novel: A Study of the 1980s*. New Delhi: Allied Publishers, 1990.

———. *A Feminist Study of Her Fiction*. New Delhi, B.R. Publishing Corporation, 1998.

Kukreti, Sumitra. "Female Protagonist in Shashi Deshpande's Novels". *The Fiction of Shashi Deshpande*. Ed. R.S. Pathak. New Delhi: Creative Books, 1998, 30.

Lal, Malashri. *Women, Literature and Culture in India: Perspectives*. New Delhi: JMI, 2008.

Lalita, K. (Ed). *Women Writing in India: 600 BC to the Early 20th Century*. Delhi: OUP, 1991.

Madan, T.N. "The Structural Implications of Marriage among Kashmiri Brahmins." *Contributions to Indian Sociology*, Vol. 9.

Miller, Jean Baker. *Towards a New Psychology of Women*. Boston: Beacon Press, 1976.

Mohan, Indra T.M.J. *Shashi Deshpande: A Critical Spectrum*. Delhi: Atlantic Publishers and Distributors, 2004.

Moi, Toril. *Sexual/Textual Politics: Feminist Literary Theory*. London: Routledge, 1988.

Mukherjee, Meenakshi. *The Anxiety of Indianness.* New Delhi: Vision Books, 1998.

Nabar, Vrinda. *Caste as Woman.* New Delhi: Penguin Books, 1995.

Palkar, Sarla. "Breaking the Silence: Shashi Deshpande's *That Long Silence.*" *Indian Women Novelist.* (Ed.) R.K. Dhawan, New Delhi: Prestige Books, 1991: 169, Set 1; Vol. V.

Pathak, R.S. *Recent Indian Fiction.* New Delhi: Prestige, 1994.

———. *The Fiction of Shashi Deshpande.* New Delhi: Creative Books, 1998.

Radha, K. *Feminism and Literature.* Trivandum: University of Kerala, 1987.

Ramamoorthy, P. "My Life is My Own: A Study of Shashi Deshpande's Women". *Indian Women Novelist.* (Ed.) R.K. Dhawan. New Delhi: Prestige Books, 1991: 169, Set 1; Vol. V.

———. "A Study of Shashi Deshpandey's Women". In *Feminism and Recent Fiction in English.* (Ed.) Sushila Singh. New Delhi: Prestige Books, 1991.

Rani, T. Ashoka (Ed.). *Woman in Women's Writing.* Tirupati: Sri Padmavati Mahila Visvavidyalam, 1995.

Reddy, Y.S. Sunitha. *A Feminist Perspective on the Novels of Shashi Deshpande.* New Delhi: Prestige Books, 2001.

Register, Cheri. "American Feminist Literary Criticism: A Bibliographical Introduction" in Josephine Donovan (Ed.), *Feminist Literary Criticism*, The University of Kentucky Press, 1979.

Rich Adrienne. *Of Woman Born: Motherhood as Experience and Institution.* New York: W.W. Norton and Company, 1976.

Riemenschneider, Dieter. "Indian Women Writing in English: The Short Story". *WLWE* (25:2): 1985.

Roy, Arundhati. *The God of Small Things.* New Delhi: India Ink, 1998.

Second Sex. 1974: 500. Translated and ed. H.M. Parshley, New York: Vintage Books, 1974.

"Shashi Deshpande as a Feminist and Novelist", *Indian English Fiction, 1980-90: An Assessment* (Ed.) Nilufer E. Barucha and Vilas Sarang. New Delhi: B.R. Publications, 1994: 127.

Sandhu, Sarabjit K. *Image of Women in the Novels of Shashi Deshpande*.

Stimpson, Catherine, R. "Gertrude Stein and the Transportation of Gender". *The Poetics of Gender*. (Ed.) Nany K. Miller, New York: Columbia Univ. Press, 1986: 1.

Taylor, Debby. *Women: A World Report, A New International Book*. London: Oxford, 1985.

Tong, Rosemarie. *Feminist Thought*. London: Routledge, 1993.

"The Crisis of Feminine: Shashi Deshpande's *The Long Silence*", *Commonwealth Quarterly*. Vol. 18, No. 46, December-March, 1993: 30.

Tripathi, J.P. "The Binding Vine and Indian Ethos." *The Fiction Shashi Deshpande*. (Ed.) R.S. Pathak. New Delhi: Prestige Books, 1998.

Tripathi, Nalinabh. "Gender Identity and Inner Space in The Darks Holds No Terrors". *The Fiction of Shashi Deshpande*. (Ed.) R.S. Pathak. New Delhi: Prestige Books, 1998: 73.

Woolf, Virginia (1925). *A Room of One's Own* rpt. London: Granada, 1977.

———. *Women and Fiction*. New York: Hard Court Brace, 1958.

Periodicals

Ananad Laxmi, S. "The Female Child in a Family Setting" in *The Indian Journal of Social Work*. Vol. LII, No. 1, January 1991.

Cunningham, John. "Indian Writer's Block", *The Indian Post* March 6, 1988.

"The Crisis of Feminine: Shashi Deshpande's *That Long Silence*", *Commonwealth Quarterly*. Vol. 18, No. 46, December-March 1993: 30.

Singh, Madhu. "Intimate and Soul Searching Portrayals of Marriage". In *Indian Book Chronicle*. July 1993.

"The Sunday Observer", Stanley Carvalho, 11 Feb. 1990. *Eve's Weekly*, 18-24 June 1988: 28.

Interviews

"Femina" May 1993 Vanamala, Vishwanatha, Interview Literature Alive, 1:3 (Dec. 1987): 8-14.

Holmstrom, Lakshmi. "Shashi Deshpande Talks to Lakshmi Holmstrom". *The Fiction of Shashi Deshpande*. (Ed.) R.S. Pathak. New Delhi, Prestige Books, 1998: 247.

Interview with Geeta Gangadharan, "Denying the Otherness", Indian Communication. *Sunday Magazine* (20 Nov. 1994): II-III.

Interview with Shashi Deshpande by Malini Nair "The Message is Incidental," *Times of India*, No. 25, Nov. 1989.

Vishwanatha, Vanamala, A. Woman's World (...). All the Way! (Interview). *The Fiction of Shashi Deshpande*. (Ed.) R.S. Pathak. New Delhi: Prestige Books, 1998.

Newspapers

Iyenger, Pushpa. "Girls in Salem are Born to Die". *The Times of India*, Aug. 23, 1992.

Khan, Sakina Yusuf. *No Minor Offence. The Times of India,* May 9, 1993.

Mangalwadi, Vishar. *Indian Express*. Sep. 19, 1987.

Milton, Edith. *The Boston Globe*. May 3, 1998.

RA Nehal